Fifth Workshop on Computational Models of Reference, Anaphora and Coreference (CRAC 2022)

Held at COLING 2022

Gyeongju, South Korea
16-17 October 2022

ISBN: 978-1-7138-6150-8

Printed from e-media with permission by:

Curran Associates, Inc.
57 Morehouse Lane
Red Hook, NY 12571

Some format issues inherent in the e-media version may also appear in this print version.

Printed with permission by Curran Associates, Inc. (2023)

For permission requests, please contact the Association for Computational Linguistics at the address below.

Association for Computational Linguistics
209 N. Eighth Street
Stroudsburg, Pennsylvania 18360

Phone: 1-570-476-8006
Fax: 1-570-476-0860

acl@aclweb.org

Additional copies of this publication are available from:

Curran Associates, Inc.
57 Morehouse Lane
Red Hook, NY 12571 USA
Phone: 845-758-0400
Fax: 845-758-2633
Email: curran@proceedings.com
Web: www.proceedings.com

COLING

International Conference on Computational Linguistics

Proceedings of the Conference and Workshops

COLING

Volume 29 (2022), No. 7

Proceedings of The Fifth Workshop on Computational Models of Reference, Anaphora and Coreference (CRAC 2022)

The 29th International Conference on Computational Linguistics

October 16–17, 2022
Gyeongju, Republic of Korea

Message from the Program Chairs

This is the fifth edition of the Workshop on Computational Models of Reference, Anaphora and Coreference (CRAC). CRAC was first held in New Orleans four years ago in conjunction with NAACL HLT 2018. But the workshop series dates back to its predecessor, the Coreference Resolution Beyond OntoNotes (CORBON) that started in 2016, and has arguably become the primary forum for coreference researchers to present their latest results since the demise of the Discourse Anaphora and Anaphor Resolution Colloquium series in 2011. While CORBON focused on under-investigated coreference phenomena, CRAC has a broader scope, covering all cases of computational modeling of reference, anaphora, and coreference.

CRAC 2022 continued to attract a large number of very high quality papers. Specifically, we received 14 submissions which were rigorously reviewed by three program committee members. Based on their recommendations, we accepted 10 papers and conditionally accepted one paper. The one conditionally accepted paper was eventually accepted to the workshop after we made sure that the authors adequately addressed the reviewers' comments in the final camera-ready version. Overall, we were pleased with the large number of submissions as well as the quality of the accepted papers. This time around we had a total of two papers that were withdrawn for various reasons.

This was the second year of the joint CODI-CRAC shared task on *Anaphora, Bridging, and Discourse Deixis in Dialogue*. In addition, this year debuted the CRAC shared task on *Multilingual Coreference Resolution*. Both these activities allowed researchers who did not participate in the workshop to disseminate their work to a smaller and more focused audience which should promote interesting discussions.

We are grateful to the following people, without whom we could not have assembled an interesting program for the workshop. First, we are indebted to our program committee members. This year the reviewing load was on an average of two papers per reviewer. All of them did the incredible job of completing their reviews in a short reviewing period. Second, this is the first year where we have three invited talks. We thank Sharid Loáiciga, Juntao Yu, Michal Novák, Massimo Poesio and Lori Levin for accepting our invitation to be this year's invited speakers. This year we have a shorter duration for the continued panel on the Universal Anaphora (UA) effort, a unified, language-independent markup scheme that reflects common cross-linguistic understanding of reference-related phenomena. Motivated by Universal Dependencies, UA aims to facilitate referential analysis of the similarities and idiosyncrasies among typologically different languages, support comparative evaluation of anaphora resolution systems and enable comparative linguistic studies. Finally, we would like to thank the workshop participants for joining us in this event.

We hope you will enjoy it as much as we do!

— Sameer Pradhan, Maciej Ogrodniczuk, Anna Nedoluzhko,
Massimo Poesio, and Vincent Ng

Organizers

Organizing Committee:

Maciej Ogrodniczuk, Institute of Computer Science, Polish Academy of Sciences, Poland
Sameer Pradhan, University of Pennsylvania and cemantix.org, USA
Anna Nedoluzhko, Charles University in Prague, Czechia
Massimo Poesio, Queen Mary University of London, UK
Vincent Ng, University of Texas at Dallas, USA

Program Committee:

Antonio Branco, University of Lisbon, Portugal
Arie Cattan, Bar-Ilan University, Israel
Haixia Chai, Heidelberg University, Germany
Stephanie Dipper, Ruhr-University, Germany
Elisa Ferracane, Abridge, USA
Yulia Grishina, Amazon, USA
Yansong Feng, Peking University, China
Christian Hardmeier, IT University of Copenhagen, Denmark
Lars Hellan, Norwegian University of Science and Technology, Norway
Veronique Hoste, Ghent University, Belgium
Yufang Hou, IBM, Dublin, Ireland
Ruihong Huang, Texas A&M University, USA
Sobha Lalitha Devi, Anna University of Chennai, India
Loic De Langhe, Ghent University, Belgium
Ekaterina Lapshinova-Koltunski, Saarland University, Germany
Sharid Loáiciga, University of Gothenburg, Sweden.
Costanza Navaretta, University of Copenhagen, Denmark
Michal Novák, Charles University in Prague, Czechia
Marta Recasens, Google, USA
Carolyn Rosé, Carnegie Mellon University, USA
Manfred Stede, University of Potsdam, Germany
Nobuhiro Ueda, Kyoto University, Japan
Yaqin Yang, Brandeis University, USA
Bonnie Webber, University of Edinburgh, UK
Juntao Yu, University of Essex, UK
Yilun Zhu, Georgetown University, USA
Heike Zinsmeister, University of Hamburg, Germany

Invited Talk (I)

Bringing together Anaphora Resolution and Linguistic Theory

Sharid Loáiciga, University of Gothenburg, Sweden

Abstract

Early work on anaphora resolution was intrinsically connected to linguistic theories of discourse interpretation. In later years, with the adoption of machine learning methods, great progress has been achieved in anaphora resolution as an independent task. This success has been even greater with current deep neural networks methods. However, the focus has been much more on solving the task than on acquiring new linguistic insights concerning anaphora resolution. In this talk, I present two ways in which we can gain and also utilize linguistic insights for anaphora resolution. First, I present experiments combining psycholinguistics with large-scale NLP tools. These show some of the complexities of hypothesis testing with corpus data. Second, I present the annotation of a multimodal corpus with anaphora information. The combination of images and text presents a unique opportunity to test our annotation schemes (i.e., our current linguistic knowledge) and to explore new ways to annotate what is unaccounted for in the same annotation schemes (i.e., new linguistic insights).

Speaker Bio

Sharid Loáiciga is a Researcher in the Department of Philosophy, Linguistics and Theory of Science at the University of Gothenburg, Sweden. She is also the Associate Director of CLASP (Centre for Linguistic Theory and Studies in Probability) in the same department. Her research is focused on discourse, and in particular on understanding human and machine interpretation of referring expressions. In recent work, she developed techniques for combining psycholinguistic methods with large-scale resources, and studied the discourse knowledge of pre-trained language models.

Invited Talk (II)

The Recent Developments in Universal Anaphora Scorer

Juntao Yu, University of Essex, UK
Michal Novák, Charles University, Prague, Czechia

Abstract

The Universal Anaphora initiative aims to push forward the state of the art in anaphora and anaphora resolution by expanding the aspects of anaphoric interpretation which are or can be reliably annotated in anaphoric corpora, producing unified standards to annotate and encode these annotations, deliver datasets encoded according to these standards, and developing methods for evaluating models carrying out this type of interpretation. Such expansion of the scope of anaphora resolution requires a comparable expansion of the scope of the scorers used to evaluate this work. Last year, we introduce an extended version of the Reference Coreference Scorer (Pradhan et al., 2014) that can be used to evaluate identity anaphora resolution (including singletons, split-antecedents), bridging reference resolution, non-referring expressions and discourse deixis. The scorer has been used in the two recent CODI-CRAC Shared Tasks on Anaphora Resolution in Dialogues. Recently, an extension of the UA scorer that supports also discontinuous markables has been used by Novák et al (2022) in the CRAC 2022 Shared Task on Multilingual Coreference Resolution. In this talk, we will introduce the details about the scorer on scoring the different aspects of anaphora resolutions and how has it been used in recently shared tasks. In addition, we will also discuss the work in progress for the scorers such as mention overlap ratio, anaphor-decomposable score and the adaptation for CRAFT shared task.

Speaker Bio

Juntao Yu is a Lecturer at the School of Computer Science and Electronic Engineering, University of Essex. Before joining Essex, He was a post-doctoral researcher at the Queen Mary University of London, working with Professor Massimo Poesio on his five-year DALI project (Disagreements and Language Interpretation, ERC-2015-AdG). He did his Ph.D. at the University of Birmingham, working on out-of-domain dependency parsing supervised by Dr Bernd Bohnet. His research interests include Deep Learning for NLP, Information Extraction, Coreference Resolution, Conversational AI, Dependency Parsing, Domain Adaptation, Semi-supervised Learning, and Multi-task Learning.

Michal Novák is a researcher at the Institute of Formal and Applied Linguistics at the Faculty of Mathematics and Physics, Charles University, Prague, Czech Republic. He received his Ph.D. from the same university, exploring coreference and its resolution methods from cross-lingual perspective. Recently, he has co-authored the CorefUD dataset, which in its latest release harmonizes coreference of 17 corpora in 11 languages under the same annotation scheme. Besides coreference, his research also focuses on machine translation. He has participated on the Czech-Ukrainian translation system within the Charles Translator project, which aims to narrow the communication gap between Ukrainian refugees and other people in the Czech Republic.

Invited Talk (III)

The CODI/CRAC 2022 Shared Task Corpus of Anaphora Resolution in Dialogue

Massimo Poesio, Queen Mary University of London, UK
Lori Levin, Carnegie Mellon University, USA

Abstract

Most current research on anaphoric reference focuses on news text, in particular written, and on identity anaphora (coreference). This is largely due to the lack of annotated datasets of a sufficient size to train and evaluate models for other genres, and other types of anaphoric reference. Arguably the most important among the understudied genres is conversational language in dialogue. Anaphora resolution in dialogue requires systems to handle grammatically incorrect language suffering from disfluencies and mentions jointly created across utterances (Poesio & Rieser, 2010) or whose function is to establish common ground rather than refer (Clark & Brennan, 1990; Heeman & Hirst, 1995). Dialogue involves much more deictic reference, vaguer anaphoric and discourse deictic reference, speaker grounding of pronouns and long-distance conversation structure. These complexities are normally absent from news or Wikipedia articles, which constitute the bulk of current datasets for coreference resolution (Poesio et al, to appear).

The series of CODI/CRAC Shared Tasks in Anaphora Resolution in Dialogue (Khosla et al, 2021; Yu et al, 2022) was organized to address this issue by creating datasets that our community could use to study anaphoric reference in different types of conversational setups, and to tackle less studied forms of anaphoric reference such as bridging reference or discourse deixis. The annotated corpus created for the CODI/CRAC series consists of conversations from four well-known conversational datasets: the AMI corpus (Carletta, 2006), the LIGHT corpus (Urbanek et al, 2019), the PERSUASION corpus (Wang et al, 2019) and SWITCHBOARD (Godfrey et al, 1992). These documents were annotated according to the annotation scheme for the ARRAU 3 corpus, which includes guidelines for identifying discontinuous markables and annotating split antecedent plurals, bridging reference, and discourse deixis. For this second edition, we created new test sets, but also systematically checked the data annotated for the first edition. As this annotation effort also involved annotators that had not been previously involved in the ARRAU 3 annotation, this work also involved extensive discussions about the scheme; new reliability tests of the annotation scheme were carried out, and the annotation guidelines were substantially revised.

Speaker Bio

Massimo Poesio is a full professor in Computational Linguistics at the School of Electronic Engineering and Computer Science, Queen Mary University of London, and a member of the University's Cognitive Science and Games and AI research groups. He is also a Fellow of the Turing Institute, a supervisor in the IGGI Doctoral training centre in Intelligent Games and Game Intelligence and the Wellcome Trust's Ph.D. programme in Health Data in Practice. He is co-founder and have been Associate Editor of Dialogue and Discourse since its foundation and he recently became co-editor of the Computational and Mathematical section of Language and Linguistics Compass.

Lori Levin has a Ph.D. in linguistics and has been working in the fields of computational linguistics and natural language processing since the 1980's, where she uses her expertise in linguistics in the annotation of corpora and the design of meaning representations. She specializes in NLP for low-resource and endangered languages. She is the co-founder and co-chair of the North American Computational Linguistics Open competition.

Table of Contents

Quantifying Discourse Support for Omitted Pronouns
Shulin Zhang, Jixing Li and John Hale 1

Online Neural Coreference Resolution with Rollback
Patrick Xia and Benjamin Van Durme 13

Analyzing Coreference and Bridging in Product Reviews
Hideo Kobayashi and Christopher Malon 22

Anaphoric Phenomena in Situated dialog: A First Round of Annotations
Sharid Loáiciga, Simon Dobnik and David Schlangen 31

Building a Manually Annotated Hungarian Coreference Corpus: Workflow and Tools
Noémi Vadász 38

NARC – Norwegian Anaphora Resolution Corpus
Petter Mæhlum, Dag Haug, Tollef Jørgensen, Andre Kåsen, Anders Nøklestad,
Egil Rønningstad, Per Erik Solberg, Erik Velldal and Lilja Øvrelid 48

Evaluating Coreference Resolvers on Community-based Question Answering: From Rule-based to State of the Art
Haixia Chai, Nafise Sadat Moosavi, Iryna Gurevych and Michael Strube 61

Improving Bridging Reference Resolution using Continuous Essentiality from Crowdsourcing
Nobuhiro Ueda and Sadao Kurohashi 74

Investigating Cross-Document Event Coreference for Dutch
Loic De Langhe, Orphee De Clercq and Veronique Hoste 88

The Role of Common Ground for Referential Expressions in Social Dialogues
Jaap Kruijt and Piek Vossen 99

Workshop Program

Sunday, October 16, 2022

	Welcome
13:30–13:40	*Opening and Welcome*
	CRAC—Invited Talk
13:40–14:40	*Bringing together Anaphora Resolution and Linguistic Theory* Sharid Loáiciga
	Paper Session I
14:40–15:00	*Quantifying Discourse Support for Omitted Pronouns* Shulin Zhang, Jixing Li and John Hale
15:00–15:10	*Online Neural Coreference Resolution with Rollback* Patrick Xia and Benjamin Van Durme
15:10–15:20	*Analyzing Coreference and Bridging in Product Reviews* Hideo Kobayashi and Christopher Malon
15:20–15:30	*Anaphoric Phenomena in Situated dialog: A First Round of Annotations* Sharid Loáiciga, Simon Dobnik and David Schlangen
	Short Break
15:30–16:00	*Coffee Break*

Sunday, October 16, 2022 (continued)

Paper Session II

16:00–16:20 *Building a Manually Annotated Hungarian Coreference Corpus: Workflow and Tools*
Noémi Vadász

16:20–16:40 *NARC – Norwegian Anaphora Resolution Corpus*
Petter Mæhlum, Dag Haug, Tollef Jørgensen, Andre Kåsen, Anders Nøklestad, Egil Rønningstad, Per Erik Solberg, Erik Velldal and Lilja Øvrelid

16:40–17:00 *Evaluating Coreference Resolvers on Community-based Question Answering: From Rule-based to State of the Art*
Haixia Chai, Nafise Sadat Moosavi, Iryna Gurevych and Michael Strube

17:00–17:20 *Improving Bridging Reference Resolution using Continuous Essentiality from Crowdsourcing*
Nobuhiro Ueda and Sadao Kurohashi

17:20–17:40 *Investigating Cross-Document Event Coreference for Dutch*
Loic De Langhe, Orphee De Clercq and Veronique Hoste

17:40–18:00 *The Role of Common Ground for Referential Expressions in Social Dialogues*
Jaap Kruijt and Piek Vossen

Closing

13:30–13:40 *Closing Remarks*

Monday, October 17, 2022

CRAC Shared Task Session

9:00–9:30 *Findings of the Shared Task on Multilingual Coreference Resolution*
Michal Novák, Zdeněk Žabokrtský, Miloslav Konopík, Anna Nedoluzhko, Michal Novák, Maciej Ogrodniczuk, Martin Popel, Ondřej Pražák, Jakub Sido, Daniel Zeman and Yilun Zhu

9:30–9:45 *Coreference Resolution for Polish: Improvements within the CRAC 2022 Shared Task*
Karol Saputa

9:45–10:00 *End-to-end Multilingual Coreference Resolution with Mention Head Prediction*
Ondřej Pražák and Miloslav Konopik

10:00–10:15 *ÚFAL CorPipe at CRAC 2022: Effectivity of Multilingual Models for Coreference Resolution*
Milan Straka and Jana Straková

Discussion

10:15–10:30 *Open Discussion*

Short Break

10:30–11:00 *Coffee Break*

CRAC Shared Task—Invited Talk

11:00–1200 *The Recent Developments in Universal Anaphora Scorer*
Juntao Yu and Michal Novák

Panel

12:00–12:30 *Panel Discussion—Universal Anaphora*
Sameer Pradhan

Long Break

12:30–14:00 *Lunch Break*

CODI-CRAC Joint Shared Task Session

14:00–14:05 *Welcome*

14:05–14:30 *The CODI-CRAC 2022 Shared Task on Anaphora, Bridging, and Discourse Deixis in Dialogue*
Juntao Yu, Sopan Khosla, Ramesh Manuvinakurike, Lori Levin, Vincent Ng, Massimo Poesio, Michael Strube and Carolyn Rosé

14:35–14:50 *Anaphora Resolution in Dialogue: System Description–CODI-CRAC 2022 Shared Task*
Tatiana Anikina, Natalia Skachkova, Joseph Renner and Priyansh Trivedi

14:50–15:05 *Pipeline Coreference Resolution for Anaphoric Identity in Dialogues*
Damrin Kim, Seongsik Park, Mirae Han and Harksoo Kim

15:05–15:30 *Neural Anaphora Resolution in Dialogue Revisited*
Shengjie Li, Hideo Kobayashi and Vincent Ng

Monday, October 17, 2022 (continued)

CODI-CRAC Joint Shared Task—Invited Talk

16:00–16:45	*The CODI/CRAC 2022 Shared Task Corpus of Anaphora Resolution in Dialogue* Massimo Poesio and Lori Levin

CODI-CRAC Joint Shared Task Discussion and Closing Remarks

16:45–17:45	*Open Discussion*
17:45–18:00	*Closing Remarks*

Quantifying Discourse Support for Omitted Pronouns

Shulin Zhang[1], Jixing Li[2], John Hale[1]
[1]University of Georgia, US
[2]City University of Hongkong, China
shulin.zhang@uga.edu
jixingli@cityu.edu.hk
jthale@uga.edu

Abstract

Pro-drop is commonly seen in many languages, but its discourse motivations have not been well characterized. Inspired by the topic chain theory in Chinese, this study shows how character-verb usage continuity distinguishes dropped pronouns from overt references to story characters. We model the choice to drop *vs.* not drop as a function of character-verb continuity. The results show that omitted subjects have higher character history-current verb continuity salience than non-omitted subjects. This is consistent with the idea that discourse coherence with a particular topic, such as a story character, indeed facilitates the omission of pronouns in languages and contexts where they are optional.

1 Introduction

Pro-drop is a phenomenon that pronouns can be omitted when they are inferable. It is common across the world's languages, and Mandarin Chinese is one of them (See examples (3) and (4) in Figure 1). Omitted pronouns in these languages, also called zero pronouns, are increasingly important in computational linguistics (*e.g.* Chen et al., 2021; Iida et al., 2006, 2015; Kong et al., 2019). This paper formalizes the notion of Topic Chains, introduced by Tsao (1977) and demonstrates that people omit pronouns when a certain kind of discourse salience is high. We show that this notion of salience is robust across various choices of language models, however, locality (*i.e.* clause recency) seems to be a key requirement.

The proposed formalization leverages the idea that verbs predicated on the same story-character exhibit discourse coherence (Huang, 1984, 1994; Li and Thompson, 1979). Figure 1 shows a literary example where the same character, the narrator, is explicitly referred to once using an explicit pronoun "wo". After that, the pronoun is dropped. The list of predicates (shown in red) applying to the narrator in examples (1) - (3) is ["draw", "lose", "draw"]. When faced with another omitted pronoun in example (4), the fact that the predicate is also "draw" supports the interpretation that the omitted element refers to the narrator. This is because "draw" is similar to the history verbs "draw" and "lose" which were predicated of this same character earlier in the discourse. In this short example, there are other entities such as "grownups" and the "boa constrictor", but their verb histories make them less plausible as candidate referents of the omitted pronoun.

In this paper, we use representations from three neural language models to quantify character-verb usage continuity in a literary discourse, and calculate salience values for each of 32 possible characters at the site of each omitted pronoun. Figure 2 summarizes the analytical steps of this process. Our contributions are as follows: (1) We provide a numerical description of the topic chain continuity. (2) We elaborate on the role of verbs in resolving omitted pronouns. (3) We show that verb similarity and clause range offer reliable clues about the referent of the omitted pronoun.

2 Related Work

Various linguistic theories point to discourse coherence as a factor that enables or encourages *pro*-drop. One of these is Tsao's (1977) notion of Topic Chain. As reviewed in Pu (2019a), a topic chain is a sequence of clauses sharing an identical topic that occurs overtly in one of the clauses. Topic Chains may cross several sentences and even paragraphs (Li, 2004). The multiclausal aspect of Topic Chains supports

Proceedings of the Fifth Workshop on Computational Models of Reference, Anaphora and Coreference (CRAC 2022) , pages 1–12
Gyeongju, Republic of Korea, October 16–17, 2022.

(1)	这	是	我	给	他	后来	画	出来	最好	的	一幅	画像。		
	zhe	shi	wo	gei	ta	houlai	hua	chulai	zuihao	de	yi fu	huaxiang		
	This	is	I	for	he	later	draw	out	best	DE	one	drawing		

"This is the best portrait I drew for him later on."

(2)	[我]	六	岁	时,	大人们	使	我	对	我的	画家	生涯	失去	了	勇气。
	wo	liu	sui	shi	darenmen	shi	wo	dui	wode	huajia	shengya	shiqu	le	yongqi
	[I]	Six	year	old	grown-ups	make	I	towards	my	painter	career	lose	LE	courage

"When I was six, grown-ups made me lose courage in my painter career."

(3)	[我]	除了	画	过	开着	肚皮	和	闭着	肚皮	的	蟒蛇,
	wo	chule	hua	guo	kaizhe	dupi	he	bizhe	dupi	de	mangshe
	[I]	except	draw	PASS	opening	belly	and	closing	belly	DE	boa

"Except that I had drawn boas with opening and closing belly,"

(4)	[我]	后来	再	没有	学	过	画。
	wo	houlai	zai	meiyou	xue	guo	hua
	[I]	afterwards	again	not	learn	PASS	draw

"I had never learned drawing afterwards."

Figure 1: Example of Chinese omitted pronouns in a topic chain. Omitted pronouns, shown here in green with square brackets are not actually spoken. However, their intended reference is unambiguous for native speakers. Predicates are shown in red, and the overtly expressed entities are shown in blue. Unlike in Romance languages, there is no morphological change on verbs to mark the gender or number of omitted elements in Chinese.

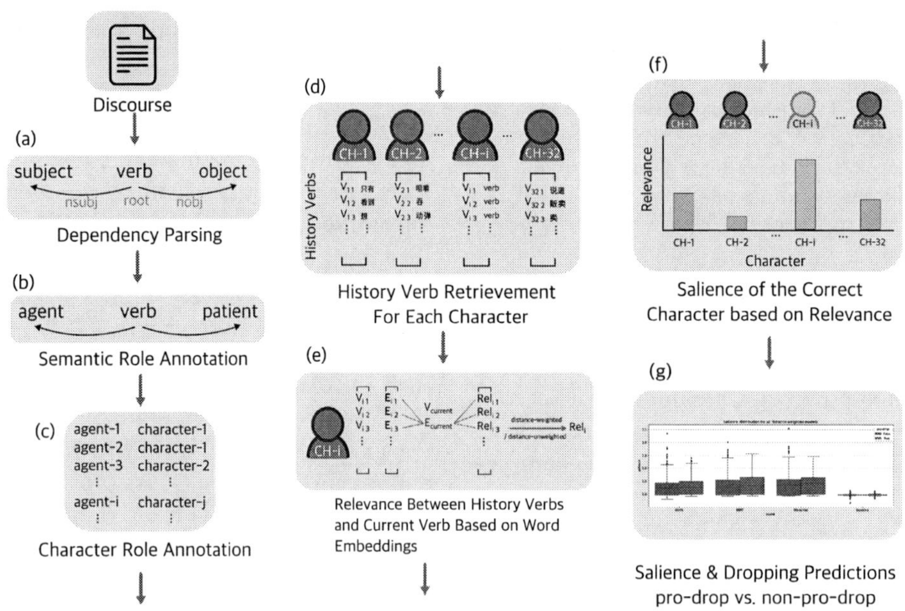

Figure 2: Analysis steps adopted in this study: (a) Grammatical subjects and objects of each main verb are identified via dependency parsing on the whole story discourse of The Little Prince (See a sentence example from Table 1, columns "S", "V", "O"); (b) Semantic role annotation: for all the subjects and objects, annotate their semantic roles as AGENT or PATIENT (See Table 1 column "V-agent" and "V-patient"); (c) Character role annotation: assign story character roles to the entities, see character occurrences in Table A1, and Table 1 column "character"; (d) History verb retrieval for each story character: for each story character, tabulate the verbs that are its main verbs being used in the discourse (See example Table A3); (e) Relevance between history verbs and a current verb: for each current verb, calculate its relevance to the history verbs, and sum with or without their distance weight (See Table 2 and A5); (f) Salience of the correct character: for each verb, calculate how "salient" the correct character is compared to all other characters (See example Table A6); (g) Group test between *pro*-drop verbs vs. non-*pro*-drop verbs, and apply logistic regression to test predictability of character salience on dropping behavior (See group results in Table 3 and Figure 3).

long-distance coreference (Sun, 2019). Taking a dynamic perspective, Pu (2019b) suggests that a topic chain "encodes a referent that is cognitively most accessible at the moment of discourse production, as enhanced by maximum discourse coherence of topic continuity and thematic coherence".

We conceptualize accessibility in Pu's sense as the relative salience of a story character that participates in a chain of predications. Instead of focusing on named entities, we form the chain based on the verbs in the preceding discourse.

3 Method

3.1 Discourse Material

The discourse material used in this study is a Chinese translation (xiaowangzi.org, 2021) of Saint-Exupéry's *The Little Prince*. It contains 2802 clauses and 16010 words, and the word tokenization was manually checked by native Chinese speakers.

3.2 Dependency Structure Retrieval and Semantic Role Annotation

We manually annotate the semantic roles Agent and Patient for each verb using dependency analyses provided by Stanza (Qi et al., 2020) and part of speech tags provided by spaCy. For most cases in the discourse, subjects are acting as agents whereas objects are acting as patients, but there are 494 exceptions (*i.e.* 218 Agents are acting as Objects, and 276 Patients are acting as Subjects) such as passives, the -BA('把') construction, the relative clause -DE('的') construction *etc.* that call for our manual annotation (See Chapter 28 and 32 in The Oxford Handbook of Chinese Linguistics (Wang and Sun, 2015) regarding these constructions).

The textual antecedents of each agent and patient are separately annotated manually. As shown in Table 1, the sentence meaning "These boas swallow their prey without chewing" has the following annotations: verbs annotated in column *V*; verbs' agents and patients annotated correspondingly in column *V-agent* and *V-patient*; pronouns or named entities' character roles are annotated in column *character*. As described below in Section 3.4,

ID	word	S	V	O	V-agent	V-patient	character
56	这些 (these)						
57	蟒蛇 (boa)	True					ch2_boa
58	把 (BA)						
59	它们 (them)						
60	的 (DE)						
61	猎获物 (prey)			True			
62	不 (not)						
63	加 (with)						
64	咀嚼 (chew)		True		57 (boa)	61 (prey)	
65	地 (DI)						
66	囫囵 (roughly)						
67	吞 (swallow)		True		57 (boa)	61 (prey)	
68	下 (down)						

Table 1: Dependency structure and semantic role annotation table. An annotation example for the sentence "These boas swallow their prey without chewing." The verbs "chew" and "swallow" are located as verbs in the column *V*. Token indices for each verb's Agent and/or Patient are annotated in the columns *V-agent* and *V-patient* respectively, and the character roles they are referring to are annotated in the column *character*.

information about characters in particular semantic roles can be used to form a dynamic usage table, reifying Pu's view of Topic Chains.

3.3 *Pro*-drop Annotation

Omitted subjects and objects are manually resolved using numerical indices from 1 to 32. As shown in Appendix Table A2, 422 Agents and 16 Patients are found omitted in the discourse, and in the following analyses, we focus on just story characters in the Agent semantic role.

3.4 Dynamic Character-Verb Usage Table

Based on the dependency annotation table, the verbs used for each character are extracted and entered in a second table, the Character-Verb Usage Table (See example in Appendix Table A3). This table includes the following features: (1) *verb*, the original text of the verb; (2) *verb_id*, the index of the verb in the whole discourse; (3) *agent/patient_character*, the verb's agent or patient story character; (4) *pro_drop*, whether the verb has *pro*-drop; (5) *ch[1-32]_prev_verbs*, for characters 1 through 32, their corresponding previous verbs and indexes are stored as lists.

The dynamic character-verb usage table includes the previous verbs for each story character until a "current verb", and this indicates the verb usage history of each character. By transforming these verb usage histories into numerical vectors, it is possible to use a simple notion of similarity to formalize discourse coherence.

3.5 History-verb and Current-verb Relevance

The idea behind comparing the history verbs and the current verb for each story character is to calculate a numerical similarity level between the current verb and preceding verbs that are part of one or another Topic Chain. Inspired by Sperber and Wilson (1986), we define a quantity called Relevance, a time-weighted function of vector similarity with preceding predicates. The Relevance evaluation process adopt three types of word embeddings (See Section 3.5.1 for details), and steps for the evaluation are introduced in Section 3.5.2.

3.5.1 Word Embeddings Methods

Word embeddings allow each word to be mapped to a single point in a vector space. Under the Distributional Hypothesis (see *e.g.* Lenci, 2018), words with similar meanings should be closer in vector space (for a textbook introduction, see Pilehvar and Camacho-Collados, 2020). We use this idea to calculate the similarity between the main verb of an omitted pronoun and the verb chains of story characters that might serve as that omitted pronoun's referent.

We use three types of word embeddings: GloVe, BERT, and Word2Vec. The GloVe model (Pennington et al., 2014) learns word embedding from the term co-occurrence matrix by minimizing the reconstruction error. GloVe has a large context window, which allows it to capture longer-term dependency features. The BERT model (Kenton and Toutanova, 2019) consists of multi-layer bidirectional transformer encoders. BERT is trained on two unsupervised tasks: predict masked tokens, and predict the next sentence, and the BERT embeddings reflect contextual corpus features. Word2Vec is a prediction-based model (Mikolov et al., 2013a,b), and the word embeddings used in this study (Li et al., 2018) were trained on a Skip-Gram with Negative Sampling (SGNS) model. All word embeddings we used were trained on large Chinese corpora, and contain contextual word knowledge that carries semantic, syntactic, and pragmatic features. Among these three word embedding models, BERT can provide contextualized features of the language compared to the others due to the tasks and processes it has been trained on.

In this study, BERT and GloVe models are applied with spaCy[1], and Word2Vec model is applied with pretrained Chinese Word Vectors[2] (Li et al., 2018). A baseline model with 300-dimension random value vectors is adopted to calculate the baseline relevance as compared to the other word embedding models.

The GloVe word embeddings are obtained from the *zh_core_web_lg* model in spaCy. The GloVe model (Pennington et al., 2014) relies on word co-occurrence in the training corpus, and considers the ratios of word-word co-occurrence probabilities to encode semantic information. The model in spaCy was trained on OntoNotes 5, CoreNLP Universal Dependencies Converter, and Explosion fastText Vectors. It has 500,000 unique vectors with a dimension size of 300. We obtained the word vectors by searching up the Chinese word in the word dictionary.

The BERT word embeddings are retrieved from the *zh_core_web_trf* model in spaCy. This transformer model was trained on OntoNotes 5, CoreNLP Universal Dependencies Converter, and bert-base-chinese. The word embedding vectors were obtained by grouping every 50 words in the discourse, and the model inputs were the 50 words combined as a string (with space between the words). The dimension of the BERT word embedding is 768. If there were more than 1 character in a word, their vectors' mean value was used as the word embedding for the whole word. For example, the word "只有" 's embedding was calculated by averaging its subwords' embedding vectors of "只" and "有".

The Word2Vec word embeddings were pretrained on Word2Vec model with a large Chinese corpus containing data from Baidu Netdisk (22.6G), and the vector dimension is 300 (Li et al., 2018).

Baseline Word Vectors were 300-dimension

[1] https://spacy.io/models/zh

[2] https://github.com/Embedding/Chinese-Word-Vectors

vectors generated randomly in the range -1 to 1. The same analysis steps are applied to this model as a baseline.

3.5.2 Relevance evaluation

The relevance between history verbs and current verbs is calculated based on their word embedding similarities (see Section 3.5.1 for details). At the same time, a weight decay function is applied to the influence of each history verb based on its distance to the current verb, and the function used here is a vanilla value decreasing function (see Equation 1), in which ω refers to the weight applying on the similarity, d refers to the clause distance between the verbs being compared, and j, k are the clause numbers the verbs are in:

$$\begin{aligned} \omega(j,k) &= 1/(d+1) \\ d &= |j-k| \end{aligned} \tag{1}$$

In this study, the "word embedding similarity" method is realized by calculating the Cosine Similarity between two word embedding vectors. As shown in Equation 2, v_{prev} refers to a word embedding vector of a previous verb, and v_{curr} refers to the one for the current verb:

$$R(v_{prev}, v_{curr}) = \frac{v_{prev} \cdot v_{curr}}{||v_{prev}||||v_{curr}||} \tag{2}$$

Therefore, the clause-distance-weighted similarity between history verbs and the current verb is shown as Equation 3, in which n refers to the number of verbs in the history verb list for a character, and *cl_prev_i* and *cl_curr* refer to the clause numbers that the previous verb and the current verb are in correspondingly.

$$R_{weighted}([v_{prev\_1}, ..., v_{prev\_n}], v_{curr}) = \sum_{i=1}^{n} \omega(cl\_prev\_i, cl\_curr) * R(v_{prev\_i}, v_{curr}) \tag{3}$$

Via Equation 3, for a current verb, each story character has a corresponding relevance value: if the value is higher, the distance-weighted word embedding similarity between history verbs and current verb is higher; and vice versa.

Appendix Table A3 shows an example of a verb and the history verbs for characters 1 through 32. The GloVe, BERT, Word2Vec, and Baseline embeddings are used to calculate the average relevance of the history verbs to each current verb for each story character.

Regressors obtained from relevance evaluation introduced in this section are shown in Table 2. The average similarity is calculated following Equation 2 and 3. Both distance-weighted and distance-unweighted relevance are explored to see whether clause distance would play a role.

Regressor Number	Regressor Name	Regressor Meaning
1	verb	the verb in the discourse acting as a main verb of a clause
2	verb-id	the word order id of this verb in the original discourse
3	agent-character	the story character referred by the agent of the verb
4	pro-drop	whether this agent is dropped in the discourse
5 - 36	ch(1-32)-prev-verbs	the previous verbs used by each story character till the current verb
37 - 68	rel-glove-ch(1-32)	relevance obtained by GloVe word embeddings
69 - 100	rel-bert-ch(1-32)	relevance obtained by BERT word embeddings
101 - 132	rel-word2vec-ch(1-32)	relevance obtained by Word2Vec word embeddings
133 - 164	rel-baseline-ch(1-32)	relevance obtained by Baseline word vectors

Table 2: Regressors obtained after the relevance calculation

As shown in Appendix Table A5, the relevance calculation results of the last verb are presented as an example.

3.6 Character Salience

With the relevance between history-current verbs computed as described in the previous section, we have a similarity value for each story character to the current verb. This character salience value refers to whether a story character stands out compared to other candidate characters. The salience level function is described in Equation 4. In Equation 4, k refers to character_k, and the relevance values were calculated based on its history-current verbs by Equation 3.

$$S(k) = \frac{\sum_{i=1}^{n} \left(\frac{R_{weighted}(k)+1}{R_{weighted}(i)+1} \right)}{n+1} \tag{4}$$

3.6.1 Ranged Character Salience

Instead of taking all 32 story characters as candidates for the salience value calculation, the

		Correct character salience pro-drop >non-pro-drop (n = 422)							
Candidates' Range		range = all		range <10 clause		range <20 clause		range <30 clause	
		t-value	*p-value*	*t-value*	*p-value*	*t-value*	*p-value*	*t-value*	*p-value*
Distance-Weighted	**GloVe**	49090.319	0.063	51137.593	0.012*	52598.233	0.003**	52121.241	0.004**
	BERT	50555.45	0.023*	45310.076	0.029*	52105.854	0.005**	51582.819	0.008**
	Word2Vec	50358.954	0.025*	51268.800	0.011*	52747.81	0.002**	52246.569	0.004**
	Baseline	44656.318	0.496	44737.336	0.483	49199.853	0.060	47875.291	0.134
Distance-Unweighted	**GloVe**	39345.494	0.959	44384.169	0.531	43818.383	0.606	43837.85	0.604
	BERT	42867.41	0.724	45310.076	0.411	45187.343	0.425	45220.75	0.421
	Word2Vec	40865.782	0.898	45236.126	0.420	44672.755	0.494	44630.117	0.498
	Baseline	43149.674	0.690	45940.625	0.330	46398.831	0.275	45552.563	0.377

Table 3: Single-sided nonparametric two-sample Wilcoxon test between *pro*-drop and non-*pro*-drop salience values among three word embedding models and the baseline model: With candidates included as all candidates, candidates within 10 clauses, 20 clauses, and 30 clauses.

		Logistic Regression Model Pro-drop Prediction Accuracy			
Candidates' Range		range = all	range <10 clause	range <20 clause	range <30 clause
Distance-Weighted	**GloVe**	**0.518**	**0.535**	**0.527**	**0.539**
	BERT	**0.538**	**0.532**	**0.536**	**0.546**
	Word2Vec	**0.534**	**0.535**	**0.537**	**0.552**
	Baseline	0.497	0.489	0.495	0.498
Distance-Unweighted	**GloVe**	**0.524**	0.487	0.490	0.485
	BERT	0.493	0.488	0.492	0.482
	Word2Vec	**0.514**	0.485	0.482	0.473
	Baseline	0.485	0.485	0.485	0.485

Table 4: *Pro*-drop prediction accuracy results of the Logistic Regression model from three word embedding models and one baseline model: salience value calculated based on all previous clauses and ranged clauses.

ranged candidates' salience compares the correct character's accumulated relevance value to the ones within a certain number of clauses. We consider candidates within 10, 20, and 30 clauses for this ranged salience.

3.7 *Pro*-drop Prediction

With the correct story character's salience level for each verb in the annotated discourse, we apply a logistic regression model to predict *pro*-drop based on the salience level. The sample sizes are chosen by the size of the smaller group (*i.e. pro*-drop), and the chosen processes are repeated 100 times to obtain the average accuracy level.

4 Results

In this study, the following analyses are applied to The Little Prince discourse to explore the effect of verb continuity on the *pro*-drop phenomenon: (1) relevance between history and current verbs for all story characters (with three types of word embeddings applied); (2) character salience of the correct character, and (3) correct character salience group comparison, and its predictability on *pro*-drop in the discourse. The following sections describe the results of (2) and (3), and (1) is an intermediate step introduced in Section 3.5.

4.1 Character Salience: *Pro*-drop vs. Non-*pro*-drop

The correct story character's salience compared to all other characters was calculated following Equation 4. For each verb, we calculated a salience value for the correct story character. See Appendix Table A6 for an example of the salience values of the last verb.

The distributions for the salience value obtained from three word embedding models and one baseline model are shown in Figure 3.

Single-sided nonparametric two-sample Wilcoxon Tests are carried out between *pro*-drop and non-*pro*-drop character salience of

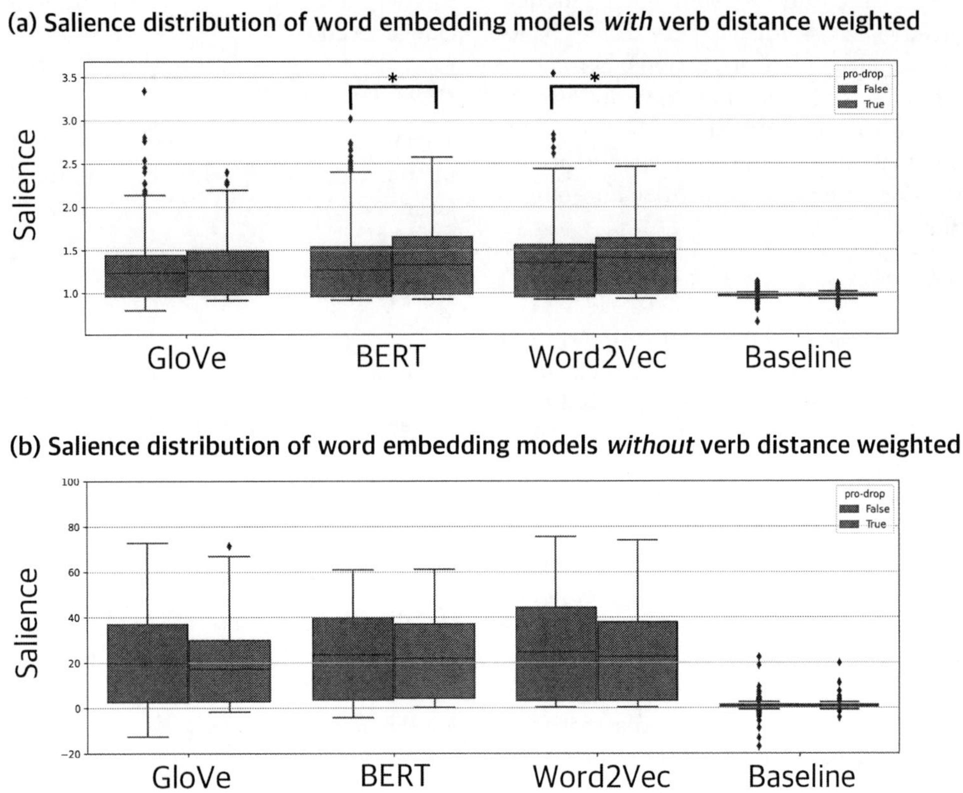

Figure 3: Salience distributions from the word embedding models: GloVe, BERT, Word2Vec, and Baseline. (a) Salience distribution based on distance-weighted models; (b) Salience distribution based on distance-unweighted models. The blue boxplots are *pro*-drop salience cases, and the red ones are non-*pro*-drop. The BERT and Word2Vec models show significant *pro*-drop > non-*pro*-drop effect, and GloVe model shows marginally significant result (See detailed Wilcoxon tests results in Table 3).

all three word embedding models and the baseline model. 422 cases are randomly selected from non-*pro*-drop salience values to match the size of the *pro*-drop ones, and this process is repeated 1000 times to gain the average statistic values. The test results are shown in Table 3. For distance-weighted models, BERT and Word2Vec show significant results ($p < 0.05$), and GloVe show marginally significant result ($p = 0.063$). For distance-unweighted models, none of them show significant results. The Wilcoxon test results based on ranged salience are shown in Table 3 in columns "range < 10/20/30 clauses" as compared to the non-ranged results in "range = all". As shown in the table, the effects of "*pro*-drop > non-*pro*-drop" on correct character salience tend to be larger when the salience is calculated based on ranged clauses. The Baseline model shows null effects on both distance-weighted and distance-unweighted models for all the ranged cases. As shown in Figure 3, the boxplots are consistent with the Wilcoxon tests.

4.2 Logistic Regression: Predict *Pro*-drop with Character Salience

With the salience values described in the previous section, the logistic regression model is applied to examine the effect of salience on *pro*-drop. 75% of the data are used as the training set, and 25% of the data are used as the testing set. See the prediction accuracy results in Table 4 based on salience values obtained from all-ranged and clause-ranged clauses. As shown in Table 4, except for the baseline model, all the distance-weighted language models' results show above chance (> 50%) accuracy.

As for distance-unweighted language models, only GloVe and Word2Vec show above chance results on all-ranged predictions. Similar to the "range-effect" shown in the previous section, it can be seen from the prediction results as well that ranged clauses' prediction accuracies tend to be slightly higher than non-ranged results.

5 Discussion

The main findings of this study are: (1) Compared with overtly expressed subjects, omitted subjects have higher verb-usage continuity. In this respect, they stand out among other story characters; (2) Clause distance plays a role in contextual information strength: With clause distance weighted, the *pro*-drop > non-*pro*-drop salience effects are statistically significant; (3) Constraining the range of candidates by clause recency appears to strengthen these effects.

These results validate Topic Chain theory (Tsao, 1977) by showing how verbs contribute to the discourse coherence that omitted pronouns depend on. The "ranged" recency effect indicates that local contextual coherence might play a more important role than whole-discourse-level coherence. This recency effect may also explain the better performance obtained by BERT and Word2Vec compared to GloVe, since GloVe word embeddings are obtained from discourse-level word co-occurrence statistical features, and BERT and Word2Vec are trained on comparably smaller scale contextual information.

It shall be noted that verb-usage continuity is not the only factor that conditions *pro*-drop. Other factors, including nonverbal lexical information and syntactic patterns *e.g.* with conjunctions, also support discourse coherence (Halliday and Hasan, 1976). In this light, it is remarkable that one factor on its own, verb-usage continuity, yields above-chance accuracy in predicting *pro*-drop.

6 Conclusion

This study quantifies character-verb usage continuity as an aspect of discourse that helps comprehenders resolve omitted pronouns. Omitted pronouns tend to show higher verb usage consistency compared to pronounced entities, and this effect is strengthened by clause recency.

Acknowledgements

This material is based upon work supported by the National Science Foundation under Grant No. 1903783.

References

Shisong Chen, Binbin Gu, Jianfeng Qu, Zhixu Li, An Liu, Lei Zhao, and Zhigang Chen. 2021. Tackling zero pronoun resolution and non-zero coreference resolution jointly. In *Proceedings of the 25th Conference on Computational Natural Language Learning*, pages 518–527.

Michael Alexander Kirkwood Halliday and Ruqaiya Hasan. 1976. Cohesion in English. *English Language Series, Longman, London.*

C-T James Huang. 1984. On the distribution and reference of empty pronouns. *Linguistic inquiry*, pages 531–574.

Yan Huang. 1994. *The syntax and pragmatics of anaphora: A study with special reference to Chinese.* Cambridge University Press.

Ryu Iida, Kentaro Inui, and Yuji Matsumoto. 2006. Exploiting syntactic patterns as clues in zero-anaphora resolution. In *Proceedings of the 21st International Conference on Computational Linguistics and 44th Annual Meeting of the Association for Computational Linguistics*, pages 625–632.

Ryu Iida, Kentaro Torisawa, Chikara Hashimoto, Jong-Hoon Oh, and Julien Kloetzer. 2015. Intra-sentential zero anaphora resolution using subject sharing recognition. In *EMNLP*, pages 2179–2189.

Jacob Devlin Ming-Wei Chang Kenton and Lee Kristina Toutanova. 2019. BERT: Pre-training of deep bidirectional transformers for language understanding. In *Proceedings of NAACL-HLT*, pages 4171–4186.

Fang Kong, Min Zhang, and Guodong Zhou. 2019. Chinese zero pronoun resolution: A chain-to-chain approach. *ACM Transactions on Asian and Low-Resource Language Information Processing (TALLIP)*, 19(1):1–21.

Alessandro Lenci. 2018. Distributional models of word meaning. *Annual review of Linguistics*, 4:151–171.

Charles N Li and Sandra A Thompson. 1979. Third-person pronouns and zero-anaphora in Chinese discourse. In *Discourse and syntax*, pages 311–335. Brill.

Shen Li, Zhe Zhao, Renfen Hu, Wensi Li, Tao Liu, and Xiaoyong Du. 2018. Analogical reasoning on Chinese morphological and semantic relations. In *Proceedings of the 56th Annual Meeting of the Association for Computational Linguistics (Volume 2: Short Papers)*, pages 138–143, Melbourne, Australia. Association for Computational Linguistics.

Wendan Li. 2004. Topic chains in Chinese discourse. *Discourse Processes*, 37(1):25–45.

Tomas Mikolov, Kai Chen, Greg Corrado, and Jeffrey Dean. 2013a. Efficient estimation of word representations in vector space. *arXiv preprint arXiv:1301.3781*.

Tomas Mikolov, Ilya Sutskever, Kai Chen, Greg S Corrado, and Jeff Dean. 2013b. Distributed representations of words and phrases and their compositionality. *Advances in neural information processing systems*, 26.

Jeffrey Pennington, Richard Socher, and Christopher D Manning. 2014. GloVe: Global vectors for word representation. In *Proceedings of the 2014 conference on empirical methods in natural language processing (EMNLP)*, pages 1532–1543.

Mohammad Taher Pilehvar and Jose Camacho-Collados. 2020. Embeddings in natural language processing: theory and advances in vector representations of meaning. *Synthesis Lectures on Human Language Technologies*, 13(4):1–175.

Ming-Ming Pu. 2019a. *Zero anaphora and topic chain in Chinese Discourse*. Routledge.

Ming-Ming Pu. 2019b. Zero anaphora and topic chain in Chinese discourse. In *The Routledge Handbook of Chinese Discourse Analysis*, pages 188–200. Routledge.

Peng Qi, Yuhao Zhang, Yuhui Zhang, Jason Bolton, and Christopher D Manning. 2020. Stanza: A python natural language processing toolkit for many human languages. In *Proceedings of the 58th Annual Meeting of the Association for Computational Linguistics: System Demonstrations*, pages 101–108.

Dan Sperber and Deirdre Wilson. 1986. *Relevance: Communication and cognition*, volume 142. Citeseer.

Kun Sun. 2019. The integration functions of topic chains in Chinese discourse. *Acta Linguistica Asiatica*, 9(1):29–57.

Fengfu Tsao. 1977. *A functional study of topic in Chinese: The first step towards discourse analysis*. Ph.D. thesis, USC, Los Angeles, California.

William SY Wang and Chaofen Sun. 2015. *The Oxford handbook of Chinese linguistics*. Oxford University Press.

xiaowangzi.org. 2021. 小王子网站. `http://www.xiaowangzi.org/`. Accessed: 2021-04-03.

A Appendix

Story character	Annotation Label	Number of Occurrence
the little prince	ch4_prince	676
the story teller	ch1_storyteller	356
the rose	ch12_rose	166
the king	ch18_king	71
the fox	ch28_fox	67
the planet	ch11_planet	62
the lamplighter	ch23_lighter	54
the sheep	ch5_sheep	48
the geologist	ch24_geologist	41
the grownups	ch3_grownups	39
the snake	ch26_snake	39
the businessman	ch22_shiyejia	37
readers	ch8_audience	30
the volcano	ch17_volcano	22
the baobab	ch9_tree	20
the drunk man	ch21_drunk	18
the conceited man	ch20_xurong	16
the travelers	ch31_traveler	15
the seed	ch10_grass	13
the explorer	ch25_explorer	13
the red-faced man	ch14_redface	11
the boa	ch2_boa	10
the switch man	ch29_switcher	10
the astronomer	ch6_universescholar	7
the echo	ch27_echo	5
the tiger	ch15_tiger	5
the drafts	ch16_wind	4
the train	ch30_train	4
the merchant	ch32_merchant	4
the children	ch13_kids	3
the general	ch19_general	3
the ruler	ch7_ruler	1

Table A1: The number of occurrence of each character in the annotated discourse

	Agent	**Patient**
***pro*-drop**	422	16
non-*pro*-drop	2032	1329
total number	2454	1345

Table A2: Distribution of annotated Agents and Patients in the whole discourse.

verb	回来
verb_id	16008
agent_character	ch4
pro_drop	False
ch1_prev_verbs	[只有, 看到, 想, 用, 画, 画, 让, 画,...]
ch2_prev_verbs	[咀嚼, 吞, 动弹, 消化, 消化, 开, 闭, 闭,...]
ch3_prev_verbs	[理解, 看, 懂, 需要, 解释, 劝, 靠, 弄,...]
ch4_prev_verbs	[朝, 望, 出现, 给, 像, 没有, 像, 干,...]
ch5_prev_verbs	[病, 需要, 像, 睡, 去, 用, 跑, 跑,...]
...	...
ch30_prev_verbs	[运载, 发, 往, 朝着, 开, 过]
ch31_prev_verbs	[寻找, 回来, 满意, 住, 追随, 追随, 睡觉, 打哈欠,...]
ch32_prev_verbs	[说道, 贩卖, 卖, 说]

Table A3: Example of Verb-Character table. (See a translation of this table in Table A4)

verb	come back
verb_id	16008
agent_character	ch4
pro_drop	False
ch1_prev_verbs	[have, see, want, use, draw, draw, let, draw,...]
ch2_prev_verbs	[chew, swallow, move, digest, digest, open, close, close,...]
ch3_prev_verbs	[understand, see, understand, need, explain, advise, lean, play,...]
ch4_prev_verbs	[turn, watch, show up, give, alike, (not) have, alike, do,...]
ch5_prev_verbs	[sick, need, alike, sleep, go, use, run, run,...]
...	...
ch30_prev_verbs	[carry, send, go, turn, drive, pass]
ch31_prev_verbs	[look up, come back, satisfy, live, follow, follow, sleep, yawn,...]
ch32_prev_verbs	[speak, sell, sell, say]

Table A4: Translation of Table A3: Example of Verb-Character table.

Relevance Regressor	(Non-weighted relevance, Weighted relevance)
rel_glove_ch1	(81.89066125531684, 0.32419914580071807)
rel_glove_ch2	(1.8756812506219913, 0.001503683756709864)
...	...
rel_glove_ch32	(0.8230171383397842, 0.001262691669193839)
rel_bert_ch1	(176.59183087820725, 0.6119750732174682)
rel_bert_ch2	(4.919826668243348, 0.0027848581443943223)
...	...
rel_bert_ch32	(0.867459723760406, 0.001329274033713714)
rel_word2vec_ch1	(134.572604613474, 0.4595537826115222)
rel_word2vec_ch2	(2.8936049625643223, 0.0020496541891822087)
...	...
rel_word2vec_ch32	(0.9999583161919829, 0.0015334960473239322)
rel_baseline_ch1	(-0.771830408650495, 0.008005141647819333)
rel_baseline_ch2	(-0.008373434318707955, 5.9110606393949324e-05)
...	...
rel_baseline_ch32	(0.08827132539725344, 0.00013526127447238275)

Table A5: Example of relevance results for the last verb

Regressor	Example value
verb	回来 (come back)
correct character	ch4
pro-drop	False
salience-glove-unweighted	45.761057
salience-bert-unweighted	57.886974
salience-word2vec-unweighted	56.125342
salience-baseline-unweighted	1.087911
salience-glove-weighted	1.206085
salience-bert-weighted	1.522071
salience-word2vec-weighted	1.427663
salience-baseline-weighted	0.979743

Table A6: Example of salience results for the last verb from three language models and one baseline model with distance-weighted/-unweighted

Online Neural Coreference Resolution with Rollback

Patrick Xia and **Benjamin Van Durme**
Human Language Technology Center of Excellence
Johns Hopkins University
{paxia, vandurme}@cs.jhu.edu

Abstract

Humans process natural language online, whether reading a document or participating in multiparty dialogue. Recent advances in neural coreference resolution have focused on offline approaches that assume the full communication history as input. This is neither realistic nor sufficient if we wish to support dialogue understanding in real-time. We benchmark two existing, offline, models and highlight their shortcomings in the online setting. We then modify these models to perform online inference and introduce *rollback*: a short-term mechanism to correct mistakes. We demonstrate across five English datasets the effectiveness of this approach against an offline and a naive online model in terms of latency, final document-level coreference F1, and average running F1.

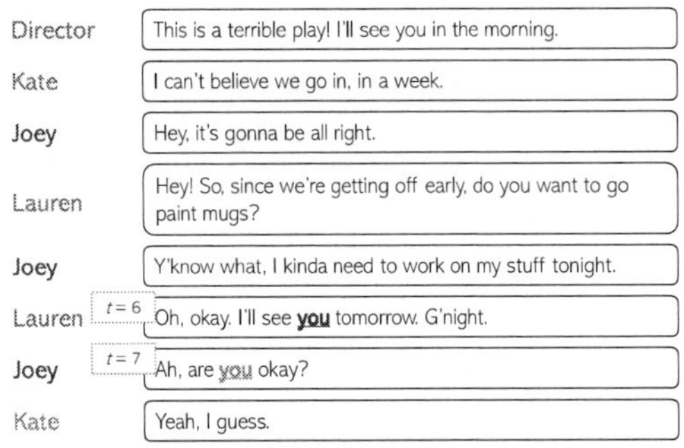

Figure 1: In this scene from *Friends*, viewers can deduce who "you" refers to at $t = 6$, and we want coreference models to be similarly capable. At $t = 7$, viewers may need more context, such as the identity of the next speaker, to be certain of who "you" refers to. Absent that context for a text-based model, its predictions will be incorrect. Our proposed *rollback* is a cheap and local revision mechanism that corrects these type of mistakes.

1 Introduction

In environments like multiparty spoken dialogue and social media streams, text in the form of tokens and sentences are available in (near) real-time. To promptly make use of this data, NLP systems often need to process text before additional tokens or sentences are available. For example, this could enable interruptions with a response or a clarification question (Boyle et al., 1994; Li et al., 2017), make decisions during a social media stream (Mathioudakis and Koudas, 2010), or recognize and translate speech live (Oda et al., 2014; Ma et al., 2020). While some language technologies operate incrementally in the *online* setting, many document-level understanding models and tasks do not.

A core task in language understanding is resolving references. Recent work has made significant progress on improving accuracy for single documents (Lee et al., 2017; Wu et al., 2020) and in the cross-document setting (Caciularu et al., 2021). However, this focus on document-level resolution makes use of global higher order inference and document-level encodings. As interest in coreference resolution is shifting back towards dialogue (Khosla et al., 2021), the *offline* setting is inconsistent with how dialogue is found in the real world. Now equipped with neural models and large-scale data, we revisit the *online* coreference resolution setting (Stoness et al., 2004; Schlangen et al., 2009).[1]

In this work, we are motivated by the human ability to resolve references *without looking into the future* (Figure 1). We simulate the online setting for two offline models (Xu and Choi, 2020; Xia et al., 2020) by making full predictions after each sentence and masking the future context. This either leads to significantly increased latency or lowered accuracy. We then modify the latter model to properly perform online inference and show that while accuracy does drop relative to the offline baselines, the latency is substantially lower. Finally, we propose *rollback*, a backtracking method which allows

[1]Xu and Choi (2022) recently explore the online setting in contemporaneous work.

Proceedings of the Fifth Workshop on Computational Models of Reference, Anaphora and Coreference (CRAC 2022), pages 13–21
Gyeongju, Republic of Korea, October 16–17, 2022.

the model to correct recently made decisions. On several coreference datasets, we show that this can recover performance comparable to that of the offline model with the latency of online models.

2 Task: Online Coreference Resolution

In offline (single doc) coreference resolution, the input is a document D, and the output is a set of clusters (or chains) of text mentions, $\mathcal{C} = \{C_1, ..., C_n\}$ such that any two mentions in a given C_i corefer. Evaluation can be performed at the document level, $S(\mathcal{C}_{\text{pred}}, \mathcal{C}_{\text{gold}})$, by comparing the predicted clusters to the gold reference clusters with an average of three corpus-level metrics, MUC (Vilain et al., 1995), B^3 (Bagga and Baldwin, 1998), and CEAF_{ϕ_4} (Luo, 2005), for the accuracy of mentions, links, and clusters. When each metric is instead computed at the corpus level instead before averaging, we refer to this as *final F1* (identical to CoNLL 2012 F1).

In the sentence-level online setting, $D = [X_1, X_2, ..., X_T]$ is a stream of sentences or utterances. After time t, we predict clusters $\mathcal{C}_{\text{pred},t} = \{C_{1,t}, ..., C_{n,t}\}$ conditioned on only $[X_1, ...X_t]$. For the reference clusters $\mathcal{C}_{\text{gold},t}$, we restrict clusters in $\mathcal{C}_{\text{gold},t}$ to contain only mentions up to sentence X_t. This may lead to empty clusters which are ignored when calculating the score.[2] To evaluate, we propose additionally using *running F1* for each document:

$$S_{\text{running}}(\mathcal{C}_{\text{pred}}, \mathcal{C}_{\text{gold}}) = \sum_{t=1}^{T} \frac{1}{T} S(\mathcal{C}_{\text{pred},t}, \mathcal{C}_{\text{gold},t}).$$

These document-level scores are subsequently averaged across the corpus (macro-average), in contrast to the already corpus-level metrics of *final F1*.

We are not the first to observe that references should be resolvable without future context. Prior work (Stoness et al., 2004; Schlangen et al., 2009; Poesio and Rieser, 2011) has also emphasized the importance of incremental (online) prediction of reference, especially in the context of dialogue. Since most models at that time already operated at the sentence level, their work is at the token-level granularity. Our work does not go as far; our goal is to first rein back *document* level neural models to the sentence level, which is still appropriate in applications where full utterances are available.

[2]Singletons may also be ignored depending on the dataset.

Dataset	Training	Dev	Test	Avg. sents
OntoNotes^{all}	2,802	343	348	26.8
OntoNotes$^{\text{conv.}}$	393	75	71	54.9
OntoNotes$^{\text{text.}}$	2,409	268	277	22.2
CI	987	122	192	19.0
LitBank	80	10	10	84.4
QBCoref	240	80	80	4.7

Table 1: Number of documents in each split for each corpus considered in this work. Avg. sents refers to number of sentences per document in the training set

Finally, we would like to compare the latency of different systems. Unlike token-level work in speech (Zhang et al., 2016) or translation (Gu et al., 2017), we are primarily interested in sentences, and we do not have readily available timestamps. Furthermore, modern models can process a single sentence in under a second, while sentences take substantially longer to be spoken or typed. Therefore, we mainly report document-level latency, which is the *wait time* between the end of the document and production of predictions. We revisit and discuss sentence-level latency in Section 4.4.

3 Method

3.1 Datasets

We select several coreference datasets to study, detailed in Table 1, that will let us analyze a variety of domains. We split the CoNLL 2012 Shared Task (OntoNotes) (Pradhan et al., 2013) into the conversational (telephone and broadcast conversations) and nonconversational text (newswire, newsgroups, broadcast news, weblogs, religious texts) genres. Character Identification (CI) (Zhou and Choi, 2018) consists of transcripts from the TV show *Friends* and is another source of social and informal conversations. LitBank (Bamman et al., 2020) is a collection of long excerpts from literature, which allows us to study latency scaling. Finally, QBCoref (Guha et al., 2015) is a collection of trivia questions where players are expected to interrupt with the answer, which is an example of a task needing a fast NLU model.

3.2 Models

We use Xu and Choi (2020) and Xia et al. (2020) as our offline baselines. We then modify the inference algorithm of the latter for our online experiments.[3]

[3]Code is available at `https://github.com/pitrack/incremental-coref`.

C2F (Xu and Choi, 2020) is a reimplementation of the coarse-to-fine coreference model (Lee et al., 2018) which detects mention spans in the entire document, scores them with each other, and finds the most likely antecedent for each span. It then uses higher order decoding strategies to promote pairwise consistency within a cluster. In this work, we do not use these decoding strategies as they are slower and only improve performance slightly. We do, however, use the extension to the training loss that accommodates singletons (Xu and Choi, 2021).

ICOREF (Xia et al., 2020) is a memory-efficient incremental coreference resolution model, itself a variant of the C2F model. They achieve this by segmenting the document into pieces that fit into a single SpanBERT (Joshi et al., 2020) window, incrementally processing each segment, and saving the set of found entity clusters after each step. Within each segment, they detect mention spans, find each span's most likely entity cluster, merge it (or form a new cluster), and update that cluster's embedding. After each text segment, the predictions for that segment are committed. This hard decision foregoes any higher-order decoding strategies, but this locality offered is exactly what we wish to extend in the sentence-level online setting.

Naive online C2F is a baseline where C2F is used to make full predictions after every sentence. For a document with n sentences, this costs n calls to the full C2F model, and effectively acts as an upper limit on model performance.

Online ICOREF For the online models, we choose to modify the inference process in ICOREF. This is because ICOREF already processes the document incrementally and it also foregoes global inference across all clusters. Like prior models, ICOREF encodes a variable number of sentences per encoder forward pass, and each sentence would have access to future contexts. To make this fully online, we modify the algorithm by segmenting the text by sentences instead of by tokens. Thus, instead of making predictions every fixed number of tokens (e.g. 512), the model makes predictions every u sentences. Setting $u = 1$ would make an online model at the sentence level.

Online ICOREF with rollback A drawback of both ICOREF and online modeling in general is the inability to correct mistakes in light of future context. We also introduce "rollback," which is run every r sentences (Algorithm 1). This process reverts all predictions made in the previous r sentence-window and remakes them all, batch-mode, with the full (r-sentence) context. The trade-off of increasing r is that the intermediate prediction quality can suffer, while decreasing r incurs additional latency.

Algorithm 1 Online coreference with rollback

Input: Sentences $S = s_1, s_2, \ldots$; update frequency u; rollback frequency r; initial clusters $\mathcal{C}_0 = \emptyset$.
for $s_t \in S$ **do**
  if $t \equiv 0 \pmod{ur}$ **then**
    $\mathcal{C}_{t-ur+1} = \text{REVERT}(\mathcal{C}_{t-1})$
    $\mathcal{C}_t = \text{ICOREF}(S[t-ur+1:t], \mathcal{C}_{t-ur+1})$
  else if $t \equiv 0 \pmod{u}$ **then**
    $\mathcal{C}_t = \text{ICOREF}(S[t-u+1:t], \mathcal{C}_{t-1})$
  else
    $\mathcal{C}_t = \mathcal{C}_{t-1}$
  yield $\mathcal{C}_t$

Δ Final F1	C2F		ICOREF	
Masked Training?	No	Yes	No	Yes
OntoNotes^{conv}	-7.8	-1.8	-8.0	-7.6
OntoNotes^{text}	-6.0	-0.3	-8.0	-6.9
LitBank	-5.3	-1.9	-5.1	-5.4
QBCoref	-4.9	-0.5	-1.1	-2.7
CI	-5.5	-1.0	-11.0	-9.6

Table 2: We train a model with and without sentence-level causal attention masks. We then report the difference in F1 between inference with and without this mask in the offline setting. Full numbers in Appendix C.

4 Experiments and Results

We first show that current models rely on future context, which is not readily available in the online setting. We demonstrate the effectiveness of online models under latency and average running F1. In particular, we analyze the benefits of rollback. Finally, we verify that for reasonable input stream speeds, online approaches are indeed appropriate.

4.1 Masking the future

We first investigate the reliance of the two baseline (offline) models, C2F and ICOREF, on future context. As shown in Figure 1, models often use future contexts to make predictions such as linking "you" with the next speaker. For each model, we consider applying a sentence-level causal mask in the encoder and remove any global decoding algorithms. The causal mask restricts each token's attention only to other tokens in its sentence or a previous one. With this mask at inference, we find that with

Metric	naive online C2F Run. F1	Fin. F1	wt (ms)	ICOREF Run. F1	Fin. F1	wt (ms)	Online ICOREF Run. F1	Fin. F1	wt (ms)	+ rollback Run. F1	Fin. F1	wt (ms)
OntoNotes^{conv}	79.2	77.0	237.8	24.9	76.2	319.3	74.8	72.7	52.0	76.6	75.2	79.0
OntoNotes^{text}	82.3	80.6	195.2	28.9	80.5	223.8	77.8	77.4	62.1	79.1	79.9	87.9
LitBank	73.8	72.2	807.4	54.5	72.7	173.3	71.9	70.6	73.5	72.6	71.3	93.7
QBCoref	76.6	70.5	107.9	15.6	71.9	82.3	72.5	71.1	45.8	72.7	71.6	54.9
CI	74.7	73.0	137.5	14.2	71.9	227.8	65.1	66.7	47.3	67.3	70.1	59.3

Table 3: Final F1, running F1, and wait time for each datasets and four inference algorithms. Our proposed rollback mechanism offers a strong compromise with higher F1s and comparable wait times vs. the fastest online models, and a final F1 comparable to offline ICOREF. Naive online C2F is the strongest method, but also the slowest.

Dataset	#Edits	Ment.	New	Existing
LitBank	453	12.1, 9.3	12.6, 10.4	27.2, 6.0
QBCoref	145	20.0, 8.3	16.6, 13.1	16.6, 7.6
CI	429	4.9, 4.4	17.0, 5.6	27.0, 13.3

Table 4: We classify the edits made in each dev set via rollback: **Ment**ion detection errors, missed **New** clusters, and incorrect links to **Existing** clusters. We report the percentage of (wrong→right, right→wrong) edits. The unreported fraction of edits are wrong→wrong. We omit OntoNotes because that dataset does not include singleton clusters, making this type of analysis difficult.

both models, performance drops considerably (Table 2). However, by training with the causal mask, the C2F model recovers from these drops in the masked setting. This suggests that coreference resolution models can be retrained to make better use of previous context and rely less on "easy" future signals. This finding is also quite promising for future investigation into *training* methods.

On the other hand, masked training does not affect the performance of the ICOREF model. Nonetheless, the incremental nature of ICOREF and ability to predict singletons is more amenable to extension to an online setting, and so we proceed with ICOREF without masking.

4.2 Online inference strategies

To properly evaluate online performance (as opposed to only simulating masking the future), we apply the modifications to ICOREF described in Section 3.2 and compare the running F1, final F1, and wait time. By increasing update sizes, u, we can interpolate between an online model ($u = 1$) and the unmasked offline ICOREF model (where u is the encoder window size). This "hybrid" mode trades off wait time for F1, as increasing u leads to longer wait times but better performance. In addition, we find that changing the rollback frequency does not correlate with wait time because larger updates are both costlier and rarer. So, we choose the best r based on each dev set.

Table 3 shows that the online models are faster than the offline ICOREF model and do better on running F1, but worse on final F1. Online with rollback is usually the best approach, as it achieves high F1 scores across all datasets, while it also has short wait times. Naive online C2F performs well on F1, but it is substantially slower on especially short or long documents.

The small margin on QBCOREF could be explained by the fact that the forward pass for online ICOREF is equal to that of a causally masked offline model and Table 2 shows that the gap between a masked and unmasked model is small.

4.3 Error correction with rollback

In Table 4, we calculate the number of predictions that are changed with rollback. In general, more edits are corrections (wrong→right) than errors (right→wrong), which demonstrates the effectiveness of rollback. For all three datasets, many of the corrections made address correctly assigning spans to existing clusters, such as the "you" in Figure 1. In QBCOREF, many corrections are un-predicting a non-mention, while in CI, many corrections are correctly predicting new starts of entity clusters.

4.4 Latency analysis

In this work, we assume that each sentence arrives after all computation has been completed for the previous sentence, which motivates our use of wait time as a metric. However, this assumption may not always be true in situations where utterances are highly frequent or short, like in online chat rooms.

To verify this empirically, we run simulations to find the token arrival speeds for which offline and online models have equivalent *sentence* latency (details in Appendix E). For all datasets, we find that this point is at over 200 words per second (wps). Additionally, if the stream is slower than 20 wps, there is never a "delay" caused by processing a sentence. This is substantially faster than the speaking (Yuan et al., 2006) and reading (Brysbaert, 2019) rates of around 3-5 wps. Therefore, sentence-level predictions are being made faster than tokens are produced, which validates our metric of wait time in this work. This may not extend to some settings with high arrival rates, like livestream comments.

5 Conclusion

We look at reining back document-level models for neural coreference resolution to the utterance level by proposing a shift towards online inference. We propose a model with the capability for making predictions online, after every sentence. This leads to lower latency than a corresponding offline model, and maintains a consistently high running F1 after each sentence. To edit predictions made without future context, we introduce a rollback mechanism which reverts and corrects recently made predictions, bringing the F1 closer to that of the offline model while maintaining its ability to make online predictions with low latency.

Future work may consider extensions to this approach by handling online processing at the word-level, revisiting the scenario considered by Schlangen et al. (2009).

Acknowledgements

We would like to thank Xutai Ma, Mahsa Yarmohammadi, and Boyuan Zheng for helpful feedback and discussion on this work. In addition, we appreciate the insightful comments and questions from the anonymous reviewers.

References

Amit Bagga and Breck Baldwin. 1998. Algorithms for scoring coreference chains. In *In The First International Conference on Language Resources and Evaluation Workshop on Linguistics Coreference*, pages 563–566.

David Bamman, Olivia Lewke, and Anya Mansoor. 2020. An annotated dataset of coreference in English literature. In *Proceedings of the 12th Language Resources and Evaluation Conference*, pages 44–54, Marseille, France. European Language Resources Association.

Elizabeth A Boyle, Anne H Anderson, and Alison Newlands. 1994. The effects of visibility on dialogue and performance in a cooperative problem solving task. *Language and speech*, 37(1):1–20.

Marc Brysbaert. 2019. How many words do we read per minute? a review and meta-analysis of reading rate. *Journal of memory and language*, 109:104047.

Avi Caciularu, Arman Cohan, Iz Beltagy, Matthew Peters, Arie Cattan, and Ido Dagan. 2021. CDLM: Cross-document language modeling. In *Findings of the Association for Computational Linguistics: EMNLP 2021*, pages 2648–2662, Punta Cana, Dominican Republic. Association for Computational Linguistics.

Jiatao Gu, Graham Neubig, Kyunghyun Cho, and Victor O.K. Li. 2017. Learning to translate in real-time with neural machine translation. In *Proceedings of the 15th Conference of the European Chapter of the Association for Computational Linguistics: Volume 1, Long Papers*, pages 1053–1062, Valencia, Spain. Association for Computational Linguistics.

Anupam Guha, Mohit Iyyer, Danny Bouman, and Jordan Boyd-Graber. 2015. Removing the training wheels: A coreference dataset that entertains humans and challenges computers. In *Proceedings of the 2015 Conference of the North American Chapter of the Association for Computational Linguistics: Human Language Technologies*, pages 1108–1118, Denver, Colorado. Association for Computational Linguistics.

Suchin Gururangan, Ana Marasović, Swabha Swayamdipta, Kyle Lo, Iz Beltagy, Doug Downey, and Noah A. Smith. 2020. Don't stop pretraining: Adapt language models to domains and tasks. In *Proceedings of the 58th Annual Meeting of the Association for Computational Linguistics*, pages 8342–8360, Online. Association for Computational Linguistics.

Mandar Joshi, Danqi Chen, Yinhan Liu, Daniel S. Weld, Luke Zettlemoyer, and Omer Levy. 2020. SpanBERT: Improving pre-training by representing and predicting spans. *Transactions of the Association for Computational Linguistics*, 8:64–77.

Mandar Joshi, Omer Levy, Luke Zettlemoyer, and Daniel Weld. 2019. BERT for coreference resolution: Baselines and analysis. In *Proceedings of the 2019 Conference on Empirical Methods in Natural Language Processing and the 9th International Joint Conference on Natural Language Processing (EMNLP-IJCNLP)*, pages 5803–5808, Hong Kong, China. Association for Computational Linguistics.

Sopan Khosla, Juntao Yu, Ramesh Manuvinakurike, Vincent Ng, Massimo Poesio, Michael Strube, and Carolyn Rosé. 2021. The CODI-CRAC 2021 shared task on anaphora, bridging, and discourse deixis in dialogue. In *Proceedings of the CODI-CRAC 2021 Shared Task on Anaphora, Bridging, and Discourse Deixis in Dialogue*, pages 1–15, Punta Cana, Dominican Republic. Association for Computational Linguistics.

Kenton Lee, Luheng He, Mike Lewis, and Luke Zettlemoyer. 2017. End-to-end neural coreference resolution. In *Proceedings of the 2017 Conference on Empirical Methods in Natural Language Processing*, pages 188–197, Copenhagen, Denmark. Association for Computational Linguistics.

Kenton Lee, Luheng He, and Luke Zettlemoyer. 2018. Higher-order coreference resolution with coarse-to-fine inference. In *Proceedings of the 2018 Conference of the North American Chapter of the Association for Computational Linguistics: Human Language Technologies, Volume 2 (Short Papers)*, pages 687–692, New Orleans, Louisiana. Association for Computational Linguistics.

Jiwei Li, Alexander H. Miller, Sumit Chopra, Marc'Aurelio Ranzato, and Jason Weston. 2017. Learning through dialogue interactions by asking questions. In *ICLR*.

Xiaoqiang Luo. 2005. On coreference resolution performance metrics. In *Proceedings of Human Language Technology Conference and Conference on Empirical Methods in Natural Language Processing*, pages 25–32, Vancouver, British Columbia, Canada. Association for Computational Linguistics.

Xutai Ma, Juan Pino, and Philipp Koehn. 2020. SimulMT to SimulST: Adapting simultaneous text translation to end-to-end simultaneous speech translation. In *Proceedings of the 1st Conference of the Asia-Pacific Chapter of the Association for Computational Linguistics and the 10th International Joint Conference on Natural Language Processing*, pages 582–587, Suzhou, China. Association for Computational Linguistics.

Michael Mathioudakis and Nick Koudas. 2010. Twittermonitor: Trend detection over the twitter stream. In *Proceedings of the 2010 ACM SIGMOD International Conference on Management of Data*, SIGMOD '10, page 1155–1158, New York, NY, USA. Association for Computing Machinery.

Yusuke Oda, Graham Neubig, Sakriani Sakti, Tomoki Toda, and Satoshi Nakamura. 2014. Optimizing segmentation strategies for simultaneous speech translation. In *Proceedings of the 52nd Annual Meeting of the Association for Computational Linguistics (Volume 2: Short Papers)*, pages 551–556, Baltimore, Maryland. Association for Computational Linguistics.

Massimo Poesio and Hannes Rieser. 2011. An incremental model of anaphora and reference resolution based on resource situations. *Dialogue Discourse*, 2:235–277.

Sameer Pradhan, Alessandro Moschitti, Nianwen Xue, Hwee Tou Ng, Anders Björkelund, Olga Uryupina, Yuchen Zhang, and Zhi Zhong. 2013. Towards robust linguistic analysis using ontonotes. In *Proceedings of CoNLL*.

David Schlangen, Timo Baumann, and Michaela Atterer. 2009. Incremental reference resolution: The task, metrics for evaluation, and a Bayesian filtering model that is sensitive to disfluencies. In *Proceedings of the SIGDIAL 2009 Conference*, pages 30–37, London, UK. Association for Computational Linguistics.

Scott C. Stoness, Joel Tetreault, and James Allen. 2004. Incremental parsing with reference interaction. In *Proceedings of the Workshop on Incremental Parsing: Bringing Engineering and Cognition Together*, pages 18–25, Barcelona, Spain. Association for Computational Linguistics.

Shubham Toshniwal, Patrick Xia, Sam Wiseman, Karen Livescu, and Kevin Gimpel. 2021. On generalization in coreference resolution. In *Proceedings of the Fourth Workshop on Computational Models of Reference, Anaphora and Coreference*, pages 111–120, Punta Cana, Dominican Republic. Association for Computational Linguistics.

Marc Vilain, John Burger, John Aberdeen, Dennis Connolly, and Lynette Hirschman. 1995. A model-theoretic coreference scoring scheme. In *Sixth Message Understanding Conference (MUC-6): Proceedings of a Conference Held in Columbia, Maryland, November 6-8, 1995*.

Wei Wu, Fei Wang, Arianna Yuan, Fei Wu, and Jiwei Li. 2020. CorefQA: Coreference resolution as query-based span prediction. In *Proceedings of the 58th Annual Meeting of the Association for Computational Linguistics*, pages 6953–6963, Online. Association for Computational Linguistics.

Patrick Xia, João Sedoc, and Benjamin Van Durme. 2020. Incremental neural coreference resolution in constant memory. In *Proceedings of the 2020 Conference on Empirical Methods in Natural Language Processing (EMNLP)*, pages 8617–8624, Online. Association for Computational Linguistics.

Patrick Xia and Benjamin Van Durme. 2021. Moving on from OntoNotes: Coreference resolution model transfer. In *Proceedings of the 2021 Conference on Empirical Methods in Natural Language Processing*, pages 5241–5256, Online and Punta Cana, Dominican Republic. Association for Computational Linguistics.

Liyan Xu and Jinho D. Choi. 2020. Revealing the myth of higher-order inference in coreference resolution. In *Proceedings of the 2020 Conference on Empirical Methods in Natural Language Processing (EMNLP)*, pages 8527–8533, Online. Association for Computational Linguistics.

Liyan Xu and Jinho D. Choi. 2021. Adapted end-to-end coreference resolution system for anaphoric identities in dialogues. In *Proceedings of the CODI-CRAC 2021 Shared Task on Anaphora, Bridging, and Discourse Deixis in Dialogue*, pages 55–62, Punta Cana, Dominican Republic. Association for Computational Linguistics.

Liyan Xu and Jinho D. Choi. 2022. Online coreference resolution for dialogue processing: Improving mention-linking on real-time conversations. In *Proceedings of the 11th Joint Conference on Lexical and Computational Semantics*, pages 341–347, Seattle, Washington. Association for Computational Linguistics.

Jiahong Yuan, Mark Liberman, and Christopher Cieri. 2006. Towards an integrated understanding of speaking rate in conversation. In *Ninth International Conference on Spoken Language Processing*.

Yu Zhang, Guoguo Chen, Dong Yu, Kaisheng Yao, Sanjeev Khudanpur, and James Glass. 2016. Highway long short-term memory rnns for distant speech recognition. In *2016 IEEE International Conference on Acoustics, Speech and Signal Processing (ICASSP)*, pages 5755–5759. IEEE.

Ethan Zhou and Jinho D. Choi. 2018. They exist! introducing plural mentions to coreference resolution and entity linking. In *Proceedings of the 27th International Conference on Computational Linguistics*, pages 24–34, Santa Fe, New Mexico, USA. Association for Computational Linguistics.

A Experimental Details

A.1 Datasets Preprocessing

We use the same preprocessing as Joshi et al. (2019) for OntoNotes, Xia and Van Durme (2021) for LitBank (first fold) and QBCoref (first fold), and Toshniwal et al. (2021) for CI. For the genre split in OntoNotes, we split the full dataset into a conversational and text-based component. Some weblog documents are conversations on message boards. We maintain this split because they are less conversational than spoken dialogue, and it is consistent with the split originally used in by ICOREF. While OntoNotes does have non-English splits, we only study English data in this work. To our knowledge, the datasets and codebases were released intended to advance research in coreference resolution, which is aligned with the focus of this work.

Since ICOREF does not readily take speaker embeddings, we augment the underlying text of CI with speakers by prepending each utterance with the name of the speaker(s), following the strategy outlined by Wu et al. (2020), and we only filter out these mentions before evaluation. We note that there could be other ways of representing the speakers, especially in plural situations, which we do not explore as it is beyond the scope of the work. While this follows the same preprocessing as Toshniwal et al. (2021), we do not do this for C2F, as this model uses the speakers as a feature. We do not evaluate CI following the metrics outlined in Zhou and Choi (2018) as we are primarily interested in exploring online coreference by using the dialogue and conversational nature of the dataset and not in the plural mentions and multiparty aspect.

A.2 Hyperparameters

We maintain all the default hyperparameters for both the C2F model[4] and ICOREF model.[5] For C2F, we train with and without mention detection loss (coefficient=1), depending on the dataset. At inference, we would also include positive scoring mentions in the predicted clusters. In addition, we follow the previous findings on continued training (Gururangan et al., 2020; Xia and Van Durme, 2021) by continuing training from the publicly released OntoNotes checkpoints of each model. We train each model once. Again, the goal of our short paper is to highlight online coreference resolution, specifically, online *inference*.

To that end, we explore several values of $u \in [1,2,3,4,5,6,7,8]$ and $r \in [2,4,5,6,8,\text{no rollback}]$ for each of the datasets. We plot u in Figure 2 to interpolate between the online and offline models. We select $r = 4$ for QBCoref, $r = 6$ for LitBank, and $r = 8$ for the other splits. Furthermore, following the findings in Section 4.1, we train all models with and without the causal mask. Models without the mask performs better.

For each test set and model (i.e. point in Figure 2), we run inference three times and take the *minimum* time rather than the average. We use minimum because in rare cases, one of the runs would be significantly slower, which would disproportionately affect the average. Overall, the mean difference between the max and min wait time across all datasets is around 10.5ms, or 12% relative to the min wait time, and the median is 5.8ms.

A.3 Computing Revisions

To compute revisions due to rollback in Section 4.3, we split each mention identified by the model either before or after rollback based on its gold reference antecedent: not a mention, first mention of a cluster, or part of another cluster. We count the number of revisions for the first two classes. For the third, we consider a cluster link correct if the

[4]`https://github.com/lxucs/coref-hoi`

[5]`https://github.com/pitrack/incremental-coref/`

Δ Final F1	C2F				ICOREF			
Masked Training?	No		Yes		No		Yes	
Masked Inference?	Yes	No	Yes	No	Yes	No	Yes	No
OntoNotes^{conv}	69.2	77.0	75.0	76.7	68.2	76.2	68.4	76.0
OntoNotes^{text}	74.7	80.6	79.9	80.2	72.5	80.5	73.4	80.3
LitBank	66.9	72.2	68.8	70.7	67.6	72.7	67.5	72.9
QBCoref	64.9	69.8	70.0	70.5	70.8	71.9	69.7	72.5
CI	67.6	73.0	71.8	72.8	60.9	71.9	61.2	70.9

Table 5: This is the full version of Table 2, on the test set. Each entry instead shows the score with mask and the score without mask instead of the difference

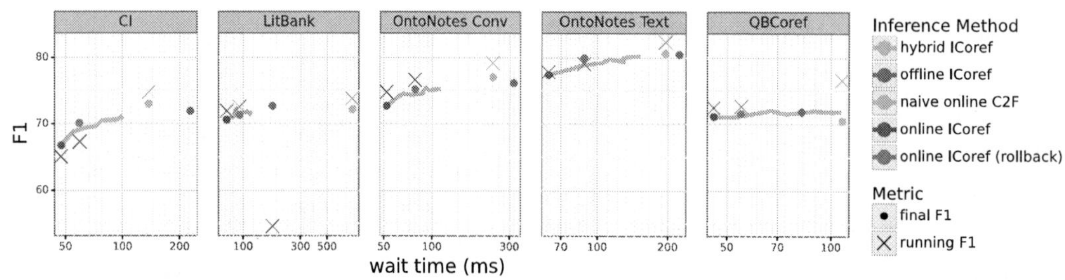

Figure 2: We plot the average wait time against the final F1 (test) and the running F1 (×) for select models. By varying the update frequency, we interpolate between **online** and **offline** ICOREF models in both final F1 and wait time.

majority of the predicted cluster overlaps with the reference cluster.

A.4 Compute

We run all experiments on a single NVIDIA RTX Quadro 6000 GPU. Training each model completes in under 24 hours, with some datasets like QBCoref taking significantly less times (under an hour). Inference runs in 1-5 minutes per trial. Because our focus was not on training (we trained each model only once and we leveraged continued training), we estimate we use around 15 GPU-days for all results presented in this paper, and not substantially (at most 3x) more than that in the development of this work. Each model is dominated by the size of SpanBERT-large (334M). C2F models have 381M parameters and ICOREF has 373M.

B Usage

Like any improvements to information extraction or natural language understanding technologies, malicious users can more easily automate harmful applications (e.g. illegal web scraping). For this work in particular, introducing an online coreference resolution model could make such applications even faster and shift the paradigm further towards harmful (algorithmically) online applications. Nonetheless, these coreference resolution models themselves are not a complete technology, and so the harms of this work are minimal. Both of the baseline models we use in this work and the subsequently released code are licensed under Apache 2.0.

C Masked Training and Inference

Table 5 is a more complete version of Table 2 from Section 4.1.

D Visual comparison of strategies

We can also visualize Table 3 in Figure 2, which shows several inference procedures. This figure more clearly shows that by modifying the rollback frequency, a hybrid inference method can be chosen to favor a purely online approach or a slower, offline approach.

E Latency

To compute sentence-level latency, we assume each (sub)token arrives uniformly at a specified rate. When the last token of a sentence arrives, if the model decides to process the preceeding chunk, we simulate running inference over the previous sentence(s). In parallel, we assume tokens continue arriving.

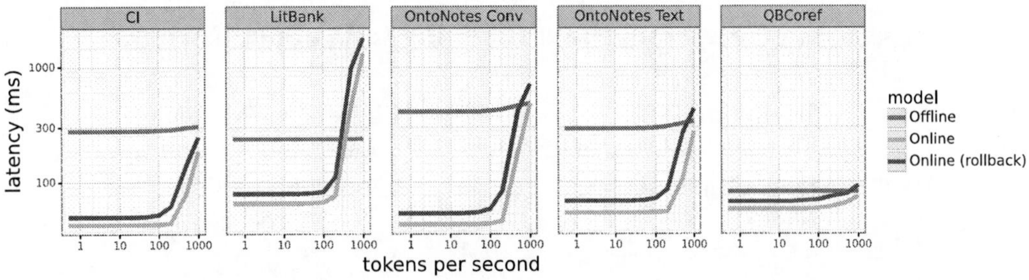

Figure 3: Simulated mean sentence-level latency given different token arrival rates.

We compute the latency between the end of *each sentence* and when the predictions *for that sentence* are produced by the simulated model. Since ICOREF is sequential, if the model is due to process a segment before the previous one is completed, the next segment is blocked until the previous one is complete.

We run inference once to obtain the size of the job for each of these segments, and then simulate sentence-level latency with different rates. We do this for just the online and offline ICOREF models, as the goal is to gain some intuition over token arrival rates and these were usually the fastest and slowest. The results are plotted in Figure 3

Analyzing Coreference and Bridging in Product Reviews

Hideo Kobayashi*
Human Language Technology Research Institute
University of Texas at Dallas
Dallas, TX USA
hideo@hlt.utdallas.edu

Christopher Malon
NEC Laboratories America
Princeton, NJ USA
malon@nec-labs.com

Abstract

Product reviews may have complex discourse including coreference and bridging relations to a main product, competing products, and interacting products. Current approaches to aspect-based sentiment analysis (ABSA) and opinion summarization largely ignore this complexity. On the other hand, existing systems for coreference and bridging were trained in a different domain. We collect mention type annotations relevant to coreference and bridging for 498 product reviews. Using these annotations, we show that a state-of-the-art factuality score fails to catch coreference errors in product reviews, and that a state-of-the-art coreference system trained on OntoNotes does not perform nearly as well on product mentions. As our dataset grows, we expect it to help ABSA and opinion summarization systems to avoid entity reference errors.

1 Introduction

To help consumers and businesses make sense of high volumes of product reviews, the NLP community has developed techniques for aspect based sentiment analysis (ABSA) (Pontiki et al., 2014, 2016), and, more recently, opinion summarization (Amplayo et al., 2022). These techniques have developed mostly without addressing challenges in coreference (Aone and William, 1995) or bridging (Clark, 1975).

In aspect based sentiment analysis (ABSA), aspect categories and associated polarities are extracted (Pontiki et al., 2016). In one subtask of SemEval 2016 Task 5, this is done on a per-sentence basis without awareness of the product being reviewed. In the other, the full review is available, but entity comparisons are not explicitly peformed. This approaches poses a danger when a customer mentions a competing product or interacting product in the review, because aspects pertaining to the competing product may be falsely associated with the main product.

As a multi-document summarization task with extractive (Angelidis et al., 2021) and abstractive (Chu and Liu, 2019; Suhara et al., 2020) approaches, opinion summarization may create coreference errors by quoting a pronoun out of context (extractive) or hallucinating a sentence with entities confused (abstractive). Factuality checking (Laban et al., 2022; Scialom et al., 2021) promises more correct summaries, either by postprocessing outputs judged to be logically inconsistent (Cao et al., 2020), or by providing a training signal for contrastive learning (Wan and Bansal, 2022). As we show in section 4, a state-of-the-art natural language inference (NLI)-based factuality score often fails to capture coreference errors.

Because existing ABSA and factuality scores do not learn to catch coreference or bridging errors adequately, a new resource is necessary. De Clercq and Hoste (2020) released coreference annotations on restaurant reviews, but this domain mostly lacked the mentions of competitors and interacting products found in product reviews. In this paper, we define a mention classification task for product reviews which simplifies the coreference and bridging resolution tasks. Our simplified task reduces labeling burden compared to labeling all pairs of mentions. Minimally trained crowdworkers are able to assign our labels with good agreement. We collected labels for 8,894 mentions in 498 reviews already, and plan to continue collecting labels from 3,000 reviews. The size of the dataset currently may be adequate only for evaluation, but we plan to collect more data which will make it useful for development.

Our contributions are: (1) simplifying coreference and bridging for product reviews into a task for which we can obtain quality labels from crowdworkers, (2) constructing a dataset for this task, (3) showing the weakness of a state-of-the-art factu-

*Work performed at NEC Laboratories America.

Proceedings of the Fifth Workshop on Computational Models of Reference, Anaphora and Coreference (CRAC 2022), pages 22–30
Gyeongju, Republic of Korea, October 16–17, 2022.

ality score on detecting confused entity mentions in product reviews, and (4) preliminary analysis of an existing coreference system applied to our annotated data. Once enough data for training is collected, we envision that ABSA or NLI systems might use predicted mention types as features, so that *e.g.* an ABSA system would recognize a sentence discussing an attribute of a competing product and not report it as an aspect of the product being reviewed, or a factuality score would catch entity inconsistency between source and generated text.

2 Dataset

We annotated 498 electronics reviews from the Amazon Review Dataset (McAuley et al., 2015; He and McAuley, 2016), consisting of reviews posted from May 1996 to July 2014. We use the electronics category as we expect the reviews in this category to include competing products and interacting items frequently. The rating for each review is given, and we retrieved the product name from the Rainforest API.[1]

3 Annotation

3.1 Annotation Scheme

Rather than asking workers to annotate mention pairs, we identify the *main product* by the name of the product being reviewed, and ask the workers to annotate every mention in the review by whether it is identical to the *main* product, a *competing* product, a product *interacting* with the main product or competitors, or a *generic* term for the category of the main product. Four corresponding bridging-related mention types are annotated for mentions that refer to a *part or attribute* of one of these categories. Every other mention is annotated with the ninth type, *others*. Appendix A gives detailed definitions of our nine mention types, with examples.

In this way, a mention type specifies less information than a true coreference or bridging relation. We expect the antecedent of every coreference relation to be labeled with the same mention type, and the antecedent of every bridging relation to be labeled with a corresponding mention type. While the "main product" type usually will consist of a single coreference cluster, multiple, non-identical competing products or interacting products may be mentioned.

For each of the 498 reviews, we automatically extract mentions and crowdworkers annotate mention types. We use the mention detection sieve in the Stanford's Multi-Pass Sieve Coreference Resolution System (Lee et al., 2013; Recasens et al., 2013) to extract mentions, including singletons. We filter out personal mentions[2] because our annotation scheme is not concerned with them.

3.2 Annotation Procedure & Agreement

Reviews with Mixed Sentiments. To collect competing, generic, and interacting mentions more efficiently, we filter the source reviews as follows. A review with 2 to 4 stars overall could have mixed sentiments because it talks about both pros and cons of the main product, but we expect that 1 or 5 star reviews with mixed sentiments say only negative (or positive) things about the main product so that positive (or negative) sentiments must refer to a competing, generic, or interacting product. Thus, we take the mixed-sentiment reviews with 1 or 5 stars to obtain source data likely to include more competing, generic, or interacting products.

Hence, we train a sentence-level sentiment analysis classifier to find reviews containing sentences with mixed sentiments. We employ RoBERTa-base and pre-train the model on a noisy-labeled training datasets, which consists of electronics reviews from the Amazon review dataset. We use 4 or 5 stars as positive and 1 or 2 stars as negative instances. These are noisy data because positive (or negative) instances could include negative (or positive) sentences. Then, we fine-tune the model on a clean sentence-level sentiment dataset generated by Wang et al. (2019) using SemEval 2016 Task 5 (Pontiki et al., 2016). We use their laptop domain. As a result, 61.1% of 1 star reviews and 46.7% of 5 star reviews are classified as ones with mixed sentiments.

Crowdsourcing Task We collect annotations via crowdsourcing on Amazon Mechanical Turk (AMT).[3] Workers are given a review that contains 15 to 20 mentions, where we add a sentence, "I bought {product name}," at the beginning of the review to help the annotator understand the review text. Then, we ask three workers to select a mention type for each mention in a review. Workers are required to pass a qualification test and are soft-

[1] https://www.rainforestapi.com

[2] We filter out personal pronouns and relative person noun phrases (e.g., *The husband)* using a lexical resource in Hou et al. (2014).

[3] https://www.mturk.com

Docs	Sentences	Tokens	Mentions
498	3,883	63,184	8,894

Table 1: Statistics on dataset.

Mention Type	Counts
Main	2864
P/A of Main	1512
Competing	429
P/A of Competing	103
Generic	193
P/A of Generic	18
Interacting	853
P/A of Interacting	308
Others	2127

Table 2: Distribution of mention types for agreed mentions (including the given product title, which is automatically labeled).

blocked if their agreement with majority labels is worse than 85%. We focus on *agreed* mentions, meaning those on which a majority (2 of 3) of workers agreed on a label.

Our annotated dataset is available as supplementary data to the paper.

3.3 Resulting Dataset & Agreement Study

Table 1 shows dataset statistics. In total, eleven crowdworkers annotated 8,894 mentions in 498 reviews. The resulting distribution of labels is shown in Table 2. As can be seen, bridging labels are less frequent than their non-bridging counterparts. For both kinds, the interacting is the second most frequent and the competing is the third most frequent label.

We use Cohen's kappa (Cohen, 1960) to measure inter-annotator agreement. For each mention, we order three annotators in the order of submission time, and use all pairs of three annotators for calculating agreement. Over all pairs, the agreement between the earlier annotator and the later annotator is substantial: kappa is .681 [4].

4 Do factuality scores detect coreference errors?

Using our dataset, we can construct examples that test a factuality score's ability to accept coreference-consistent substitution of entities and reject inconsistent substitions. For NLI-based factuality checking, we apply the SummaC zero shot (ZS) system (Laban et al., 2022). We consider one version in which it computes implication using each sentence individually, and another version in which the whole review document is used as a single premise for implication. Although the original paper suggested that sentence-level granularity could be beneficial, the document-level granularity may have a better chance of following coreference and bridging relations across sentences. Both versions are trained on MNLI (Williams et al., 2018) plus Vitamin C (Schuster et al., 2021).

Orig.	Repl.	Consis.	Inconsis.
Main	Main	100%	
Main	Competing		83%
Main	Interacting		93%
Competing	Competing	75%	
Competing	Main		82%
Competing	Interacting		93%
Interacting	Interacting	45%	
Interacting	Main		100%
Interacting	Competing		100%

Table 3: Rates at which substitutions were manually verified as consistent or inconsistent.

Original	Replacement	Label	Accuracy
Main	Main	Consis.	100%
Main	Competing	Inconsis.	20%
Main	Interacting	Inconsis.	38%
Competing	Competing	Consis.	87%
Competing	Main	Inconsis.	44%
Competing	Interacting	Inconsis.	50%
Interacting	Interacting	Consis.	89%
Interacting	Main	Inconsis.	32%
Interacting	Competing	Inconsis.	100%

Table 4: SummaC-ZS results.

We test the SummaC-ZS score on our annotated product reviews as follows. For the mention categories "Main product," "Competing product," and "Interacting product," we take sentences that contain the second or subsequent mentions of these categories (so that coreference antecedents are likely), and construct one sentence in which we replace that mention with the main product name, or the first mention of a competing product, or the first mention of an interacting product. The task is to determine whether this generated sentence is factually correct or not. One consistent replacement and one inconsistent replacement was generated from each of 60 reviews. Replacements whose type agrees with the original mention are usually expected to be correct and replacement across categories are expected to be incorrect, but in case they are not,

[4]See Appendix B for more agreement study

	MUC			B3			CEAF4			
	P	R	F1	P	R	F1	P	R	F1	AVG F1
OntoNotes	85.9	85.5	85.7	79.0	78.9	79.0	76.7	75.2	75.9	80.2
Main	68.3	59.5	63.6	63.1	48.3	54.7	50.5	68.1	58.0	58.8
Competing	37.1	27.4	31.6	43.7	28.8	34.7	57.7	40.6	47.7	38.0
Generic	22.2	11.8	15.4	32.3	14.0	55.0	19.6	18.8	28.0	21.0

Table 5: Coreference results. The metrics are MUC, B^3, and $CEAF_{\phi 4}$ as well as the average F1 of these metrics.

the ground truth is manually checked by an author and disagreements are filtered out. Examples of the replacements are shown in Appendix C.

Table 3 reports the rate at which each substitution was verified by an author to be consistent. One major reason a replacement within the same category can fail to be consistent is the presence of non-identical mentions within the category. This occurs with 20% of Competing and 55% of Interacting substitutions. The remaining 5% of disagreements on Competing substitutions are due to the annotation error. A major reason why a replacement with another category fails to be inconsistent is that machine's replacements are correctly done, but the resulting sentence is still consistent based on human's interpretation. This occurs with all disagreements on Main, 9% of Competing replaced with Main, and all of Competing replaced with Interacting. The other 9% of Competing replaced with Main are due to annotation error.

The SummaC-ZS models were tested on the manually verified NLI pairs. Table 4 shows the accuracies achieved with document granularity on test examples of replacements of each mention type, using a score threshold of .5. Inconsistent substitutions are mostly not caught. Varying the threshold of the models to alter the bias, we obtained an AUC of .721 using sentence granularity and .770 using document granularity.

Everything in the generated text but the entity mention exactly matches the source text. Hence, there are no semantic challenges apart from the entity resolution. Therefore, this result shows significant room for improvement in distinguishing non-coreferent entities.

5 Evaluating Pre-trained Coreference

We evaluate the coreference clusters output by the system of Xu and Choi (2020) against the clusters consisting of all mentions of three types: main, competing, and generic. Generally these mention types will consist of a union of coreference clusters. To associate coreference clusters output by the system to one of these mention types, we take the union of all the clusters intersecting the mention type. Therefore recall failures will occur only when a mention fails to be detected or is not recognized as an anaphor to be linked to anything. Good recall means that the mentions of the category were recognized as potential anaphors. A precision failure with respect to these mention types indicates an error in which the coreference system links a mention with an antecedent of a different type.

We use the coreference model in Xu and Choi (2020) with the SpanBERT-Large encoder trained on OntoNotes 5.0[5] and set all parameters as in the original paper. Table 5 reports MUC, B^3, and $CEAF_{\phi 4}$ for types that have more than mention.

The model achieves lower AVG F1 in Competing and Generic compared to Main. From the mention distribution in Table 2, we see that randomly chosen product mentions are more likely to be annotated as Main, making it easier to get higher precision than Competing or Generic, which correctly match fewer mentions. Additionally, there may be non-identical mentions within the Competing and Generic categories, possibly contributing singleton cluster predictions which are filtered out even if the mention type overall contains multiple entities. Although Main is likely to have identical mentions, the model still underperforms in AVG F1 compared to OntoNotes, possibly due to difficulty recognizing the lengthy product names as anaphora, or other challenges applying a model trained on news articles to the product review domain.

6 Conclusion

We presented a new corpus of 498 electronics product reviews with a relaxed form of coreference and bridging annotation. We tested an OntoNotes-based coreference system on the reviews, and used the annotations to measure how much a factuality score failed to detect coreference errors on product

[5]https://catalog.ldc.upenn.edu/LDC2013T19

reviews. As more data is collected, we hope the resource will be useful to help ABSA and opinion summarization systems avoid entity reference errors in analyzing product reviews.

References

Reinald Kim Amplayo, Arthur Bravzinskas, Yoshihiko Suhara, Xiaolan Wang, and Bing-Quan Liu. 2022. Beyond opinion mining: Summarizing opinions of customer reviews. *Proceedings of the 45th International ACM SIGIR Conference on Research and Development in Information Retrieval.*

Stefanos Angelidis, Reinald Kim Amplayo, Yoshihiko Suhara, Xiaolan Wang, and Mirella Lapata. 2021. Extractive opinion summarization in quantized transformer spaces. *Transactions of the Association for Computational Linguistics*, 9:277–293.

Chinatsu Aone and Scott William. 1995. Evaluating automated and manual acquisition of anaphora resolution strategies. In *33rd Annual Meeting of the Association for Computational Linguistics*, pages 122–129.

Meng Cao, Yue Dong, Jiapeng Wu, and Jackie Chi Kit Cheung. 2020. Factual error correction for abstractive summarization models. In *Proceedings of the 2020 Conference on Empirical Methods in Natural Language Processing (EMNLP)*, pages 6251–6258, Online. Association for Computational Linguistics.

Eric Chu and Peter J. Liu. 2019. Meansum: A neural model for unsupervised multi-document abstractive summarization. In *ICML*.

Herbert H Clark. 1975. Bridging. In *Theoretical issues in natural language processing*.

Jacob Cohen. 1960. A coefficient of agreement for nominal scales. *Educational and psychological measurement*, 20(1):37–46.

Orphée De Clercq and Veronique Hoste. 2020. It's absolutely divine! can fine-grained sentiment analysis benefit from coreference resolution? In *Proceedings of the Third Workshop on Computational Models of Reference, Anaphora and Coreference*, pages 11–21.

Ruining He and Julian McAuley. 2016. Ups and downs: Modeling the visual evolution of fashion trends with one-class collaborative filtering. In *proceedings of the 25th international conference on world wide web*, pages 507–517.

Yufang Hou, Katja Markert, and Michael Strube. 2014. A rule-based system for unrestricted bridging resolution: Recognizing bridging anaphora and finding links to antecedents. In *Proceedings of the 2014 Conference on Empirical Methods in Natural Language Processing (EMNLP)*, pages 2082–2093.

Philippe Laban, Tobias Schnabel, Paul N. Bennett, and Marti A. Hearst. 2022. SummaC: Re-visiting NLI-based models for inconsistency detection in summarization. *Transactions of the Association for Computational Linguistics*, 10:163–177.

Heeyoung Lee, Angel Chang, Yves Peirsman, Nathanael Chambers, Mihai Surdeanu, and Dan Jurafsky. 2013. Deterministic coreference resolution based on entity-centric, precision-ranked rules. *Computational linguistics*, 39(4):885–916.

Julian McAuley, Christopher Targett, Qinfeng Shi, and Anton Van Den Hengel. 2015. Image-based recommendations on styles and substitutes. In *Proceedings of the 38th international ACM SIGIR conference on research and development in information retrieval*, pages 43–52.

Maria Pontiki, Dimitris Galanis, Haris Papageorgiou, Ion Androutsopoulos, Suresh Manandhar, Mohammad AL-Smadi, Mahmoud Al-Ayyoub, Yanyan Zhao, Bing Qin, Orphée De Clercq, Véronique Hoste, Marianna Apidianaki, Xavier Tannier, Natalia Loukachevitch, Evgeniy Kotelnikov, Nuria Bel, Salud María Jiménez-Zafra, and Gülşen Eryiğit. 2016. SemEval-2016 task 5: Aspect based sentiment analysis. In *Proceedings of the 10th International Workshop on Semantic Evaluation (SemEval-2016)*, pages 19–30, San Diego, California. Association for Computational Linguistics.

Maria Pontiki, Dimitris Galanis, John Pavlopoulos, Harris Papageorgiou, Ion Androutsopoulos, and Suresh Manandhar. 2014. SemEval-2014 task 4: Aspect based sentiment analysis. In *Proceedings of the 8th International Workshop on Semantic Evaluation (SemEval 2014)*, pages 27–35, Dublin, Ireland. Association for Computational Linguistics.

Marta Recasens, Marie-Catherine De Marneffe, and Christopher Potts. 2013. The life and death of discourse entities: Identifying singleton mentions. In *Proceedings of the 2013 conference of the North American chapter of the association for computational linguistics: human language technologies*, pages 627–633.

Tal Schuster, Adam Fisch, and Regina Barzilay. 2021. Get your vitamin C! robust fact verification with contrastive evidence. In *Proceedings of the 2021 Conference of the North American Chapter of the Association for Computational Linguistics: Human Language Technologies*, pages 624–643, Online. Association for Computational Linguistics.

Thomas Scialom, Paul-Alexis Dray, Sylvain Lamprier, Benjamin Piwowarski, Jacopo Staiano, Alex Wang, and Patrick Gallinari. 2021. QuestEval: Summarization asks for fact-based evaluation. In *Proceedings of the 2021 Conference on Empirical Methods in Natural Language Processing*, pages 6594–6604, Online and Punta Cana, Dominican Republic. Association for Computational Linguistics.

Yoshihiko Suhara, Xiaolan Wang, Stefanos Angelidis, and Wang-Chiew Tan. 2020. OpinionDigest: A simple framework for opinion summarization. In *Proceedings of the 58th Annual Meeting of the Association for Computational Linguistics*, pages 5789–5798, Online. Association for Computational Linguistics.

David Wan and Mohit Bansal. 2022. FactPEGASUS: Factuality-aware pre-training and fine-tuning for abstractive summarization. In *Proceedings of the 2022 Conference of the North American Chapter of the Association for Computational Linguistics: Human Language Technologies*, pages 1010–1028, Seattle, United States. Association for Computational Linguistics.

Hao Wang, Bing Liu, Chaozhuo Li, Yan Yang, and Tianrui Li. 2019. Learning with noisy labels for sentence-level sentiment classification. *arXiv preprint arXiv:1909.00124*.

Adina Williams, Nikita Nangia, and Samuel Bowman. 2018. A broad-coverage challenge corpus for sentence understanding through inference. In *Proceedings of the 2018 Conference of the North American Chapter of the Association for Computational Linguistics: Human Language Technologies, Volume 1 (Long Papers)*, pages 1112–1122, New Orleans, Louisiana. Association for Computational Linguistics.

Liyan Xu and Jinho D Choi. 2020. Revealing the myth of higher-order inference in coreference resolution. *arXiv preprint arXiv:2009.12013*.

A Examples of Mention Types

Main Product. The main product is a phrase that refers to the product being reviewed.

(1) I bought *a Canon EOS 90D camera*. I love **this product** so much. **It** has amazing lenses.

Competing Product. The competing product is a phrase that refers to something a reviewer might purchase (or already did purchase) as an alternative to the main product.

(2) I bought *Sennheiser Headphone*. The sound quality is poor. **My Phillips headphones** have better sound quality.

(3) I bought *Anker speaker*. After going through reviews of **the different products**, I decided to go with this little monster.

Generic Term. The generic term is a phrase that refers to a general class of products to which the main product belongs.

(4) I bought *Sony speaker*. So I was thinking about getting **a small portable bluetooth speaker** for some time.

Part-of/Attribute-of Main Product. This indicates a phrase that is a part or attribute of the product being reviewed.

(5) I bought *Sennheiser Headphone*. But, **the cable** easily get tangled.

(6) I bought *Apple iPhone 13 Silicone Case*. I like **its color**.

Part-of/Attribute-of Competing Product. This indicates a phrase that is a part or attribute of the competing product.

(7) I bought *a Surface Laptop*. I like my old macbook because **its keyboard** is easy to type.

Part-of/Attribute-of Generic Term. This indicates a phrase that is a part or attribute of the general class to which the main product belongs, not specifically the main product.

(8) I bought *a Surface Laptop 11-inch*. I've been thinking to buy a 11-inch laptop, but I was worried if **the screen** is too small. Turned out it's good enough.

Interacting Item. The interacting item is a phrase that refers to an item that are used with the main product, competing product, or generic term.

(9) I bought *Samsung monitor*. I used **my HDMI cable** to connect with a laptop, but **the cable** was broken.

Part-of/Attribute-of Interacting Item. This indicates a phrase that is a part or attribute of the interacting item.

(10) I bought *Samsung monitor*. I used my laptop with this monitor, but it did not work. I typed on **the keyboard** of the laptop ...

Others. This indicates a phrase that is not any of above types.

B Agreement Study

To investigate which parts of our annotation scheme are well-defined and well understood, Table 6 shows the confusion matrix for annotations on agreed mentions, where rows correspond to workers' annotations and columns correspond to the majority label. Many generic mentions are thought to refer to the main product, and a part or attribute of a generic mention may be confused with a particular (main or competing) product.

C Examples of substitutions for factuality checking

Here we give some examples that we constructed to test whether SummaC-ZS recognized consistent and inconsistent substitution of entities.

C.1 Substitutions we tested

Generally, we expect substitution by the same mention type to result in consistent hypotheses and substitution by different mention types to result in inconsistent hypotheses. Here are two such examples that were included in our test dataset:

Replacing competing product by competing product:

- *Review*: I bought Creative Labs Vado Pocket Video Camcorder (Pink) OLD MODEL (Discontinued by Manufacturer). I purchased this as a gift for a business associate and I had planned to buy a pile more to create some low budget video fun. Sadly, the Vado was better in theory than in reality. The video was super

	Main	P/A of Main	Com	P/A of Com	Gen	P/A of Gen	Int	P/A of Int	Oth
Main	95.05	1.68	1.71	0.65	5.35	0	0.78	0.11	0.96
P/A of Main	2.09	89.2	0.62	4.85	1.55	5.56	1.37	5.09	3.98
Com	0.54	0.13	90.6	1.29	4.84	3.7	0.55	0.22	0.25
P/A of Com	0.04	0.4	1.48	83.82	0.52	3.7	0.16	0.87	0.41
Gen	0.62	0.35	2.87	0.97	84.11	3.7	0.86	0.87	0.24
P/A of Gen	0.03	0.26	0.08	2.27	1.21	81.48	0.04	0.43	0.16
Int	0.45	0.99	0.7	0.32	0.86	0	91.01	7.58	1.22
P/A of Int	0.11	1.54	0.16	1.94	0.35	0	3.09	80.52	1.22
Oth	1.07	5.45	1.79	3.88	1.21	1.85	2.15	4.33	91.57

Table 6: Confusion matrix on agreed mentions.

fuzzy and seemed out of focus. My associate and I played with it for a couple days trying to get the video to be in focus but we never got it to look right. **I bought a Flip and it worked great.** Sadly the Flip used AA batteries and was more expensive but at least the video was in focus...

- *Hypothesis*: I bought a Flip and **a Flip** worked great.
- *Human judgment*: Consistent

Replacing competing product by main product:

- *Review*: I bought Creative Labs Vado Pocket Video Camcorder (Pink) OLD MODEL (Discontinued by Manufacturer). I purchased this as a gift for a business associate and I had planned to buy a pile more to create some low budget video fun. Sadly, the Vado was better in theory than in reality. The video was super fuzzy and seemed out of focus. My associate and I played with it for a couple days trying to get the video to be in focus but we never got it to look right. **I bought a Flip and it worked great.** Sadly the Flip used AA batteries and was more expensive but at least the video was in focus...
- *Hypothesis*: I bought a Flip and **Creative Labs Vado Pocket Video Camcorder** worked great.
- *Human judgment*: Inconsistent

C.2 Substitutions eliminated from testing

Our automatic procedure also constructed substitutions such as the following, but based on human validation, they were not tested. In the first example, even though the mention types agreed, the authors judged the resulting hypothesis as inconsistent:

Replacing competing product by competing product:

- *Review*: I bought Olympus Camedia D535 3.2 MP Digital Camera with 3x Optical Zoom. Cute, nice display but apparently too easy to delete pix. 90 shots disappeared. I am no amateur. I have owned Casio, HP, (3) Sony Mavicas, Nikon 4300, and some cheapo that I threw away. **Still use the Mavicas and Nikon.** The tiny xD memory chip is small and difficult to handle, and it is in the battery case and you drop out batteries. Either the memory stick deleted itself or the delete sequence was initiated without my knowledge or realization. This is something I have never had happen before. Not happy camper.
- *Hypothesis*: Still use **Casio, HP** and Nikon.
- *Human judgment*: Inconsistent

In the second example, even though the mention types disagreed, the authors judged the resulting hypothesis as consistent:

Replacing competing product by interacting product:

- *Review*: I bought Hakuba DMSP-SD4 Media-case for Digital Memory. I have three Hakuba cases, and as Amazon conveniently pointed out, I've ordered this very before. Unfortunately, what I received this time around is not what was pictured. **Instead it is black (definitely NOT the color I would have wanted (too difficult to see in my gear), does not have a retaining strap of any sort (though, for me, this is unecessary), and finally it certainly doesn't seem like it's as "substantial" as my other Hakuba cases.** If this is what is available, then so be it. However, please understand that when shopping online, pictures are all we have to decide what product to purchase. Given a choice between what I received and what was pictured, I would have never chosen what I received.

- *Hypothesis*: Instead it is black (definitely NOT the color I would have wanted (too difficult to see in my gear), does not have a retaining strap of any sort (though, for me, this is unecessary), and finally it certainly doesn't seem like it's as "substantial" as **my gear**.

- *Human judgment*: Consistent

Anaphoric Phenomena in Situated Dialog: A First Round of Annotations

Sharid Loáiciga[1] **Simon Dobnik**[1] **David Schlangen**[2]
[1]CLASP, Department of Philosophy, Linguistics and Theory of Science,
University of Gothenburg, Sweden
[2]Computational Linguistics, Department of Linguistics, University of Potsdam, Germany
`{sharid.loaiciga, simon.dobnik}@gu.se`,
`david.schlangen@uni-potsdam.de`

Abstract

We present a first release of 500 documents from the multimodal corpus *Tell-me-more* (Ilinykh et al., 2019) annotated with coreference information according to the ARRAU guidelines (Poesio et al., 2021). The corpus consists of images and short texts of five sentences. We describe the annotation process and present the adaptations to the original guidelines in order to account for the challenges of grounding the annotations to the image. 50 documents from the 500 available are annotated by two people and used to estimate inter-annotator agreement (IAA) relying on Krippendorff's α.

1 Introduction

Coreference resolution—linking together all referring expressions that refer to the same discourse entity—has a long tradition in computational linguistics. The progress is undeniable as evidenced by recent systems (Joshi et al., 2019; Kirstain et al., 2021), particularly in the text domain, rich in news data. Coreference resolution work for dialog and spoken data in general, on the other hand, has been less predominant, as the phenomena in this genre are broader and harder to tackle (Khosla et al., 2021). However, interest in tackling these challenges is possible thanks to the creation of new resources. Situated dialog corpora—dialog about an image presented as common ground to the dialog participants—is part of these recent resources. Dialog text approximates natural conversations, while the image constraints an otherwise unlimited choice of entities and events in the dialog.

In this paper, we present a first release of a portion of the multimodal corpus *Tell-me-more* (Ilinykh et al., 2019) annotated with coreference information according to the ARRAU guidelines (Poesio et al., 2021). The *Tell-me-more* corpus consists of images accompanied with a short English text of five complete sentences, collected by asking participants to describe the image to a friend. An example is presented in (1). The genre of these texts is therefore in between standard text (as found in news text for example) and dialog data which reflects the features found in conversations rather than written conventions. The simplicity of the text is essential for our purposes, as it allows us to test the limits of the guidelines to account for reference and grounding. In contrast, standard situated dialog is very rich in changes of point of reference, spacial references, and dynamic references depending on the participant's cognitive state that are very challenging to ground to the image.

(1) 1. There is four chair red laquer dining set shown in the image. 2. There are opened white french doors leading to the outside showing. 3. There is a pool with blue water showing through the french doors. 4. The pools is surrounded by green shrubbery. 5. The wood floor is covered with white paint.[1]

We discuss some of the changes to the baseline guidelines necessary to account for the challenges of grounding the annotations while following standard anaphora annotation. This release comprises 500 documents. From those, 50 documents are double annotated and used to estimate inter-annotator agreement (IAA).[2]

[1]Note that the examples have been transcribed with their original spelling errors and disfluencies. The English speakers who provided the data were recruited through Amazon Mechanical Turk and their IP addresses limited to the US.

[2]The annotations are publicly available at `https://`

Proceedings of the Fifth Workshop on Computational Models of Reference, Anaphora and Coreference (CRAC 2022), pages 31–37
Gyeongju, Republic of Korea, October 16–17, 2022.

2 Related Work

Anaphora resolution for situated dialog is a relatively unexplored area, reflected in the few resources available for it. The insufficiency of corpora hinders the learning from gold data which is standard in machine learning and has driven researchers to propose alternative strategies. Working with the VisDial dataset (Das et al., 2017), Kottur et al. (2018) use automatic coreference links generated with an out-of-the-box system[3], while Yu et al. (2019) annotate 5000 documents using workers recruited through crowd-sourcing. Li and Moens (2021), on their part, propose an unsupervised approach relying on heuristics by adding POS tags embeddings and sentence position embeddings in order to guide the system into learning noun antecedents. Note that these three papers deal with pronouns only, since they are frequent in the dialog genre.

Liu and Hockenmaier (2019) and Plummer et al. (2017), on their part, propose automatic methods to ground the entities in the text to specific regions in the image.

There exist other corpora whose textual part comprises question answer pairs (Antol et al., 2015; Goyal et al., 2017). Unlike dialog data, question answer pairs are short, with few opportunities for re-mention of the different objects in the image and hence coreference. There is also corpora designed towards navigation and location involving videos and long dialog interactions between an instruction giver and an instruction follower. Examples include the SCARE corpus (Stoia et al., 2008) and the corpus by Thomason et al. (2019). On a similar venue, recent work has used Minecraft[4] to collect dialog where an architect gives instructions to a builder about how to move and position some pieces in order to achieve a target structure (Narayan-Chen et al., 2019; Jayannavar et al., 2020). Due to the multiple changes in reference perspective and very long dialog games, this type of corpora is more difficult to annotate than the corpus used in this paper. In this sense, we see our work as a stepping stone towards achieving the annotation of more complex data in the future.

doi.org/10.5281/zenodo.7084861

[3]https://github.com/huggingface/neuralcoref

[4]https://www.minecraft.net/en-us

Average	Annotator A	Annotator B
tokens	48.16	48.16
mentions	13.72	17.08
singletons	9.38	12.4
chains	1.74	1.84
non-referring	1.86	2.02
bridging	2.64	3.4

Table 1: Annotators statistics averaged over 50 documents. We consider each set of 5 sentences a document.

3 The Annotation Process

The annotation was carried out by two annotators with a background in computational linguistics. The MMAX annotation tool (Müller and Strube, 2006) was chosen with the aim to replicate the ARRAU scheme easily.

3.1 Markables

Text Mentions. Annotators start by identifying the referring expressions or mentions to annotate. Following ARRAU, we consider all noun phrases (NPs) and instruct annotators to mark the complete NP with all its modifiers and not just its head. This includes NPs which are non-referring such as pleonastic NPs and also NPs not re-mentioned later in the text (singletons). The mentions also include personal pronouns and demonstrative pronouns used as deictics (to refer back to non-nominal antecedents).

Unlike ARRAU, the mention identification process is done entirely by hand. The absence of automatic preprocessing to detect the mentions resulted in a different number of mentions per annotator, as shown in Table 1. In addition, the annotators had a relatively high disagreement rate on the mentions boundaries, but not on the overall number of mentions, as the documents are short and simple. We analyze these disagreements further in Section 4.

Image Objects. The image, on its part, is processed automatically in order to detect objects and mark them with bounding boxes. In *Tell-me-more*, the object labels are part of the underlying ADE20K data (Zhou et al., 2017), extracted using tools from Schlangen (2019).

Mention Attributes. The morphosyntactic properties of the mention are annotated, including gender (female, male, neutre)[5], number (singular, plural, mass) and person (1st, 2nd, 3rd), and its semantic type (person, animate, concrete, space, time, plan (for actions), abstract, or unknown). We include all these categories used in ARRAU.

An additional attribute of our own is *cardinality*. This accounts for a common strategy consisting on grouping things in order to refer to them collectively. In other words, objects can be created dynamically as the dialog progresses. The *cardinality* attribute has the values *unique* and *group*. The first refers to single individual objects while groups refer to entities composed by several objects. The value *group* is used for cases where the speaker refers to a specific region of the image containing several entities together, for example, *a four chair red laquer [sic] dinning set* in example (1) which is grammatically singular but conceptually plural.

3.2 Reference

As mentioned, ARRAU covers a broad range of anaphoric relations including both non-referring and referring NPs. Distinguishing between these two is non-trivial, and research around ARRAU have argued in favour of annotating both types (Poesio, 2016; Yu et al., 2020).

Non-referring. This includes mentions with a specific syntactic or semantic function: predication, expletive, idiom, incomplete or fragmentary expression, quantifier, and coordination. Following ARRAU, we keep all these types of non-referential mentions.

Referring. If a mention is identified as referring, then its information status needs to be annotated as *discourse-new* or *discourse-old*; discourse-old information needs to point to an antecedent.[6] This distinction signals whether an entity is mentioned a first or a subsequent time.

Referring mentions can form coreference chains, a group of mentions pointing to the same entity, a central construct in the anaphora resolution domain. Built on top of the document as a unit, this notion relies on and in turn informs theories about accessibility hierarchy and salience of entities (Ariel, 1988, 2004; Grosz et al., 1995).

One key principle in these theories is that some referring expressions are used to introduce entities (discourse-new) and some others to refer back to them (discourse-old). In situated dialog, in addition to the textual context, the image provides additional context, constraining the amount of referents and their perceived status by the participants depending on the task in which they are presented (Allopenna et al., 1998). We illustrate this contrast with (2) below. Typically, pronouns are the form of choice for discourse-old entities that have been previously introduced by another expression with lexical meaning. The text in (2), however, starts with *It*. This is possible because the image provides the context and this source of reference ought to be accounted for differently in the annotation than a typical discourse-old case referring back to a *phrase* or *segment* antecedent such as the *it* in sentence 2.

(2) 1. It s a well-lit kitchen with stainded wooden cupboards. 2. There's a microwave mounted over the stove, which has a red tea kettle on it. 3. The appliances are black and stainless steel in the kitchen. 4. The countertops look like they're black granite. 5. The window has sunlight streaming in and it 's very brightly light.

In order to keep these cases distinct, we introduced the value *task* for the *It* in sentence 1. This means that a discourse-old entity can have distinct types of antecedents: *phrase*, *segment*, or *task*. Our reasoning is that although the pronoun *It* does not have an antecedent in the text, it appears in the first position of the first sentence because the speaker was probably referring back to the *the image* in the instructions "Describe the image to a friend...".

3.2.1 Bridging

Another referential relationship included in the ARRAU guidelines is bridging, an associative relationship between two mentions (Versley et al., 2016). When a mention is referential, our annotation indicates whether it is also a related object of some other entity. The *Tell-me-more* corpus is rich in examples of the *part-of* bridging relationship: "An object that stands in a part-of relation to an object previously mentioned" (Artstein and Poesio, 2006). Since the corpus uses pictures of different rooms in a house, after a room is introduced, a series of objects belonging to that room follow, creating many opportunities for using a bridging reference mechanism. For instance, imagine your surprise if the second sentence of example (3) started with *the toaster* instead of *the bed*. Coherence will be immediately broken.

[5] Since the texts are in English, most NPs are marked as neutre.

[6] An antecedent can always be annotated as *ambiguous* if a clear entity cannot be identified for a particular mention.

(3) 1. This is a bedroom with a twin sized bed in it. 2. The bed has a blue bag laying on it and a green bad on the floor at the foot of the bed. 3. There is a nightstand aside of the bed with a water bottle on it. 4. There is an arched closet space on one wall and an arched shelving area too. 5. There is a small lamp attached to the wall at the head of the bed.

3.3 Grounding

The ARRAU scheme provides a basic grounding scheme that serves our purposes well (Artstein and Poesio, 2006). In this scheme, the objects in an image have a pre-determined id which can be associated with the text mentions of that object. In our annotation, we take the labels of the bounding boxes as the objects ids. We also differentiate between visible objects with a bounding box and visible objects without a bounding box. For all objects with a corresponding bounding box, the specific object id is linked to its mention in the text.

For bridging references, mentions in a *part-of* relation which do not have a bounding box of their own are grounded to the object that they are a part-of. For example, if the object 'the base of the bathtub' does not have a bounding box, but the object 'the bathtub' does, then 'the base of the bathtub' is grounded to 'the bathtub'.

4 Measuring Agreement

This release contains 500 annotated documents by one annotator and 50 annotated by two. In this section, we detail the computation of the inter-annotator agreement (IAA) using the 50 documents which have been doubled annotated.

Computing IAA for coreference resolution is non-trivial, as annotators need to decide on the mentions boundaries and also which ones belong together in a chain. Following Passonneau (2004), we report Krippendorff's α with weighted δ:

$$\alpha = 1 - \frac{pD_O}{pD_E} = 1 - \frac{rm-1}{m-1} \frac{\sum_i \sum_b \sum_{c>b} n_{b_i} n_{c_i} \delta_{bc}}{\sum_b \sum_c n_b n_c \delta_{bc}} \quad (1)$$

Where m is the number of annotators, and r is the number of coding units, i.e., mentions. For every pair of mentions b and c, δ_{bc} is the distance between the sets formed by their tokens; n_{b_i} is the number of times the value b was assigned by each annotator to each mention i. The distance between the mentions' tokens is 0 when the mentions' tokens are identical, 0.33 when one set subsumes the other, 0.67 when one intersects the other, and 1 when they are disjoint.

To compute Eq. 1, we code our annotations as described in Passonneau (2004), who relies on a predefined number of coding units in order to compute the set distance δ between mentions. Since we do not have predefined mentions because annotators were asked to identify the mentions boundaries by hand, we compute IAA at the token level. This means that our scores are potentially penalized because irrelevant tokens are treated as their own sets.[7]

We compute Krippendorff's α per document and obtained an average of 0.5550. There is a lot of variation, however, with the lowest $alpha$ value at 0 and the maximum at 1, and $\sigma = 0.2263$. Results per document are reported in Table 2.

Doc. id	α	Doc. id	α
8	0.6925	220	0
10	0.4669	237	0.5635
15	0.5641	245	0.6277
26	0.5807	249	0.6212
34	1	251	0
40	0	253	0.6285
53	0.5084	260	0.5921
55	0.7038	266	0.6061
57	0.5955	302	0.6293
62	0.622	311	0.8971
74	0.723	316	0.6737
81	0.6864	340	0.6748
83	0.393	372	0.6146
93	0.6359	387	0.6215
102	0.5319	406	0.1689
107	0	411	0.7609
115	0.4806	416	0.5965
136	0.6077	440	0.5316
163	0.6058	444	0.7366
167	0.6214	445	0.6853
168	0	457	0.4266
176	0.6434	465	0.717
186	0.3105	477	0.7302
196	0.6759	488	0.6225
198	0.7137	500	0.661
average	0.5550		

Table 2: Krippendorff-α for 50 documents double annotated with coreference information following the ARRAU corpus guidelines.

The IAA results obtained are very mixed. The low scores of some documents are partly explained by our choice to do the mention identification completely by hand. This means that the annotators had to decide the boundaries of each mention, yielding

[7]As an illustration, consider the example in (4). Here the tokens *{Mostly, is, is, has, a, and, and, , is, on, is}* are left non-annotated by annotator A; while *{Mostly, is, is, has, and, and, is, on, is}* by annotator B. This is expected as they do not form part of any of their identified mentions, but by scoring at the token level, each set would then be taken as forming a "mention" and hence compared.

imperfect matches even if they agreed on the underlying mention. In the future, we plan to process the text with an automatic mention detection tool and measure our annotations with respect to the tool's output.

4.1 Examples

In this section we present two examples of documents with αs of 0.5807 and 0.

(4) 1. Mostly [[this room]] is [[a bed]]. 2. [[There]] is [[a lamp on a small white nightstand next to the bed.]] 3. [[The bed]] has [a [light blue bed skirt]] and [[white comforter]] and [[4 white pillows]]. 4. [[There]] is [[a blue dresser with a lamp] on [it]]. 5. [[There]] is [[a full length window with vertical shades]].

In this example, we consider the maximal spans for each annotator.[8] Annotator A's annotations are shown with cyan brackets while Annotator B's with blue ones. The example shows that they agree in almost all the boundaries, with disagreements only on sentence 3 *a* and sentence 4 *it*. This also creates a disagreement with the corresponding coreferential chain: for annotator A, the *it* in sentence 4 is coreferential with *a blue dresser with a lamp*; for annotator B, this is part of the singleton *a blue dresser with a lamp on it*.

An α score of 0 occurs when the document does not have any chains, or when at least one of the annotators decided not to annotate anything. This scenario happens when the quality of the text data is unsatisfactory (5).

(5) 1. two beds 2. blue wall 3. three paintings 4. one window 5. tan wall

5 Differences with ARRAU

The annotation guidelines for ARRAU were designed to include a broad range of anaphoric phenomena found in many genres. Our documents are much simpler and the scale of our annotation much smaller, at least at the moment. Issues included in ARRAU but not included here comprise genericity, min words arguments (the head word of a mention), grammatical function, embedded arguments, and any type of complex structure requiring automatic parse of the texts.

[8]Mentions may contain embedded mentions.

6 Conclusion

In this paper, we presented the first release of a portion of the *Tell-me-more* corpus manually annotated with anaphora information according to standard guidelines used for the task of coreference resolution. We also presented IAA scores on 50 documents annotated by two people with training in computational linguistics. Our resource is the first of its kind, although its size is small. However, we believe that it can support linguistic studies about the relationship between textual anaphora and reference to objects, and that it can contribute to research on bridging reference. In addition, it can be used as validation data for automatic methods developed for grounding the entities in the text to the image. This is still work in progress and we look forward to future cycles of revisions and updates of our guidelines in the near-future.

Acknowledgements

The authors thank Sebastiano Gigliobianco for his support setting up the MMAX tool and annotating a large portion of the data. We also thank Philine Huß for her annotation work.

References

Paul D. Allopenna, James S. Magnuson, and Michael K. Tanenhaus. 1998. Tracking the time course of spoken word recognition using eye movements: Evidence for continuous mapping models. *Journal of Memory and Language*, 38(4):419–439.

Stanislaw Antol, Aishwarya Agrawal, Jiasen Lu, Margaret Mitchell, Dhruv Batra, C. Lawrence Zitnick, and Devi Parikh. 2015. VQA: Visual Question Answering. In *Proceedings of the IEEE International Conference on Computer Vision (ICCV)*.

Mira Ariel. 1988. Referring and accessibility. *Journal of Linguistics*, 24(1):65–87.

Mira Ariel. 2004. Accessibility marking: Discourse functions, discourse profiles, and processing cues. *Discourse Processes*, 37(2):91–116.

Ron Artstein and Massimo Poesio. 2006. Arrau annotation manual (trains dialogues).

Abhishek Das, Satwik Kottur, Khushi Gupta, Avi Singh, Deshraj Yadav, José MF Moura, Devi Parikh, and Dhruv Batra. 2017. Visual dialog. In *Proceedings of the IEEE Conference on Computer Vision and Pattern Recognition*, pages 326–335.

Yash Goyal, Tejas Khot, Douglas Summers-Stay, Dhruv Batra, and Devi Parikh. 2017. Making the V in VQA matter: Elevating the role of image understanding in Visual Question Answering. In *Conference on Computer Vision and Pattern Recognition (CVPR)*.

Barbara J. Grosz, Aravind K. Joshi, and Scott Weinstein. 1995. Centering: A framework for modelling the local coherence of discourse. *Computational Linguistics*, 2(21):203–225.

Nikolai Ilinykh, Sina Zarrieß, and David Schlangen. 2019. Tell me more: A dataset of visual scene description sequences. In *Proceedings of the 12th International Conference on Natural Language Generation*, pages 152–157, Tokyo, Japan. Association for Computational Linguistics.

Prashant Jayannavar, Anjali Narayan-Chen, and Julia Hockenmaier. 2020. Learning to execute instructions in a Minecraft dialogue. In *Proceedings of the 58th Annual Meeting of the Association for Computational Linguistics*, pages 2589–2602, Online. Association for Computational Linguistics.

Mandar Joshi, Omer Levy, Luke Zettlemoyer, and Daniel Weld. 2019. BERT for coreference resolution: Baselines and analysis. In *Proceedings of the 2019 Conference on Empirical Methods in Natural Language Processing and the 9th International Joint Conference on Natural Language Processing (EMNLP-IJCNLP)*, pages 5803–5808, Hong Kong, China. Association for Computational Linguistics.

Sopan Khosla, Juntao Yu, Ramesh Manuvinakurike, Vincent Ng, Massimo Poesio, Michael Strube, and Carolyn Rosé. 2021. The CODI-CRAC 2021 shared task on anaphora, bridging, and discourse deixis in dialogue. In *Proceedings of the CODI-CRAC 2021 Shared Task on Anaphora, Bridging, and Discourse Deixis in Dialogue*, pages 1–15, Punta Cana, Dominican Republic. Association for Computational Linguistics.

Yuval Kirstain, Ori Ram, and Omer Levy. 2021. Coreference resolution without span representations. In *Proceedings of the 59th Annual Meeting of the Association for Computational Linguistics and the 11th International Joint Conference on Natural Language Processing (Volume 2: Short Papers)*, pages 14–19, Online. Association for Computational Linguistics.

Satwik Kottur, José M. F. Moura, Devi Parikh, Dhruv Batra, and Marcus Rohrbach. 2018. Visual coreference resolution in visual dialog using neural module networks. In *The European Conference on Computer Vision (ECCV)*.

Mingxiao Li and Marie-Francine Moens. 2021. Modeling coreference relations in visual dialog. In *Proceedings of the 16th Conference of the European Chapter of the Association for Computational Linguistics: Main Volume*, pages 3306–3318, Online. Association for Computational Linguistics.

Jiacheng Liu and Julia Hockenmaier. 2019. Phrase grounding by soft-label chain conditional random field. In *Proceedings of the 2019 Conference on Empirical Methods in Natural Language Processing and the 9th International Joint Conference on Natural Language Processing (EMNLP-IJCNLP)*, pages 5112–5122, Hong Kong, China. Association for Computational Linguistics.

Christoph Müller and Michael Strube. 2006. Multi-level annotation of linguistic data with MMAX2. In Sabine Braun, Kurt Kohn, and Joybrato Mukherjee, editors, *Corpus Technology and Language Pedagogy: New Resources, New Tools, New Methods*, pages 197–214. Peter Lang, Frankfurt a.M., Germany.

Anjali Narayan-Chen, Prashant Jayannavar, and Julia Hockenmaier. 2019. Collaborative dialogue in Minecraft. In *Proceedings of the 57th Annual Meeting of the Association for Computational Linguistics*, pages 5405–5415, Florence, Italy. Association for Computational Linguistics.

Rebecca J. Passonneau. 2004. Computing reliability for coreference annotation. In *Proceedings of the Fourth International Conference on Language Resources and Evaluation (LREC'04)*, Lisbon, Portugal. European Language Resources Association (ELRA).

Bryan A. Plummer, Liwei Wang, Chris M. Cervantes, Juan C. Caicedo, Julia Hockenmaier, and Svetlana Lazebnik. 2017. Flickr30k entities: Collecting region-to-phrase correspondences for richer image-to-sentence models. *International Journal of Computer Vision*, 123:74 – 93.

Massimo Poesio. 2016. Linguistic and cognitive evidence about anaphora. In Massimo Poesio, Roland Stuckardt, and Yannick Versley, editors, *Anaphora Resolution: Algorithms, Resources and Applications*, pages 23–54. Springer-Verlag, Berlin Heidelberg.

Massimo Poesio, Maris Camilleri, Paloma Carretero-Garcia, and Ron Artstein. 2021. Arrau 3 annotation manual.

David Schlangen. 2019. Natural language semantics with pictures: Some language & vision datasets and potential uses for computational semantics. In *Proceedings of the 13th International Conference on Computational Semantics - Long Papers*, pages 283–294, Gothenburg, Sweden. Association for Computational Linguistics.

Laura Stoia, Darla Magdalene Shockley, Donna K. Byron, and Eric Fosler-Lussier. 2008. SCARE: a situated corpus with annotated referring expressions. In *Proceedings of the Sixth International Conference on Language Resources and Evaluation (LREC'08)*, Marrakech, Morocco. European Language Resources Association (ELRA).

Jesse Thomason, Michael Murray, Maya Cakmak, and Luke Zettlemoyer. 2019. Vision-and-dialog navigation. In *Conference on Robot Learning (CoRL)*.

Yannick Versley, Massimo Poesio, and Simone Ponzetto. 2016. Using lexical and encyclopedic knowledge. In Massimo Poesio, Roland Stuckardt, and Yannick Versley, editors, *Anaphora Resolution: Algorithms, Resources and Applications*, pages 397–429. Springer-Verlag, Berlin Heidelberg.

Juntao Yu, Alexandra Uma, and Massimo Poesio. 2020. A cluster ranking model for full anaphora resolution. In *Proceedings of the 12th Language Resources and Evaluation Conference*, pages 11–20, Marseille, France. European Language Resources Association.

Xintong Yu, Hongming Zhang, Yangqiu Song, Yan Song, and Changshui Zhang. 2019. What you see is what you get: Visual pronoun coreference resolution in dialogues. In *Proceedings of the 2019 Conference on Empirical Methods in Natural Language Processing and the 9th International Joint Conference on Natural Language Processing (EMNLP-IJCNLP)*, pages 5123–5132, Hong Kong, China. Association for Computational Linguistics.

Bolei Zhou, Hang Zhao, Xavier Puig, Sanja Fidler, Adela Barriuso, and Antonio Torralba. 2017. Scene parsing through ade20k dataset. In *2017 IEEE Conference on Computer Vision and Pattern Recognition (CVPR)*, pages 5122–5130.

Building a Manually Annotated Hungarian Coreference Corpus: Workflow and Tools

Noémi Vadász
Hungarian Research Centre for Linguistics
Hungary, Budapest
vadasz.noemi@nytud.hu

Abstract

This paper presents the complete workflow of building a manually annotated Hungarian corpus, KorKor, with particular reference to anaphora and coreference annotation. All linguistic annotation layers were corrected manually. The corpus is freely available in two formats. The paper gives insight into the process of setting up the workflow and the challenges that have arisen.

1 Introduction

The main motivation for building a coreference corpus was the fact that it is always interesting to investigate the behavior of a linguistic phenomenon in real texts. A manually annotated corpus is useful not only for linguists, but also for training and evaluating tools. KorKor, a Hungarian coreference corpus presented in this paper contains multiple linguistic annotation layers, such as disambiguated POS-tags, lemmata and morphological features (of two morphological tagsets) and dependency relations. All of these ordinary linguistic annotations were corrected manually, as well as the anaphora and coreference annotations.

Representativeness is an important feature of a corpus if we expect the tools trained on it to work with predictable quality in different genres and domains. However, in the current phase of the research, only two sources of texts were involved, since this phase aimed more at setting up the corpus building workflow and producing the necessary tools.

The resource is available under CC-BY 4.0 license to enhance accessibility, usability and extensibility. KorKor can be found in the following GitHub repository: `https://github.com/vadno/korkor_pilot`. Apart from the corpus itself, the whole workflow with detailed instructions, the annotation guidelines and the tools prepared in the frame of this project are also available in the GitHub repository to provide help for anyone having the necessary resources (financial resource, human labor, raw material) to continue the project or create a new, similar corpus based on it.

2 Background

2.1 Anaphora and Coreference

As a brief overview, here we discuss the definition of anaphora and coreference, which are often tangled in the literature. Resolution of both of them is required for interpreting a text, however the differences between them should be noted. An anaphora gets its interpretation from an other, previously mentioned constituent, its antecedent, therefore, it does not have an independent meaning. Coreference means that two expressions have the same referent. While anaphoric relations operate on the level of grammar, coreference belongs to the lexicon. As (van Deemter and Kibble, 1999) pointed out, coreference is a symmetric transitive relation, while anaphora is not, but it is context-dependent. An annotated corpus can contain e.g. only pronominal anaphora, but it can also be richly annotated with different relations between entities or even events. (Lapshinova-Koltunski et al., 2022) refers to the latter as "full coreference annotation", because it contains not only annotation of pronouns, but also full nominal phrases, verbal phrases and clauses and includes rich set of links with both entity and event coreference.

At the same time, in annotated corpora, occurrences in the text referring to the same entity are technically annotated similarly, and each type of anaphora is distinguished by different categories based on e.g. the type of the pronoun, as well as the different types of coreference relations. The differences between the two relation types are reflected in our annotation scheme in such a way that the type of the relation with the antecedent or previously mentioned coreferent element is marked next

Proceedings of the Fifth Workshop on Computational Models of Reference, Anaphora and Coreference (CRAC 2022), pages 38–47
Gyeongju, Republic of Korea, October 16–17, 2022.

to the token. The labels used in KorKor for the different types of anaphora relations and coreference are detailed in Section 4.8.

2.2 Coreference Corpora

First, here we present the annotation schemes of two well-known shared tasks related to our topic. The annotation scheme of CoNLL-2012 (Pradhan et al., 2012) distinguishes between two types of coreference: Indentity and Appositive. The former is used for anaphoric coreference and all other types of mentions, the latter functions as attribution. The annotation scheme of MUC-6[1] and MUC-7 (Hirschman and Chinchor, 1998) does not separate different types of coreference. In these schemes coreference annotation is similar to a hyperlinked text, where the links connect the mentions of a given entity. An important objective of these shared tasks is to achieve high interannotator agreement, and following these schemes it can be accomplished. On the other hand, it is important to keep in mind that we have much more linguistic knowledge about the linguistic phenomena of coreference and anaphora, and these information can be important e.g. in information extraction tasks.

From the perspective of our work the most interesting resources are corpora of pro-drop languages, because the dropped elements as pronouns has referential properties. Hungarian is also a pro-drop language, which means that some pronouns (namely the personal and possessive pronouns in subject, object or possessor roles) can be left out from the sentence. In these cases, the person and number of the subject and the object can be calculated from the inflection of the finite verb, and the person and number of the possessor are calculable from the inflection of the possessum.

There are multiple coreference corpora for pro-drop languages, for example OntoNotes5.0 (Weischedel et al., 2013) for Arabic and Chinese, NAIST Text corpus (Iida et al., 2017) for Japanese, AnCora-CO (Recasens and Martí, 2010) for Spanish and Catalan, PCC (Ogrodniczuk et al., 2016) for Polish, and ParCorFull2.0 (Lapshinova-Koltunski et al., 2022) contains Portuguese as well. The annotation scheme of AnCora-CO includes dropped subjects in the syntactic trees and in the coreference annotation as well. NAIST, OntoNotes5.0 and PCC also contain zero pronouns.

ZAC (Zero Anaphora Corpus) (Baptista et al., 2016) is made specifically for the task of resolving dropped pronouns and contains texts in Brazilian Portuguese. It is 35,000 words long and contains texts from various sources. Only this linguistic phenomenon is annotated in it, however, it is really detailed, as it indicates the number and person of the dropped pronoun, indicates whether it is an anaphora or cataphora, and also indicates intersentential anaphoras separately, as well as providing the antecedent token. There are almost 1,500 zero anaphoras in the corpus, which clearly shows how important it is to deal with this phenomenon in the case of pro-drop languages.

As ParCorFull2.0 is a parallel corpus containing originally English and German texts, extending it with Portuguese was a challenge, because a pro-drop language had to fit into an annotation scheme which was not prepared to deal with this linguistic phenomenon. Here, the antecedents of the zero pronouns are marked next to the verbs, which seems to be a good solution, since the inflection of the verbs shows the characteristics of the dropped pronoun. This could only be applied to Hungarian by keeping in mind that a verb can have not only a dropped subject but also a dropped object, so it may happen that two antecedents need to be marked next to the verb.

It is also a possible solution, that the dropped pronouns do not appear in the corpus, since they are not present as independent tokens in the original text. This can be explained by the fact that the input of the coreference resolver does not contain dropped pronouns, and we do not necessarily want them to appear in the output, so we do not expect the resolver's training data to contain them either. On the other hand, for information extraction tasks, it is definitely useful if we have a richer linguistic annotation (e.g. zero verbs, ellipses and dropped pronouns). It can be a good solution that the corpus contains dropped pronouns but in a way that it can be used without them.

2.3 A Hungarian Coreference Corpus

The design of the corpus was inspired by the biggest Hungarian coreference corpus, SzegedKoref (Vincze et al., 2018). It was created by enriching a smaller part of Szeged Corpus (Csendes et al., 2005) with coreference

[1] https://cs.nyu.edu/~grishman/COtask21.book_1.html

annotation. It consists of student essays and newspaper articles giving altogether 55 763 tokens. 2 456 coreference chains were found in the texts, in which anaphoric and coreference relations are also included.

But why is another Hungarian coreference corpus needed besides SzegedKoref? Manually annotated data are always very valuable resources and the more of them, the better. Both SzegedKoref and KorKor have manually corrected annotation layers, therefore both of them are useful for numerous tasks apart from anaphora and coreference resolution. However, there are some differences between the annotation principles, schemes and tagsets, for instance in morphological and syntactic annotation. Joint use of the two corpora is still feasible after harmonizing the different formats.

Nonetheless, it has to be noted that there are some further differences between the two corpora on the level of theoretical issues. Both corpora contain dropped subjects, objects and possessors, but in contrast with SzegedKoref, in KorKor zero nodes for subjects are allocated to the infinitives, because they also play a role in the anaphoric relations. Another difference is that KorKor contains zero substantive verbs and ellipted verbs as well. Moreover, the method and the tagset of coreference and anaphora are different as well.

The tagset of SzegedKoref differentiates between the following relation classes: pronominal, nominal, adverbial, verbal and derivational. The class of nominal relations is divided into further subclasses: repetition, synonym, hypernym, holonym, epithet and apposition. In contrast, the tagset of KorKor contains only two tags for all nominal relations, which distinguishes identical reference and part-whole relation. However, the tagset of KorKor differentiates multiple types of pronominal anaphora with regard to the type of the pronoun: personal, demonstrative, reciprocal, reflexive and possessive, and it contains three extra tags for generic subject, speaker and addressee. The annotation guidelines of SzegedKoref highlights, that generic pronouns are not to be marked, but in our data we saw many examples that the generic subject in the text is also able to participate in anaphoric chains. Speaker and addressee is SzegedKoref got pronominal tag as other pronouns. Adverbial, verbal and derivational relations are not annotated in KorKor.

3 Data

3.1 Formats

The corpus is available in two formats. The setup of KorKor.`xtsv` follows the format used by the latest version of `e-magyar` (Indig et al., 2019), to be cited henceforward `emtsv`. In the `tsv` files, every line represents a token and sentences are separated by a blank line. Annotations are placed in the columns, which are described in the header. The motivation of using this format is that it fits well into the frame of `emtsv`, which was used during this project and which also can be used for further development of the corpus.

The KorKor.`conllup` files use the CoNLL-U Plus format[2]. A file of this format may contain any subset of the original columns of the core CoNLL-U files plus other project-specific ones. A comment listing the actual columns is inserted as the first line. This format is widely used, therefore the corpus could reach more people.

The two versions are different not only in their format but in their content as well, see the details in Section 4.9.

3.2 Sources

Texts from two sources were selected for building the corpus, using the collection of OPUS Corpus (Tiedemann, 2012): articles from Hungarian Wikipedia, and texts from the Hungarian website of the GlobalVoices[3] newsportal. Using OPUS ensures that the corpus is available under free licence. In addition to the coreference annotated corpus, a smaller amount of data (8,600 tokens) got only manually corrected lemmata, POS tags and dependency analysis. These data await further work, but at the same time the annotation layers completed so far could also be useful for others. Table 1. summarizes the size of the two formats of the coreference annotated corpus (in number of documents and tokens).

4 The Workflow

The building process was set up as a pipeline, in which as many steps were intended to be automated as possible. Human work was used for supervising and – if needed – correcting the annotation. Certain processing steps were carried out by the

[2]`https://universaldependencies.org/ext-format.html`

[3]`https://hu.globalvoices.org`

	documents	tokens (conllup)	tokens (xtsv)
huwiki	62	16,739	18,262
globv	32	7,760	8,799
TOTAL	94	24,499	26,581

Table 1: The size of the two formats of the coreference annotated corpus.

latest version of emtsv. As emtsv is a text processing pipeline, and the output of a given module forms the input of another one, it was reasonable to check and correct annotation not only at the end of the process but at several points of the workflow. Although human annotation in multiple cycles is certainly a labour-intensive method, minor faults are easier to fix, than muddled tangles. Thus, human annotators corrected the annotations in three phases.

The steps of the workflow were the following (tools used are in parentheses – steps where no tools are given were carried out with scripts developed within the project):

1. text collection
2. emtsv process (emToken, emMorph, and emTag modules)
3. format conversion
4. manual check (Google Spreadsheets)
5. format conversion
6. emtsv process (emDep module)
7. format conversion (emCoNLL module)
8. manual check (WebAnno)
9. manual insertion of zero substantives and elipted verbs (plain text editor)
10. zero pronoun insertion (emZero module)
11. pronominal anaphora resolution
12. manual check and coreference annotation (Google Spreadsheets)
13. format conversion

The annotators have recorded the time needed for the correction of each document and each annotation layer. This information allows us to calculate the cost of the expansion of the corpus, and it could be helpful even in other corpus building projects.

annotation layer	token/hour
4. morphology	871.77
8. dependency	667.76
12. anaphora and coreference	595.86

Table 2: The time needed for manual correcting of the different annotation layers.

Table 2 shows the working hours needed to correct the different annotation layers.

The annotators reported every problem and question arising, therefore the annotation guidelines became finer and more detailed which sped up and made manual work easier.

The workflow includes multiple conversion steps between file formats, as the output of a certain step may differ from the expected input format of the following one. Each step of the workflow is specified below.

4.1 Preprocessing Texts

The selected texts consist of several sentences, because anaphora and coreference relations span through sentence boundaries. The length of the documents range from 5 to 27 sentences, the length of the sentences ranging from 3 to 71 tokens (counting punctuation marks as separate tokens). We paid special attention to add texts of manageable sizes to the corpus without truncation and wanted to include as many texts as possible from the sources. Therefore, in the case of both news and Wikipedia texts, we selected those that were of the appropriate length for our purposes, so we did not have to delete text fragments. Parts of some Wikipedia texts had to be cut out, but in these cases we made sure that the coherence and structure of the text did not change, and especially that there were no anaphoras without antecedents. The text selection was not influenced by the number of anaphora and coreference chains, as it was not checked in advance.

The texts were prepared for emtsv. Despite the fact that Wikipedia articles and news are edited texts, a lot of spelling errors had to be corrected in them. Each text forms a raw corpus document (plain text files in UTF-8 character encoding).

4.2 Tokenization, Lemmatization and POS tagging

The output of the relevant modules of `emtsv` (emToken (Mittelholcz, 2017), emMorph (Novák, 2014; Novák et al., 2016; Novák, 2003) and emTag (Orosz and Novák, 2012, 2013)) is a `tsv` file of four columns (the format was described in Section 3.1). The content of the columns are: token, all possible lemmata and morphological tags, disambiguated lemma, disambiguated morphological tag.

4.3 Manual correction

In the first phase of manual work, tokenization, disambiguated lemmata and morphological tags were checked and corrected. Google Spreadsheets were used for this task, because it fits for most of our needs.

Seven linguists have edited the output of the modules of `emtsv` mentioned above. After some preprocessing steps that made the documents appropriate for Google Spreadsheets, conditional formatting was applied to make the document easier to follow and to give instant feedback to the annotators. Tokens for which the morphological analyzer produced multiple possible labels were highlighted. In case of tokens that have only one possible analysis anyway, the disambiguator is usually not wrong either. These tokens were not highlighted, but of course the annotators had to check them as well, since mistakes can occur in these too. Based on the annotators' feedback, conditional formatting and highlighting helped their work.

Besides tokenization, the disambiguated lemmata and morphological tags (the output of `emTag`) were checked by the annotators. To correct the lemma and the tag, they could choose from all possible lemma – morphological tag pairs of the token provided by `emMorph`. If none of them were acceptable, both of them could be set manually.

To make correction of tokenization errors easier, correcting commands were written into certain cells of the spreadsheet, e.g. to join or split tokens. First, the document was exported. Second, a postprocessing script responsible for the format conversion interpreted and carried out the correcting commands (such as line deletion, line insertion with the given content, joining two or more tokens, or splitting a token). The output format of the post-processing script was again `xtsv`.

All the texts were corrected by at least two annotators, and a third one curated the documents. The inter-annotator agreement rate in terms of Cohen's κ for the morphological tags was: 96.07%.

4.4 Dependency Parsing

The corrected documents were fed into `emtsv` again for dependency parsing. As the dependency parser module (`emDep`) requires another morphological tagset in the input, the corrected tags were converted into a UD compatible tagset[4] by using a script[5]. Note that the UD tagset, in contrast with the `emMorph` tagset, does not encode derivational information, therefore the two layers differ not only in their format, but in their fineness as well. As the UD tagset is less detailed and lossless mapping is possible between them, no manual check was required. Thanks to this conversion step, end users can use two types of tagsets: emMorph, the current and most detailed Hungarian morphological tagset, and UD, which is widely used and meets an international standard.

4.5 Manual Correction and Zero Substantive Verbs

In this phase, WebAnno (Eckart de Castilho et al., 2016), a general purpose web-based annotation tool was used for manual correction, because it suited most of our needs. Link annotations as dependency edges are easy to handle with the drag-and-drop operation method, texts in different phases of analysis could be imported in various formats, and its interface allows us to check and correct already annotated documents as well. There are some additional functionalities like comparing and visualizing documents annotated by multiple annotators and calculating inter-annotator agreement. The flexibility of the tool provides that one can easily create a custom layer besides multiple built-in layers. WebAnno runs on a server and the annotators can use it via their common browser.

The output of the dependency module was converted to CoNLL-U, a file format edible for WebAnno. The conversion was done by the corresponding module of `emtsv`. Three linguists have checked and corrected the dependency edges.

[4]For details about Hungarian morphological tagsets, see (Vadász and Simon, 2019) and `https://github.com/dlt-rilmta/panmorph`.

[5]`https://github.com/vadno/emmorph2ud2`

Nevertheless, some weaknesses of the tool have turned out during the work. The tokenization was previously corrected, but still the annotators found tokenization errors in this phase as well. Unfortunately, WebAnno does not support token deletion or insertion, thus these errors had to be corrected in a separate postprocessing step.

In this postprocessing step, zero substantives and ellipted verbs were inserted as well. The reason why zero substantives and ellipted verbs were included is because they also have a subject – either overt or dropped – and ellipted verbs also have an object or other arguments.

A zero substantive was inserted in a sentence without a finite verb as a new token, where it would turn up as an overt substantive verb if the sentence was in past tense. Zero substantives got a combined ID from the ID of the preceding token. In Example 1, two zero substantives were inserted into the dependency tree.

Ellipted verbs are also insterted into the corpus, because in the absence of an overt verb, adjuncts could not be bound to their mother nodes. Ellipted verbs were also inserted manually, and as in the case of zero subordinates, they got a combined ID. In Example 2, an ellipted verb was inserted into the dependency tree.

Altogether, 419 zero substantives and 22 ellipted verbs were inserted into the corpus.

4.6 Inserting dropped pronouns

Dropped pronouns were inserted by a rule-based script[6]. The rules work on the preceding annotation layers (lemma, morphological tag and dependency analysis). Dropped pronouns are inserted in the following cases:

- subject, if a verb does not have a subject in the dependency tree;
- object, if a transitive verb does not have an object in the dependency tree;
- possessor, if a possessum does not have a possessor in the dependency tree;
- subject for an inflected or a non-inflected infinitive in the dependency tree.

Inserting dropped pronouns generates extra branches in the dependency tree. Zero subjects are placed after the verb, zero objects after the verb (and the subject), zero possessors after the possessum. All zero pronouns get a combined ID from the ID of the preceding token and the syntactic role of the zero element (SUBJ, OBJ, POSS). Not surprisingly, the POS tag of the zero pronouns is pronoun (PRON), their morphological features, like person and number, are calculated from the verb or the possessum.

Altogether, the corpus contains 867 zero subjects, 101 zero objects and 379 zero possessors.

[6]For the sake of anonymity, the link is provided only in the final version.

4.7 Inserting pronominal anaphora

Pronominal anaphora relations are also inserted by a rule-based script. The script searches for the pronouns, and a set of rules operate on the POS tag, the morphological features and the syntactic information of the other words.

For the time being, the script searches for an antecedent only for personal pronouns, all other types of pronouns (possessive, reflexive, reciprocal, demonstrative and relative) had to be inserted manually. The antecedent searching algorithm for personal pronouns works by simple rules, e.g. if the subject of a verb is covert and the inflection of the verb is identical to the verb of the previous clause, the antecedent of the subject is the subject of the verb in the previous clause.

4.8 Manual Correction and Coreference Annotation

Four linguists have checked and corrected the insertion of the dropped pronouns and pronominal anaphora and annotated the coreference relations in this phase.

There is a large range of annotation tools capable for the task of anaphora and coreference annotation and some of them can be used not only for annotating but correcting already existing annotation as well. However, no annotation tools fit perfectly our needs, principally by reason of the inserted zero elements and the generated IDs.

Hence, to perform this correction and annotation phase, Google Spreadsheets with conditional formatting was used again. Anaphora and coreference annotations were noted into two columns: one is for the ID of the head of the mother node, and one for the relation type. The following anaphora relation types are annotated in KorKor (with the tag in parentheses): personal (**prs**), demonstrative (**dem**), reciprocal (**recip**), reflexive (**refl**), relative (**rel**), possessive (**poss**).

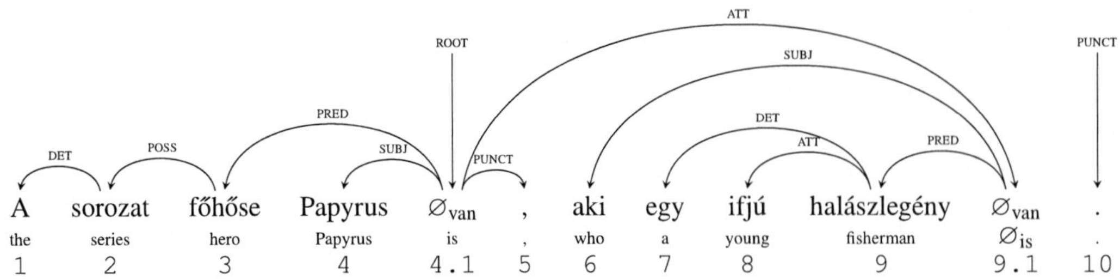

The hero of the series is Papyrus, who is a young fisherman.

Figure 1: In this complex sentence, the zero substantive verb of the subordinate clause is dependent from the zero substantive of the main clause. Original IDs and combined IDs of zero elements are under the tokens.

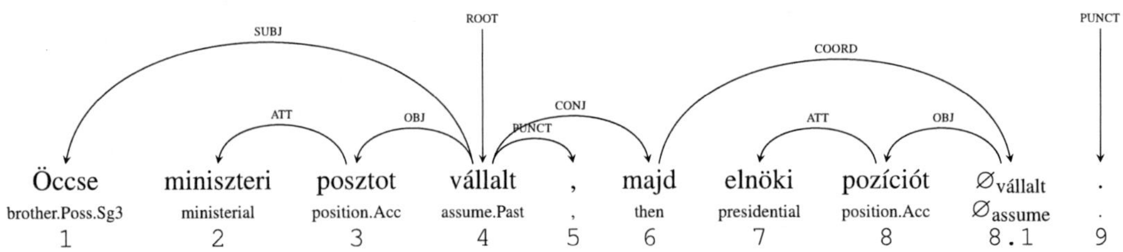

His brother undertaken a ministerial position, then a presidential one.

Figure 2: The verb of the first clause of the compound sentence occurs in the second clause covertly. A zero node is inserted, thus the arguments have a mother node to bind to.

The script that automatically inserted a link to the antecedent for the personal pronouns did not account for the other anaphora types and the relations in which they occur. For instance, the referent of a general subject – usually expressed in English by passive constructions – may be difficult to grasp. In Example 1 the verb *elítéltek* certainly has a third person plural subject, but it can not be related with any entities mentioned in the preceding text. In KorKor generic subjects are marked with the tag **arb**. General subjects do not have an antecedent, but they can be antecedents of other generic subjects.

(1) a Kínai Kommunista Párt egyik volt vezetője, akit hazaárulás miatt **elítéltek**
one of the ex-leaders of the Communist Party of China, who was ***convicted*** *for treason it was first* ***mentioned*** *in 1883 as an area donated to the Orthodox community*

Another interesting case is, when the speaker (or the writer) addresses the hearer (or the reader), as in Example 2. This type occurs rarely in the genre of news and Wikipedia, but still, some examples were found, moreover, expanding the corpus with other genres (literature, personal texts) would bring more instances.

(2) A születésnapi ajándékoknak is nagyon **örülünk**, ha **szeretnéd** támogatni a munkánkat, **küldj nekünk** adományt, vagy **vegyél** egyet az NSA-s karácsonyi **üdvözlőlapjaink** közül, amelyet a Creative Time-nál dolgozó **barátaink** terveztek.
We*'re also very happy for birthday gifts, if* ***you*** *want to support* ***our*** *work, send us a donation, or buy one of our NSA Christmas cards designed by* ***our*** *friends at Creative Time.*

Two further tags were introduced to handle these special types of subjects: **addr** for the addressee, and **speak** for the speaker (writer). Bringing the addressee and the speaker/writer into the set of the participants of the event put down by the text allows us to mark if a pronoun refers back to these participants.

In coreference corpora, multiple types of coreference are usually annotated, such as repetition, variation, synonym, hypernym, hyponym, and holonym. While working out the design of KorKor and setting the annotation principles, we have faced some difficulties in connection with the different relation types, namely that it was challenging to write a guideline that could precisely define and differentiate the coreference types, because it is sometimes too hard for the annotators to distinguish the certain types. As a result, only two tags are used for marking coreference relations in KorKor. The tag **coref** is for the relation tpye when the two elements have identical reference (e.g. in the case of repetition, synonym, hiper- and hyponym). The tag **holo** is used when a part–whole connection holds between the two entities. It is important to distinguish these two types, because we found examples for "branching" coreference chains as in Example 3.

While in a coreference relation both participants are overt, the antecedent of a pronoun can be either a dropped pronoun or an overt phrase, therefore anaphoric and coreference relations make up a tangled net with branches, instead of a simple chain.

Table 3 summarizes the total number of each relation type in the corpus (counted in KorKor.`xtsv`).

relation type	occurrence
prs	1 306
dem	121
recip	10
refl	16
rel	294
poss	0
arb	274
speak	4
addr	1
coref	1 365
holo	180

Table 3: The total number of anaphoric and coreference relations in KorKor.

4.9 Converting to CoNLL-U Plus

The version of KorKor.`conllup` was converted from KorKor.`xtsv`. Although the two formats are interoperable, it was not only a simple format conversion. Firstly, zero elements are not listed as separate tokens in KorKor.`conllup`, which means that the affected dependency trees and anaphoric relations had to be revised and modified. Dropped pronouns are annotated in a different manner: if a verb has a covert subject or object, or if a possessum has a covert possessor, it is annotated in specific a column. Person and number of dropped subjects, objects and possessors are calculated from the inflection of the verb or the possessum. In the current state of the corpus these dropped pronouns are left out from the coreference chains, their antecedents are not marked and they can not be the antecedents of an other element.

Additionally, in KorKor.`conllup`, the coreferent elements form a simple chain, in which the elements having the same referent are linked linearly, instead of a tangled net structure with branches.

Consequently, the two versions fit for different users. KorKor.`xtsv` is suitable for examining the nature of anaphora from the linguistic point of view. The presence of zero elements allow the user to formulate queries about, for example, what events a participant in the text has attended. On the other hand, as KorKor.`conllup` is closer to to the usual coreference corpora, it is more applicable as a training or a test dataset, therefore is can form a base of a higher level information retrieval task, for example.

4.10 Further Questions

We made an interesting observation regarding Wikipedia articles, the annotation of which we often encountered serious difficulties. Illustrative example, when an article refers to an animal species, e.g. describes a certain type of chicken. First, it writes about the animal's features and habits in general, where it occurs, what it eats, etc., and then it covers the animal's body parts and their properties. The situation gets even more complicated if these are followed by presenting in detail separately the hen and the rooster (in first person sinular). These cases are marked as holonyms in KorKor, but this solution can be disputed.

Some problematic issues have emerged in connection with coreference, for which neither us, nor the literature have provided any answers yet. In Example 3, the state of the referent changes can be seen. What kind of relationship exists between a human and his/her dead body?

(3) Három hónap telt el **az újságíró házaspár**, Sagar Sarwar és felesége, Meherun Runi meggyilkolása óta. **A holttesteket** már exhumálták is, hogy megismételjék a boncolást. *Three months have passed since the murder of* ***the journalist couple****, Sagar Sarwar and*

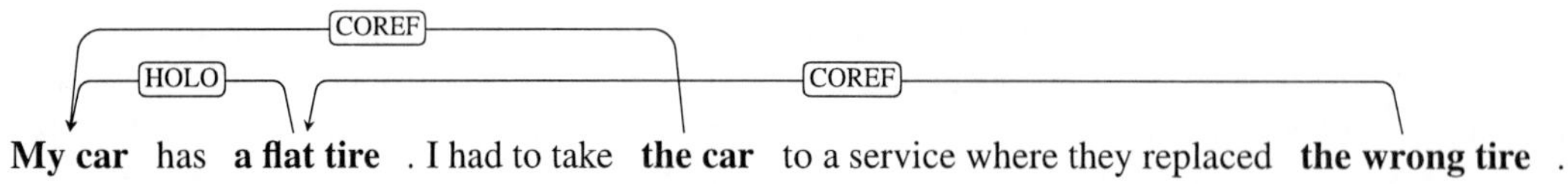

Figure 3: Branching coreference chains: a whole-part relation holds between *the car* and *the tire*, and both of them are repeated later in the text.

his wife. ***The bodies*** *are already exhumated to repeat the autopsy.*

Example 4 illustrates the issue of split antecedents.

(4) **Papyrus** bátor és megmenti **Thèti-Chèri-t**. **A két egymásra lelt barát** küldetést kap az istenektől, hogy védelmezzék meg a fáraót.
Papyrus *is brave and saves* ***Thèti-Chèri***. ***The two friends found each other*** *got a mission from the gods to guard the pharaoh.*

According to our annotation principles, only one antecedent could be connected to a word, however the phrase *the two friends found each other* relates and refers to *Papyrus* and *Thèti-Chèri* at the same time. It would not help, if *Papyrus* and *Thèti-Chèri* were coordinated. In this case, the annotation would technically achievable, but it would be ambiguous, because the referring phrase could be either the whole coordination, or only the head of it.

Our annotation scheme does not cover the problem of these problematic cases, they are still waiting for solution and are part of our future plans, as is further expansion of the corpus.

References

J. Baptista, Simone Pereira, and Nuno J. Mamede. 2016. Zac : Zero anaphora corpus a corpus for zero anaphora resolution in portuguese. In *Proceedings of Workshop on Corpora and Tools for Processing Corpora, PROPOR 2016*.

Dóra Csendes, János Csirik, Tibor Gyimóthy, and András Kocsor. 2005. The Szeged Treebank. In *Proceedings of the 8th International Conference, TSD 2005*, pages 123–131, Karlovy Vary, Czech Republic. Springer.

Richard Eckart de Castilho, Éva Mújdricza-Maydt, Seid Muhie Yimam, Silvana Hartmann, Iryna Gurevych, Anette Frank, and Chris Biemann. 2016. A web-based tool for the integrated annotation of semantic and syntactic structures. In *Proceedings of the Workshop on Language Technology Resources and Tools for Digital Humanities (LT4DH)*, pages 76–84, Osaka, Japan. The COLING 2016 Organizing Committee.

Lynette Hirschman and Nancy Chinchor. 1998. Appendix F: MUC-7 coreference task definition (version 3.0). In *Seventh Message Understanding Conference (MUC-7): Proceedings of a Conference Held in Fairfax, Virginia, April 29 - May 1, 1998*.

Ryu Iida, Mamoru Komachi, Naoya Inoue, Kentaro Inui, and Yuji Matsumoto. 2017. Naist text corpus: Annotating predicate- argument and coreference relations in japanese. In *Handbook of Linguistic Annotation*, pages 1177–1196, Dordrecht. Springer Netherlands.

Balázs Indig, Bálint Sass, Eszter Simon, Iván Mittelholcz, Noémi Vadász, and Márton Makrai. 2019. One format to rule them all – the `emtsv` pipeline for Hungarian. In *Proceedings of the 13th Linguistic Annotation Workshop*, pages 155–165, Florence, Italy. Association for Computational Linguistics.

Ekaterina Lapshinova-Koltunski, Pedro Augusto Ferreira, Elina Lartaud, and Christian Hardmeier. 2022. Parcorfull2.0: A parallel corpus annotated with full coreference. In *Proceedings of the 13th Conference on Linguistic Resources and Evaluation (LREC)*, pages 805–813. European Language Resources Association (ELRA). Null ; Conference date: 20-06-2022 Through 25-06-2022.

Iván Mittelholcz. 2017. `emToken`: Unicode-képes tokenizáló magyar nyelvre (`emToken`: A unicode-compatible tokenizer for Hungarian). In *XIII. Magyar Számítógépes Nyelvészeti Konferencia (MSZNY2017)*, pages 70–78, Szeged. Szegedi Tudományegyetem Informatikai Tanszékcsoport.

Attila Novák. 2003. Milyen a jó Humor? (What good humor is like?). In *I. Magyar Számítógépes Nyelvészeti Konferencia*, pages 138–144, Szeged. SZTE.

Attila Novák. 2014. A new form of Humor – Mapping constraint-based computational morphologies to a finite-state representation. In *Proceedings of the Ninth International Conference on Language Resources and Evaluation (LREC'14)*, Reykjavik, Iceland. European Language Resources Association (ELRA).

Attila Novák, Borbála Siklósi, and Csaba Oravecz. 2016. A new integrated open-source morphological analyzer for Hungarian. In *Proceedings of the Tenth International Conference on Language Resources and*

Evaluation (LREC 2016), Paris, France. European Language Resources Association (ELRA).

Maciej Ogrodniczuk, Katarzyna Głowińska, Mateusz Kopeć, Agata Savary, and Magdalena Zawisławska. 2016. Polish coreference corpus. In *Human Language Technology. Challenges for Computer Science and Linguistics*, pages 215–226, Cham. Springer International Publishing.

György Orosz and Attila Novák. 2012. PurePos 2.0 – an open source morphological disambiguator. In *Proceedings of the 9th International Workshop on Natural Language Processing and Cognitive Science*, pages 53–63, Wroclaw.

György Orosz and Attila Novák. 2013. PurePos 2.0: a hybrid tool for morphological disambiguation. In *Proceedings of the International Conference Recent Advances in Natural Language Processing RANLP 2013*, pages 539–545, Hissar, Bulgaria. INCOMA Ltd. Shoumen, BULGARIA.

Sameer Pradhan, Alessandro Moschitti, Nianwen Xue, Olga Uryupina, and Yuchen Zhang. 2012. CoNLL-2012 shared task: Modeling multilingual unrestricted coreference in OntoNotes. In *Joint Conference on EMNLP and CoNLL - Shared Task*, pages 1–40, Jeju Island, Korea. Association for Computational Linguistics.

Marta Recasens and Antonia Martí. 2010. Ancora-co: Coreferentially annotated corpora for spanish and catalan. *Language Resources and Evaluation*, 44:315–345.

Jörg Tiedemann. 2012. Parallel data, tools and interfaces in opus. In *Proceedings of the Eight International Conference on Language Resources and Evaluation (LREC'12)*, Istanbul, Turkey. European Language Resources Association (ELRA).

Noémi Vadász and Eszter Simon. 2019. Konverterek magyar morfológiai címkekészletek között (Converters between Hungarian morphological tagsets). In *XV. Magyar Számítógépes Nyelvészeti Konferencia (MSZNY 2019)*, pages 99–112, Szeged. Szegedi Tudományegyetem Informatikai Tanszékcsoport.

Kees van Deemter and Rodger Kibble. 1999. What is coreference, and what should coreference annotation be? In *Coreference and Its Applications*, pages 90–96.

Veronika Vincze, Klára Hegedűs, Alex Sliz-Nagy, and Richárd Farkas. 2018. SzegedKoref: A Hungarian coreference corpus. In *Proceedings of the 11th Language Resources and Evaluation Conference*, Miyazaki, Japan. European Language Resource Association.

Ralph Weischedel, Martha Palmer, Mitchell Marcus, Eduard Hovy, Sameer Pradhan, Lance Ramshaw, Nianwen Xue, Ann Taylor, Jeff Kaufman, Michelle Franchini, Mohammed El-Bachouti, Robert Belvin, and Ann Houston. 2013. OntoNotes Release 5.0.

NARC – Norwegian Anaphora Resolution Corpus

Petter Mæhlum,[1] Dag Haug,[2] Tollef Jørgensen,[3] Andre Kåsen,[4] Anders Nøklestad,[5] Egil Rønningstad,[1] Per Erik Solberg,[4] Erik Velldal,[1] and Lilja Øvrelid[1]

[1]University of Oslo, Language Technology Group
[2]Department of Philosophy, Classics, History of Arts and Ideas, University of Oslo
[3]Department of Computer Science, Norwegian University of Science and Technology
[4]The Norwegian Language Bank, National Library of Norway
[5]Department of Linguistics and Scandinavian Studies, University of Oslo

Abstract

We present the Norwegian Anaphora Resolution Corpus (NARC), the first publicly available corpus annotated with anaphoric relations between noun phrases for Norwegian[1]. The paper describes the annotated data for 326 documents in Norwegian Bokmål, together with inter-annotator agreement and discussions of relevant statistics. We also present preliminary modelling results which are comparable to existing corpora for other languages, and discuss relevant problems in relation to both modelling and the annotations themselves.

1 Introduction

Coreference resolution (CR) is a central NLP task which enables a wide range of applications aiming to extract and aggregate various types of information from text, e.g. relations, events and opinions. While a number of datasets for CR have been developed for a range of different languages, no such openly available dataset is currently available for Norwegian.

In this paper, we describe the annotation of the Norwegian Anaphora Resolution Corpus (NARC). The annotation effort enriches the existing annotation of the Norwegian Dependency Treebank (NDT) (Solberg et al., 2014), which has been converted to the Universal Dependencies standard (Øvrelid and Hohle, 2016; Velldal et al., 2017) and has further been annotated with named entities in a separate effort, resulting in the NorNE dataset (Jørgensen et al., 2020). Norwegian has two written standards: Bokmål and Nynorsk, and the dataset consists of 300,000 tokens from each.[2]

The paper is organized as follows: we start out by reviewing related work, then we describe the annotation effort, summarize the annotation procedure, explain guidelines developed for the project and the inter-annotator agreement scores. Finally, corpus statistics and initial experiments with Norwegian CR are presented, before concluding the paper.

2 Related Work

In this section we review some related work, both in terms of existing datasets with coreference annotation and research on coreference modelling based on these datasets.

2.1 Datasets

Early datasets for CR were MUC (Grishman and Sundheim, 1996) and ACE (Doddington et al., 2004), which enabled considerable research on this task, further spurred by the CoNLL-2011 and 2012 shared tasks on CR (Pradhan et al., 2011, 2012) based on the widely used OntoNotes dataset (Weischedel et al., 2011).

There are now a wide range of annotated coreference datasets. A majority of these are in English, such as Quiz Bowl Coreference (Guha et al., 2015), Character Identification, (Chen and Choi, 2016), WikiCoref (Ghaddar and Langlais, 2016), GUM (Zeldes, 2017), BASHI (Rösiger, 2018), PreCo (Chen et al., 2018), GAP (Webster et al., 2018), ARRAU (Uryupina et al., 2020) and LitBank (Bamman et al., 2020).

There is also a growing number of non-English corpora being made available to the research community, including datasets for Catalan/Spanish (Recasens and Martí, 2010), Czech (Nedoluzhko et al., 2016), Danish (Korzen and Buch-Kromann, 2011), Dutch (Hendrickx et al., 2008), German (Lapshinova-Koltunski et al., 2018; Bourgonje and Stede, 2020), Hungarian (Vincze et al., 2018), Lithuanian (Žitkus and Butkiene, 2018), Polish (Ogrodniczuk et al., 2016) and Russian (Toldova and Ionov, 2017). The recent Universal Anaphora

[1]`https://github.com/ltgoslo/NARC`

[2]We here focus on the annotation of the Bokmål part of the NDT, however, annotation of the Nynorsk part of the treebank follows the same guidelines and is currently close to completion. The final version of the corpus will include statistics and data for both written standards.

Proceedings of the Fifth Workshop on Computational Models of Reference, Anaphora and Coreference (CRAC 2022), pages 48–60
Gyeongju, Republic of Korea, October 16–17, 2022.

initiative[3] constitutes an important step towards the harmonization of different annotation standards for corpora annotated with various types of anaphoric information. A dataset of particular relevance to the current work is BREDT (Borthen et al., 2007) – annotated with coreference and other anaphoric relations in Norwegian. BREDT covers in total 12 different kinds of relations, all linguistically motivated. The data has been previously used both to test a rule-based (Holen, 2007) and a machine learning-based system (Nøklestad, 2009) for Norwegian CR. Unfortunately, however, the BREDT dataset is not openly available.

2.2 Modelling

A variety of CR approaches have been published using the MUC and ACE datasets, ranging from linear programming, probabilistic and rule-based mention–pair models (Ng and Cardie, 2002; Luo et al., 2004; Culotta et al., 2007; Denis and Baldridge, 2007; Finkel and Manning, 2008; Haghighi and Klein, 2009). These datasets were of limited size, and Poon and Domingos (2008) found that unsupervised models were comparable to supervised models at the time – an important observation for low-resource languages. After the SemEval 2010 (Recasens et al., 2010) and CoNLL shared tasks (Pradhan et al., 2011, 2012), more extensive models were proposed, such as the ranking models by Björkelund and Farkas (2012); Durrett and Klein (2013), the sieve-based deterministic model by Lee et al. (2013) and other machine learning-based methods (Clark and Manning, 2015, 2016). Recent state-of-the-art models, however, such as those by Agarwal et al. (2019); Wu et al. (2020); Kantor and Globerson (2019); Xu and Choi (2020); Joshi et al. (2020); Kirstain et al. (2021) and Dobrovolskii (2021) have mostly been evaluated on the OntoNotes dataset. This is perhaps due to lack of compatability in terms of formats, annotation styles, and genres across datasets. Consequently, there are several concerns regarding real-world use of models that are not evaluated on other domains, especially regarding domain generalizability and robustness (Guha et al., 2015; Moosavi, 2020; Sukthanker et al., 2020). The same issues will likely translate to NARC, as data sources are limited (see Section 3.1). To tackle these issues, cross-domain adaptability will be a central topic for future evaluation.

[3]https://github.com/UniversalAnaphora

For computing preliminary benchmark results for NARC – as presented in Section 5 – we adopt the approach for word-level coreference resolution developed by Dobrovolskii (2021)[4]. Rather than directly predicting coreference links between word spans, the problem is split into two sub-tasks; first predicting coreference links between individual words, and then predicting the corresponding spans. This substantially reduces the computational complexity while still maintaining SotA performance when evaluated on OntoNotes for English, owing in particular to gains in recall (Dobrovolskii, 2021).

3 Annotation

We here detail the annotation effort and present the underlying data for annotation, the pre-annotation of markables, the annotated NARC mentions and relations, as well as the review and curation process and inter-annotator agreement.

3.1 Data source

As mentioned above, the underlying data for the annotation effort is the Norwegian Dependency Treebank (NDT), a richly annotated dataset (Solberg et al., 2014; Øvrelid and Hohle, 2016; Jørgensen et al., 2020). The original treebank contains manually annotated syntactic and morphological information for both varieties of written Norwegian – Bokmål and Nynorsk – comprising roughly 300,000 tokens of each and a total of around 600,000 tokens. The corpus contains a majority of news texts (comprising around 85% of the corpus), but also other types of texts, such as government reports, parliamentary transcripts and blog data.

3.2 Pre-annotation

In order to alleviate the annotators' job of locating potential mentions for coreference, we make use of the existing syntactic annotation of the data to perform a pre-annotation step. In particular, we formulate simple heuristics over parts-of-speech and dependency relations which derive noun phrases from the dependency syntax of the treebank. Using the dependency syntax, we extract all nominal heads that are either i) nouns (both common and proper nouns), ii) referential personal pronouns [5],

[4]Information on the modelling setup is available from the data repository.

[5]The NDT annotation identifies so-called formal subjects/objects, which are non-referential or expletive uses of the pronoun *det* 'it'.

iii) possessive pronouns, or iv) adjectives in a nominal syntactic function (subject, object or prepositional complement). The full NP is constructed by traversing all syntactic dependents of these nominal heads. For coordination, we extract the full coordinated phrase as well as potential markables for individual nominal conjuncts. The annotators are instructed to treat the pre-annotated markables as suggestions only, since the syntactic units do not always correspond to coreference mentions (Popel et al., 2021).

3.3 Annotation guidelines

The annotation guidelines were developed during an initial pilot phase, where the documents used for training of the annotators were annotated by two of the project PIs. The guidelines were based largely on the guidelines from Ontonotes and the previous Norwegian BREDT dataset, as described in section 2.1 above, and were continuously refined following discussions and inputs from the annotators. The full set of annotation guidelines are released along with the dataset.

3.4 NARC markables

The annotators are presented with the pre-annotated markables for annotation. As mentioned above, these include nouns, referential personal and possessive pronouns, as well as adjectives in a nominal function. Below we describe some of the specific cases regarding the annotation of markables in NARC.

Markable boundaries Compounding is highly productive in Norwegian and compounds are written as one word, e.g. *innebandylag* 'field hockey team'. Even so, markables in NARC always correspond to full tokens and are never sub-token units. Additional information that is often provided in parentheses behind a noun, e.g. *John (53)* is part of the noun phrase and therefore also part of the markable in NARC. Both relative clauses and appositions are also included in the span of the markable that they modify.

Nested markables NARC allows for nested markables, i.e., when a nominal markable is contained within a larger markable. When considering pre-annotated markables that were nested, the annotators were instructed to assess whether it is possible for the individual nominals making up the larger markable to have a reference that is independent of the markable as a whole. Only in cases where this is in fact possible should nesting of markables be allowed. Proper nouns are always considered to be atomic and they are not annotated as nested even if it is possible to identify composite proper nouns within the names, such as e.g., *Oslo* in the proper name *University of Oslo*. This treatment is also in line with the flat annotation of such names in both the original treebank (Solberg et al., 2014) and NorNE (Jørgensen et al., 2020), the named entity annotated version of the treebank as described above.

3.5 NARC relations

Three relations are used in NARC: COREFERENCE, BRIDGING and SPLIT-ANTECEDENT.[6] In the following we describe the annotation of these relations in NARC, relating to annotation efforts for other datasets wherever possible.

3.5.1 Coreference

COREFERENCE is the relation reserved for coreferring markables. The annotation guidelines are to a large extent based on those of OntoNotes (Weischedel et al., 2011). Two broad categories of coreferring expressions are recognised in NARC: *anaphors* and what we might called *repeated coreferring entities*. Anaphors, or anaphoric expressions, usually need to be resolved to an antecedent to be interpreted. This includes third person pronouns and possessive determiners such as *hun*, 'she' and *hans*, 'his', but also definite nouns such as *bilen*, 'the car'. The second category, *repeated coreferring entities*, are markables such as proper names and first and second personal pronouns, which are not inherently anaphoric, but which still can corefer with a markable in the previous text. Indefinite nominals, including many quantified expressions, are not assumed to be coreferent with a markable in the previous text, but they can be antecedents of anaphors.

Markables are generally linked to the nearest coreferring markable to the left. Figure 1 illustrates this: The spans marked with boxes are the markables of the text. The pronoun *han*, 'he', has a coreferent relation to *Henrik Bjørnstad* in the preceding sentence. This is, however, not always the case. In some instances, pronouns may resolve to markables that *follow* rather than precede – a

[6] Unlike OntoNotes, there is no relation for appositives (BBN Technologies, 2007, 1.2). Instead, the adjacent, coreferring nouns in an appositive construction are taken as part of the same markable span.

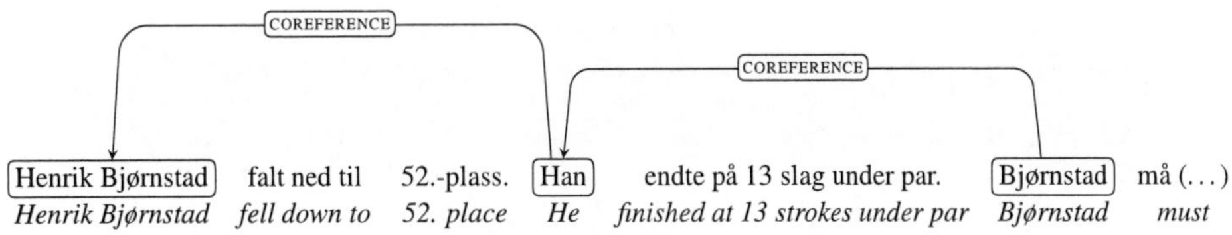

Figure 1: Example of a coreference relation in NARC.

phenomenon called *cataphora*. In cataphoric expressions, the markable is linked to the nearest antecedent to the right. This is shown in Figure 2, where the antecedent of the pronoun appears after the reference.

OntoNotes permits certain markables which are neither nominals nor determiners. Firstly, coreference relations are drawn between anaphoric expressions and verbs in OntoNotes. This means that e.g. event-denoting definite descriptions such as *the large growth* can refer back to a verb such as *grew*, which thereby becomes a markable. In NARC, however, all markables are nominal. Secondly, temporal adverbials such as *now* and *then* may participate in coreference chains in OntoNotes (BBN Technologies, 2007, 1.1.4; 2.8), whereas we only annotate temporal expressions that are nominal.

In NARC, we have chosen not to include verbs and adverbs in the set of possible markables. While this may leave certain anaphoric markables without an antecedent, it makes the annotation task easier and removes a potential source of inconsistencies. It is, for example, not always clear if the actual antecedent of an anaphoric expression is a verb or an entire proposition.

3.5.2 Split antecedent

The anaphoric possibilities of plural pronouns and definite nouns are a bit broader than for singular anaphors. They may corefer with a plural nominal or a coordinated structure in the textual context, in which case it is annotated with a COREFERENCE relation in NARC. Quite often, however, the reference of the plural anaphor is not coreferent with one single markable, but rather has multiple 'partial' antecedents in the discourse. Such cases are treated differently in different datasets. In OntoNotes, they are not annotated at all. In the ARRAU corpus, they are handled as a kind of bridging (Uryupina et al., 2020, pp. 106-107). In NARC, we use a special relation in such cases: SPLIT-ANTECEDENT. A split antecedent relation is drawn from the anaphor to each of its partial antecedents. This is shown in figure 3.

3.5.3 Bridging

BRIDGING indicates an anaphoric relation between two markables that are *not* coreferent, but associated in such a way that the correct identification of the anaphoric referent requires that the hearer establishes the relation to the antecedent. For example, in Figure 4, *rattet* 'the wheel' refers to the steering wheel of the mentioned car, *den gullfargede Roveren* 'the gold-colored Rover'. Typical relations involved in bridging are part–whole relations and various types of possession (Clark, 1977). Bridging can also involve verbal antecedents, where a following definite nominal is understood to have filled a particular thematic role: *John was murdered yesterday. The knife laid nearby*. In line with our decision to exclude verbal antecedents, we do not annotate these.

There are fewer corpora with bridging annotation compared to those which annotate coreference. For example, OntoNotes does not include bridging annotation, although two later efforts, IS-notes (Markert et al., 2012) and BASHI (Rösiger, 2018), each added this for 50 WSJ articles from OntoNotes. The ARRAU corpus (Uryupina et al., 2020) also includes bridging annotations.

Bridging is a complex phenomenon, with several sub-types and no established annotation standard; see the discussion in Roesiger et al. (2018). For our purposes, we adopted a very simple heuristic: when encountering a definite NP, annotators were asked first to look for a coreferent antecedent. If there is none, they should look for a related but not coreferent NP (e.g. bearing a part–whole relation or a possessive relation) and consider whether that related NP explains the use of the definite article by imagining the text without the antecedent. If this makes the definite infelicitous, it should be marked with BRIDGING. We make no attempt to identify sub-types of bridging.

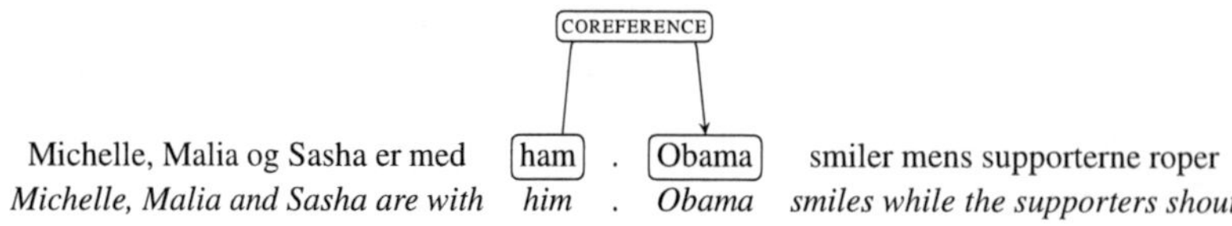

Figure 2: Example of a cataphora relation in NARC.

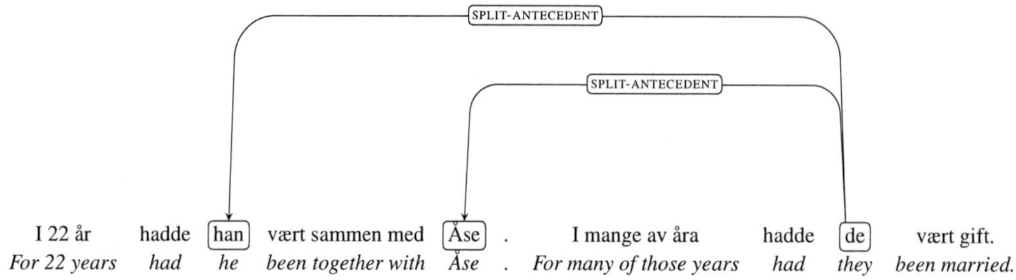

Figure 3: Example of a split antecedent relation in NARC.

3.6 Annotation Procedure

Annotation was performed using the Brat annotation tool (Stenetorp et al., 2012). Six students with a background in NLP and linguistics annotated the Norwegian Bokmål part of the corpus. The students received financial remuneration for their annotation work. All annotators completed an initial training round where they were tasked with annotation of the same set of documents, followed by a round of discussion and consolidation, along with updates to the annotation guidelines.

Due to restrictions in the annotation software, and the time needed to annotate, documents of over 150 sentences in length were split into smaller sections and annotated separately. All other documents were sorted into groups of 10 which were balanced according to length to ensure a constant workload for the annotators across the annotation period. During weekly meetings, the annotators had the opportunity to discuss challenges encountered when annotating or unclarities in the guidelines, so that these could be resolved, and the guidelines updated. Note that the documents set aside for measuring inter-annotator agreement were exempt from these discussions.

3.6.1 Review and Curation

Following the initial annotation process, all documents were re-annotated in one of two ways. The documents annotated by a single annotator were *reviewed* by a second annotator in a subsequent step. In this case, the second annotator only corrected errors from the first annotation round. In the case of documents annotated for inter-annotator agreement, a third annotator would base the curation of the document on one annotation, and then make changes based on the other, ensuring that both annotations are taken into account, while at the same time making sure there are no errors. Although both addition and removal of annotations were seen in the review process, the average changes were positive in all cases. These differences in numbers for the relations are summarized in Table 1.

Markables	Relations	Coref.	Bridg.
1.7	5.9	4.5	1.5

Table 1: Differences in numbers before and after review. Numbers are average differences between documents.

3.7 Inter-Annotator Agreement

59 documents, divided into 5 groups of 10 and one group of 9, were set aside for inter-annotator agreement towards the end of the annotation period. Each document group was annotated by two annotators. All annotators annotated at least one group for IAA, while some annotated more, due to differences in capacity. These documents were chosen as they are believed to represent a point in time where annotators should be familiar with the guidelines and the annotation task. In order to get a reliable indication of which areas are the most problematic, we look at agreement scores for different components separately. We follow Nedoluzhko et al. (2016) in using an F_1 score to look at the

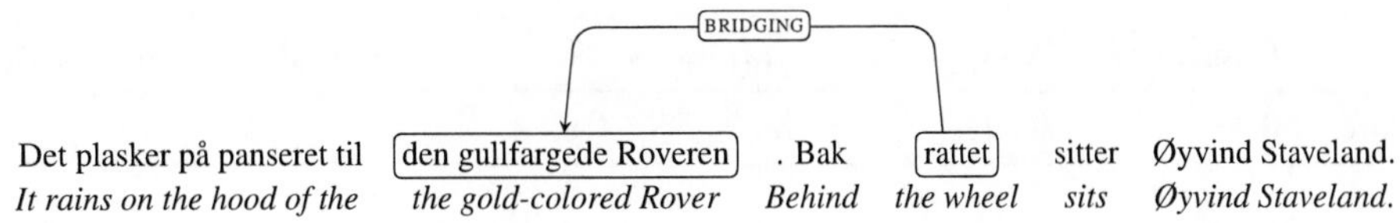

Figure 4: Example of a bridging relation in NARC.

agreement for all relations, and Cohen's κ for the specific labels. We also use the F_1 score for the markable agreement, following Kopeć and Ogrodniczuk (2014).

We see that annotators largely agree on the markables in the document, with some minor differences. On average, there was a difference of 2.2 markables per document, giving an F_1 score of 0.99. We see this as a confirmation that the pre-annotation provided a satisfactory basis for the annotation. Notably, 17% of the disagreement is due to the word *seg* 'oneself', which was known to fall outside of the pre-annotations in certain cases.

For the relations, we measure an overall F_1 score of 0.83. We see that although annotators tend to agree on many relations, there was still disagreement that had to be addressed during the review phase. When calculating the observed Cohen's κ, we follow Kopeć and Ogrodniczuk (2014), who notes that Cohen's κ must be calculated separately for each document, then averaged across documents in order to avoid including the probability of annotating across documents. The agreement score was calculated based on the markables that were already used in some relation by the annotators, and the relations for each annotator. The resulting values are presented in Table 2. We note that IAA scores are relatively high, especially for COREFERENCE. Both SPLIT-ANTECEDENT and especially BRIDGING have lower scores than COREFERENCE, but they also have fewer annotated examples. The low score for BRIDGING is also not surprising, based on the observation that this is a much more difficult annotation task.

4 Corpus statistics

Table 3 summarizes the most important statistics for the dataset [7]. We see that unsurprisingly the most common type of relation by far is the COREFERENCE relation, followed by BRIDGING and SPLIT-ANTECEDENT. However, some of these low numbers for BRIDGING can be explained by the difficulty of identifying bridging in the first place. We see that despite a large number of possible markables from the pre-annotation process, only 37% are used in relations. Relations are overwhelmingly anaphoric, with only 1.3% being cataphoric. As we do not pose any restrictions on how far back a relation can be drawn in a document, there are some relations with long edges. Looking at the distance based on tokens, the mode distance is 6, but the distribution has a long tail to the right with many long-distance relations. An example of this is in one of the documents with more than 150 sentences, where a relation was drawn from near the end of the document to an antecedent near the start, separating the elements of the relation by 5629 tokens. These cases do require that no relevant antecedent be mentioned in between. Due to the long tail, the average distance is 70.4, while the median is 19.0 for COREFERENCE. For BRIDGING, the average is 32.1 while the median is 16.0. Note that the annotators were told to think about whether the removal of the antecedent in a BRIDGING relation would change the viability of the definite form believed to have a BRIDGING relation. This might have caused an implicit restriction on bridging-relation lengths. For COREFERENCE there were no such restrictions, and annotators were asked to mark all COREFERENCE relations where possible. The median for the split antecedent relations is 22.0.

Clusters are collections of relations that have markables in common. The average length for COREFERENCE clusters is 4.7 tokens, while for BRIDGING it is 2 tokens. Most clusters, regardless of type, are of length 2, i.e. from a single antecedent to an anaphoric or bridging expression. Despite the low average, there are still some very long clusters.

Finally, we also analyzed the data to investigate what types of expressions occur as anaphoric expressions. As noted earlier, there are primarily two types of relations that fall under COREFERENCE.

[7] These statistics correspond to the first version of the NARC corpus. Subsequent releases of the dataset will contain the full Bokmål part of NDT as well as the Nynorsk part of the corpus.

	Overall F_1	Anaphor κ	Cataphor κ	Coref. κ	Bridging κ	Split Ant. κ
Scores	0.83	0.82	0.80	0.84	0.44	0.66

Table 2: IAA scores for the 59 documents annotated for agreement. The overall score is in F_1, while the others are represented by Cohen's κ, showing scores for specific directions (anaphor and cataphor) and labels (coreference, bridging, split antecedent).

Type	Value
Documents	326
Sentences	15125
Tokens	231363
Total markables	6979
Used markables	26005
Singletons	43788
Single word markables	34
Discontinuous markables	499
COREFERENCE relations	19420
BRIDGING relations	990
SPLIT-ANTECEDENT relations	292
COREFERENCE clusters	5350
BRIDGING clusters	962
Anaphor relations	20425
Cataphor relations	277
Sentences per document	46.4
Tokens per document	709.7
Markables per document	214
Avg. COREFERENCE cluster length	4.7
Avg. BRIDGING cluster length	2.0
Avg. COREFERENCE distance	70.4
Avg. BRIDGING distance	32.1
Avg. SPLIT-ANTECEDENT distance	53.9

Table 3: Counts and average values for some key statistics in the dataset. Singletons are markables that are not used in any relation. The last three values are the average distance between the antecedent and the referring expression in tokens.

The most common COREFERENCE expressions are pronouns, but both true anaphoric pronouns and pronouns referring to repeated entities are common. About 38% of all COREFERENCE relations are from a pronoun. As only third person pronouns and definite nouns can give rise to BRIDGING relations, this is naturally reflected in the types of expressions found. The most common is the pronoun *de* 'they', but another notable feature of the BRIDGING relations is that we see word forms such as *hodet* 'the head' *øynene* 'the eyes' *hånden* 'the hand' and *skuldrene* 'the shoulders' among the most common words. These are all typical of inalienable body parts, a type of bridging mentioned specifically in BREDT (Borthen et al., 2007).

5 Experiments

This section presents preliminary benchmarking experiments on the new dataset. Below we describe the distribution format of the data, the framework used for modelling and evaluation, and the results.

5.1 Format

Prior to modelling, the resulting files from the annotation tool (Brat) were converted to the format JSON Lines. This format has been common in coreference modelling since Lee et al. (2018) described the minimization process from the OntoNotes' CoNLL-format to JSON Lines, stripped of PoS-tags, lemmas and word sense information. For NARC, the annotations represent tokens structured in sentences along with coreference mention clusters, similar to LitBank (Bamman et al., 2020), GUM (Zeldes, 2017) and PreCo (Chen et al., 2018). Singleton mentions, i.e. markables not included in a coreference chain (see Table 3), have been discarded from the post-processing tasks, but may be used separately to model the impact of a separate mention detection system, as briefly studied by Chen et al. (2018), or a variation of the mention-ranking systems by Clark and Manning (2016). The dataset will include the data as JSON Lines and CoNLL, with and without singleton mentions. Furthermore, aligning NARC with the Norwegian Dependency Treebank (NDT), we will release the dataset in the CorefUD (Coreference Universal Dependencies) format, as described by Nedoluzhko et al. (2022).

5.2 Modelling framework

We apply the framework for word-level coreference resolution (wl-coref) developed by Dobrovolskii (2021), as mentioned in Section 2. This two-stage approach first predicts candidate antecedents for each token, before reconstructing the full spans by predicting the most likely start- and end-tokens in

Model	MUC			B^3			$CEAF_e$			LEA			CoNLL
	P	R	F_1	P	R	F_1	P	R	F_1	P	R	F_1	Mean F_1
NorBERT2	**90.40**	79.35	84.52	**63.15**	**62.71**	**62.93**	**55.52**	33.54	41.82	**61.94**	**61.50**	**61.72**	**63.09**
XLM-R	84.97	**84.51**	**84.74**	61.09	49.09	54.44	51.17	**51.17**	**51.17**	58.87	47.11	52.34	**63.45**

Table 4: Evaluation of predictions on the held-out test split of NARC.

the same sentence. To create the required training data, the syntactic head for each annotated span is added to the dataset through the Norwegian parser available with spaCy[8]. On the basis of this, two training sets are created; one for predicting the word-level coreference links and one for predicting the corresponding spans (Dobrovolskii, 2021).

The original wl-coref system was trained with a 48 GB GPU resource. Our model was trained using a 40 GB GPU resource, which was sufficient to run the *base* model of XLM-RoBERTa with the same hyperparameters as Dobrovolskii (2021), but not the *large* version.

For evaluation we use the standard coreference metrics as computed by the CoNLL 2012 scoring script, including the MUC metric proposed by Vilain et al. (1995), B^3 as proposed by Bagga and Baldwin (1998), $CEAF_e$ as proposed by Luo (2005), and finally the aggregated score of Mean F_1 as proposed by Pradhan et al. (2012), referred to as the CoNLL-F_1. We also evaluate with the Link-based Entity-Aware metric (LEA) by Moosavi and Strube (2016), using standard settings for entity importance scores.

Training a model for Norwegian text limits the options for pretrained language models. We chose four transformer-based language models for introductory testing on a subset of the data, two Norwegian and two multilingual, namely NorBERT2 (Kutuzov et al., 2021), NB-BERT (Kummervold et al., 2021), XLM-RoBERTa (XLM-R base) (Conneau et al., 2020) and multilingual BERT (mBERT) (Devlin et al., 2019).

Dobrovolskii (2021) report the choice of pretrained language models to be important for the system's performance. They use large, monolingual versions of RoBERTa, SpanBERT and Longformer. Such models are presently not available for Norwegian.

5.3 Results

The four language models were evaluated using wl-coref. Based on these initial results, as seen

mBERT	nb-BERT	nor-BERT2	XLM-R
51.3	51.8	54.0	56.1

Table 5: The four preliminary selected pretrained language models and their F_1 scores according to the wl-coref evaluation.

in Table 5, the NorBERT2 and XLM-RoBERTa models were selected for further experimentation. We proceeded with fine-tuning the two models on the training set, comprising 80% of the data. Two other splits – dev and test – were used for evaluation and a held-out test set respectively. Results on the test set are shown in Table 4. The high MUC scores indicate that the model was able to properly group mention clusters. The somewhat lower recall scores shows that there are still some lacking clusters, regardless of the groups they were linked to. B^3 and $CEAF_e$ scores are significantly lower, meaning that while a lot of mentions were found, the models discovered fewer entities and was unable to correctly assign mention clusters. The LEA score also represents the lack of entity assignment within the discovered clusters, and the higher score compared to $CEAF_e$ of the NorBERT2 model is likely due to LEA supporting a weighted one-to-many assignment of clusters.

Regardless, we find that the scores are comparable to existing work on CR, with the main difference being the MUC values scoring higher than current state-of-the-art models on the OntoNotes dataset. The reason for lower scores on the following metrics are, as discussed, likely due to issues with entity resolution and assignment, and this is thus an important takeaway for future work.

6 Conclusion

This paper has introduced a new corpus for coreference resolution: the Norwegian Anaphora Resolution Corpus (NARC). It is the first openly available corpus of this kind for Norwegian and represents the result of a large annotation effort which en-

[8]https://spacy.io/

riches the Norwegian Dependency Treebank (Solberg et al., 2014; Øvrelid and Hohle, 2016) with annotation of document-level coreference resolution, including the annotation of split antecedents and bridging. The paper has detailed the annotation effort, including a summary of guidelines, annotion procedure, inter-annotator agreement and resulting dataset statistics, as well as provided results from initial modelling experiments. While this paper focuses on the annotation of the Bokmål section of the corpus, the final corpus will contain the full treebank dataset, including also its Nynorsk sections, corresponding to the second written standard of Norwegian. NARC, including the annotation guidelines, will be made freely available[9]. It will further be aligned with the underlying treebank, allowing for smooth interaction with the other annotation layers such as PoS, dependency syntax and named entities, thus constituting a richly annotated resource for Norwegian NLP in the future.

Acknowledgements

We want to express our gratitude to the many annotators involved with annotating the datasets: Fredrik Aas Andreassen, Marie Emerentze Fleisje, Jennifer Juveth, Annika Willoch Olstad, Anne Oortwijn, Stian Ramstad, Lilja Charlotte Storset, Veronica Dahlby Tveitan and Alexandra Wittemann. We are grateful for the initial funding from Teksthub, and to Språkbanken for the main funding of the project.

References

Oshin Agarwal, Sanjay Subramanian, Ani Nenkova, and Dan Roth. 2019. Evaluation of named entity coreference. In *Proceedings of the Second Workshop on Computational Models of Reference, Anaphora and Coreference*, pages 1–7, Minneapolis, USA. Association for Computational Linguistics.

Amit Bagga and Breck Baldwin. 1998. Algorithms for scoring coreference chains. In *Proceedings of the First International Conference on Language Resources and Evaluation, Workshop on Linguistics Coreference*, pages 563–566, Granada, Spain.

David Bamman, Olivia Lewke, and Anya Mansoor. 2020. An annotated dataset of coreference in English literature. In *Proceedings of the 12th Language Resources and Evaluation Conference*, pages 44–54, Marseille, France. European Language Resources Association.

[9] `https://github.com/ltgoslo/NARC`

BBN Technologies. 2007. Co-reference guidelines for English OntoNotes version 7.0. Technical report, BBN Technologies.

Anders Björkelund and Richárd Farkas. 2012. Data-driven multilingual coreference resolution using resolver stacking. In *Joint Conference on EMNLP and CoNLL - Shared Task*, pages 49–55, Jeju Island, Korea. Association for Computational Linguistics.

Kaja Borthen, Lars G. Johnsen, and Christer Johansson. 2007. Coding anaphor-antecedent relations; the annotation manual for bredt. In *Proceedings from the first Bergen Workshop on Anaphora Resolution (WAR1)*, pages 86–111. Cambridge Scholars Publishing.

Peter Bourgonje and Manfred Stede. 2020. The Potsdam commentary corpus 2.2: Extending annotations for shallow discourse parsing. In *Proceedings of The 12th Language Resources and Evaluation Conference*, pages 1061–1066, Marseille, France. European Language Resources Association.

Hong Chen, Zhenhua Fan, Hao Lu, Alan Yuille, and Shu Rong. 2018. PreCo: A large-scale dataset in preschool vocabulary for coreference resolution. In *Proceedings of the 2018 Conference on Empirical Methods in Natural Language Processing*, pages 172–181, Brussels, Belgium. Association for Computational Linguistics.

Yu-Hsin Chen and Jinho D. Choi. 2016. Character identification on multiparty conversation: Identifying mentions of characters in TV shows. In *Proceedings of the 17th Annual Meeting of the Special Interest Group on Discourse and Dialogue*, pages 90–100, Los Angeles. Association for Computational Linguistics.

Herbert H Clark. 1977. Bridging. In Philip N. Johnson-Laird and Peter C. Wason, editors, *Thinking: Readings in Cognitive Science*, pages 311–326. Cambridge University Press, Cambridge.

Kevin Clark and Christopher D. Manning. 2015. Entity-centric coreference resolution with model stacking. In *Proceedings of the 53rd Annual Meeting of the Association for Computational Linguistics and the 7th International Joint Conference on Natural Language Processing (Volume 1: Long Papers)*, pages 1405–1415, Beijing, China. Association for Computational Linguistics.

Kevin Clark and Christopher D. Manning. 2016. Improving coreference resolution by learning entity-level distributed representations. In *Proceedings of the 54th Annual Meeting of the Association for Computational Linguistics (Volume 1: Long Papers)*, pages 643–653, Berlin, Germany. Association for Computational Linguistics.

Alexis Conneau, Kartikay Khandelwal, Naman Goyal, Vishrav Chaudhary, Guillaume Wenzek, Francisco Guzmán, Edouard Grave, Myle Ott, Luke Zettlemoyer, and Veselin Stoyanov. 2020. Unsupervised cross-lingual representation learning at scale. In *Proceedings of the 58th Annual Meeting of the Association for Computational Linguistics*, pages 8440–8451, Online. Association for Computational Linguistics.

Aron Culotta, Michael Wick, and Andrew McCallum. 2007. First-order probabilistic models for coreference resolution. In *Human Language Technologies 2007: The Conference of the North American Chapter of the Association for Computational Linguistics; Proceedings of the Main Conference*, pages 81–88, Rochester, New York. Association for Computational Linguistics.

Pascal Denis and Jason Baldridge. 2007. Joint determination of anaphoricity and coreference resolution using integer programming. In *Human Language Technologies 2007: The Conference of the North American Chapter of the Association for Computational Linguistics; Proceedings of the Main Conference*, pages 236–243, Rochester, New York. Association for Computational Linguistics.

Jacob Devlin, Ming-Wei Chang, Kenton Lee, and Kristina Toutanova. 2019. BERT: Pre-training of deep bidirectional transformers for language understanding. In *Proceedings of the 2019 Conference of the North American Chapter of the Association for Computational Linguistics: Human Language Technologies, Volume 1 (Long and Short Papers)*, pages 4171–4186, Minneapolis, Minnesota. Association for Computational Linguistics.

Vladimir Dobrovolskii. 2021. Word-level coreference resolution. In *Proceedings of the 2021 Conference on Empirical Methods in Natural Language Processing*, pages 7670–7675, Online and Punta Cana, Dominican Republic. Association for Computational Linguistics.

George Doddington, Alexis Mitchell, Mark Przybocki, Lance Ramshaw, Stephanie Strassel, and Ralph Weischedel. 2004. The automatic content extraction (ACE) program – tasks, data, and evaluation. In *Proceedings of the Fourth International Conference on Language Resources and Evaluation (LREC'04)*, Lisbon, Portugal. European Language Resources Association (ELRA).

Greg Durrett and Dan Klein. 2013. Easy victories and uphill battles in coreference resolution. In *Proceedings of the 2013 Conference on Empirical Methods in Natural Language Processing*, pages 1971–1982, Seattle, Washington, USA. Association for Computational Linguistics.

Jenny Rose Finkel and Christopher D Manning. 2008. Enforcing transitivity in coreference resolution. In *Proceedings of ACL-08: HLT, Short Papers*, pages 45–48, Columbus, Ohio, USA. Association for Computational Linguistics.

Abbas Ghaddar and Philippe Langlais. 2016. Coreference in Wikipedia: Main concept resolution. In *Proceedings of The 20th SIGNLL Conference on Computational Natural Language Learning*, pages 229–238, Berlin, Germany. Association for Computational Linguistics.

Ralph Grishman and Beth M Sundheim. 1996. Message understanding conference-6: A brief history. In *COLING 1996 Volume 1: The 16th International Conference on Computational Linguistics*, pages 466–471.

Anupam Guha, Mohit Iyyer, Danny Bouman, and Jordan Boyd-Graber. 2015. Removing the training wheels: A coreference dataset that entertains humans and challenges computers. In *Proceedings of the 2015 Conference of the North American Chapter of the Association for Computational Linguistics: Human Language Technologies*, pages 1108–1118, Denver, Colorado. Association for Computational Linguistics.

Aria Haghighi and Dan Klein. 2009. Simple coreference resolution with rich syntactic and semantic features. In *Proceedings of the 2009 conference on empirical methods in natural language processing*, pages 1152–1161, Singapore. ACL and AFNLP.

Iris Hendrickx, Gosse Bouma, Frederik Coppens, Walter Daelemans, Veronique Hoste, Geert Kloosterman, Anne-Marie Mineur, Joeri Van Der Vloet, and Jean-Luc Verschelde. 2008. A coreference corpus and resolution system for Dutch. In *Proceedings of the Sixth International Conference on Language Resources and Evaluation (LREC'08)*, Marrakech, Morocco. European Language Resources Association (ELRA).

Gordana Ilić Holen. 2007. Automatic anaphora resolution for norwegian (ARN). In *Anaphora: Analysis, Algorithms and Applications*, pages 151–166, Berlin, Heidelberg. Springer Berlin Heidelberg.

Fredrik Jørgensen, Tobias Aasmoe, Anne-Stine Ruud Husevåg, Lilja Øvrelid, and Erik Velldal. 2020. NorNE: Annotating named entities for Norwegian. In *Proceedings of the 12th Language Resources and Evaluation Conference*, pages 4547–4556, Marseille, France. European Language Resources Association.

Mandar Joshi, Danqi Chen, Yinhan Liu, Daniel S. Weld, Luke Zettlemoyer, and Omer Levy. 2020. SpanBERT: Improving pre-training by representing and predicting spans. *Transactions of the Association for Computational Linguistics*, 8:64–77.

Ben Kantor and Amir Globerson. 2019. Coreference resolution with entity equalization. In *Proceedings of the 57th Annual Meeting of the Association for Computational Linguistics*, pages 673–677, Florence, Italy. Association for Computational Linguistics.

Yuval Kirstain, Ori Ram, and Omer Levy. 2021. Coreference resolution without span representations. In *Proceedings of the 59th Annual Meeting of the Association for Computational Linguistics and the 11th International Joint Conference on Natural Language*

Processing (Volume 2: Short Papers), pages 14–19, Online. Association for Computational Linguistics.

Mateusz Kopeć and Maciej Ogrodniczuk. 2014. *Inter-annotator Agreement in Coreference Annotation of Polish*, pages 149–158. Springer International Publishing, Cham.

Iorn Korzen and Matthias Buch-Kromann. 2011. Anaphoric relations in the copenhagen dependency treebanks. In *Proceedings of DGfS Workshop, Göttingen, Germany*, pages 83–98.

Per E Kummervold, Javier De la Rosa, Freddy Wetjen, and Svein Arne Brygfjeld. 2021. Operationalizing a national digital library: The case for a Norwegian transformer model. In *Proceedings of the 23rd Nordic Conference on Computational Linguistics (NoDaLiDa)*, pages 20–29, Reykjavik, Iceland (Online). Linköping University Electronic Press, Sweden.

Andrey Kutuzov, Jeremy Barnes, Erik Velldal, Lilja Øvrelid, and Stephan Oepen. 2021. Large-scale contextualised language modelling for Norwegian. In *Proceedings of the 23rd Nordic Conference on Computational Linguistics (NoDaLiDa)*, pages 30–40, Reykjavik, Iceland (Online). Linköping University Electronic Press, Sweden.

Ekaterina Lapshinova-Koltunski, Christian Hardmeier, and Pauline Krielke. 2018. ParCorFull: a parallel corpus annotated with full coreference. In *Proceedings of the Eleventh International Conference on Language Resources and Evaluation (LREC 2018)*, Miyazaki, Japan. European Language Resources Association (ELRA).

Heeyoung Lee, Angel Chang, Yves Peirsman, Nathanael Chambers, Mihai Surdeanu, and Dan Jurafsky. 2013. Deterministic coreference resolution based on entity-centric, precision-ranked rules. *Computational Linguistics*, 39(4):885–916.

Kenton Lee, Luheng He, and Luke Zettlemoyer. 2018. Higher-order coreference resolution with coarse-to-fine inference. In *Proceedings of the 2018 Conference of the North American Chapter of the Association for Computational Linguistics: Human Language Technologies, Volume 2 (Short Papers)*, pages 687–692, New Orleans, Louisiana. Association for Computational Linguistics.

Xiaoqiang Luo. 2005. On coreference resolution performance metrics. In *Proceedings of Human Language Technology Conference and Conference on Empirical Methods in Natural Language Processing*, pages 25–32, Vancouver, British Columbia, Canada. Association for Computational Linguistics.

Xiaoqiang Luo, Abe Ittycheriah, Hongyan Jing, Nanda Kambhatla, and Salim Roukos. 2004. A mention-synchronous coreference resolution algorithm based on the bell tree. In *Proceedings of the 42nd Annual Meeting of the Association for Computational Linguistics (ACL-04)*, pages 135–142, Barcelona, Spain.

Katja Markert, Yufang Hou, and Michael Strube. 2012. Collective classification for fine-grained information status. In *Proceedings of the 50th Annual Meeting of the Association for Computational Linguistics (Volume 1: Long Papers)*, pages 795–804, Jeju Island, Korea. Association for Computational Linguistics.

Nafise Sadat Moosavi. 2020. *Robustness in Coreference Resolution*. Ph.D. thesis, Neuphilologische Fakultät > Institut für Computerlinguistik – Heidelberg University, Heidelberg.

Nafise Sadat Moosavi and Michael Strube. 2016. Which coreference evaluation metric do you trust? A proposal for a link-based entity aware metric. In *Proceedings of the 54th Annual Meeting of the Association for Computational Linguistics (Volume 1: Long Papers)*, pages 632–642, Berlin, Germany. Association for Computational Linguistics.

Anna Nedoluzhko, Michal Novák, Silvie Cinková, Marie Mikulová, and Jiří Mírovský. 2016. Coreference in Prague Czech-English Dependency Treebank. In *Proceedings of the Tenth International Conference on Language Resources and Evaluation (LREC'16)*, pages 169–176, Portorož, Slovenia. European Language Resources Association (ELRA).

Anna Nedoluzhko, Michal Novák, Martin Popel, Zdeněk Žabokrtský, Amir Zeldes, Daniel Zeman, Peter Bourgonje, Silvie Cinková, Jan Hajič, Christian Hardmeier, Pauline Krielke, Frédéric Landragin, Ekaterina Lapshinova-Koltunski, M. Antònia Martí, Marie Mikulová, Maciej Ogrodniczuk, Marta Recasens, Manfred Stede, Milan Straka, Svetlana Toldova, Veronika Vincze, and Voldemaras Žitkus. 2022. Coreference in universal dependencies 1.0 (CorefUD 1.0). LINDAT/CLARIAH-CZ digital library at the Institute of Formal and Applied Linguistics (ÚFAL), Faculty of Mathematics and Physics, Charles University.

Vincent Ng and Claire Cardie. 2002. Improving machine learning approaches to coreference resolution. In *Proceedings of the 40th Annual Meeting of the Association for Computational Linguistics*, pages 104–111, Philadelphia, Pennsylvania, USA. Association for Computational Linguistics.

Anders Nøklestad. 2009. *A machine learning approach to anaphora resolution including named entity recognition, PP attachment disambiguation, and animacy detection*. Ph.D. thesis, University of Oslo.

Maciej Ogrodniczuk, Katarzyna Głowińska, Mateusz Kopeć, Agata Savary, and Magdalena Zawisławska. 2016. Polish coreference corpus. In *Human Language Technology. Challenges for Computer Science and Linguistics*, pages 215–226, Cham. Springer International Publishing.

Lilja Øvrelid and Petter Hohle. 2016. Universal Dependencies for Norwegian. In *Proceedings of the Tenth International Conference on Language Resources and Evaluation (LREC'16)*, pages 1579–1585, Portorož, Slovenia. European Language Resources Association (ELRA).

Hoifung Poon and Pedro Domingos. 2008. Joint unsupervised coreference resolution with Markov Logic. In *Proceedings of the 2008 Conference on Empirical Methods in Natural Language Processing*, pages 650–659, Honolulu, Hawaii. Association for Computational Linguistics.

Martin Popel, Zdeněk Žabokrtský, Anna Nedoluzhko, Michal Novák, and Daniel Zeman. 2021. Do UD trees match mention spans in coreference annotations? In *Findings of the Association for Computational Linguistics: EMNLP 2021*, pages 3570–3576. Association for Computational Linguistics.

Sameer Pradhan, Alessandro Moschitti, Nianwen Xue, Olga Uryupina, and Yuchen Zhang. 2012. CoNLL-2012 shared task: Modeling multilingual unrestricted coreference in OntoNotes. In *Joint Conference on EMNLP and CoNLL-Shared Task*, pages 1–40, Jeju Island, Korea. Association for Computational Linguistics.

Sameer Pradhan, Lance Ramshaw, Mitchell Marcus, Martha Palmer, Ralph Weischedel, and Nianwen Xue. 2011. CoNLL-2011 shared task: Modeling unrestricted coreference in OntoNotes. In *Proceedings of the Fifteenth Conference on Computational Natural Language Learning: Shared Task*, pages 1–27, Portland, Oregon, USA. Association for Computational Linguistics.

Marta Recasens, Lluís Màrquez, Emili Sapena, M. Antònia Martí, Mariona Taulé, Véronique Hoste, Massimo Poesio, and Yannick Versley. 2010. SemEval-2010 task 1: Coreference resolution in multiple languages. In *Proceedings of the 5th International Workshop on Semantic Evaluation*, pages 1–8, Uppsala, Sweden. Association for Computational Linguistics.

Marta Recasens and M Antònia Martí. 2010. AnCora-CO: Coreferentially annotated corpora for Spanish and Catalan. *Language resources and evaluation*, 44(4):315–345.

Ina Roesiger, Arndt Riester, and Jonas Kuhn. 2018. Bridging resolution: Task definition, corpus resources and rule-based experiments. In *Proceedings of the 27th International Conference on Computational Linguistics*, pages 3516–3528, Santa Fe, New Mexico, USA. Association for Computational Linguistics.

Ina Rösiger. 2018. BASHI: A corpus of Wall Street Journal articles annotated with bridging links. In *Proceedings of the Eleventh International Conference on Language Resources and Evaluation (LREC 2018)*, Miyazaki, Japan. European Language Resources Association (ELRA).

Per Erik Solberg, Arne Skjærholt, Lilja Øvrelid, Kristin Hagen, and Janne Bondi Johannessen. 2014. The Norwegian dependency treebank. In *Proceedings of the Ninth International Conference on Language Resources and Evaluation (LREC'14)*, pages 789–795, Reykjavik, Iceland. European Language Resources Association (ELRA).

Pontus Stenetorp, Sampo Pyysalo, Goran Topić, Tomoko Ohta, Sophia Ananiadou, and Jun'ichi Tsujii. 2012. brat: a web-based tool for NLP-assisted text annotation. In *Proceedings of the Demonstrations at the 13th Conference of the European Chapter of the Association for Computational Linguistics*, pages 102–107, Avignon, France. Association for Computational Linguistics.

Rhea Sukthanker, Soujanya Poria, Erik Cambria, and Ramkumar Thirunavukarasu. 2020. Anaphora and coreference resolution: A review. *Information Fusion*, 59:139–162.

Svetlana Toldova and Max Ionov. 2017. Coreference resolution for Russian: the impact of semantic features. *Computational Linguistics and Intellectual Technologies: Proceedings of the International Conference "Dialogue 2017"*, pages 339–348.

Olga Uryupina, Ron Artstein, Antonella Bristot, Federica Cavicchio, Francesca Delogu, Kepa J Rodriguez, and Massimo Poesio. 2020. Annotating a broad range of anaphoric phenomena, in a variety of genres: the ARRAU corpus. *Natural Language Engineering*, 26(1):95–128.

Erik Velldal, Lilja Øvrelid, and Petter Hohle. 2017. Joint UD parsing of Norwegian Bokmål and Nynorsk. In *Proceedings of the 21st Nordic Conference on Computational Linguistics*, pages 1–10, Gothenburg, Sweden. Association for Computational Linguistics.

Marc Vilain, John Burger, John Aberdeen, Dennis Connolly, and Lynette Hirschman. 1995. A model-theoretic coreference scoring scheme. In *Proceedings of the Sixth Message Understanding Conference (MUC-6)*, Columbia, Maryland.

Veronika Vincze, Klára Hegedűs, Alex Sliz-Nagy, and Richárd Farkas. 2018. SzegedKoref: A Hungarian coreference corpus. In *Proceedings of the Eleventh International Conference on Language Resources and Evaluation (LREC 2018)*, Miyazaki, Japan. European Language Resources Association (ELRA).

Kellie Webster, Marta Recasens, Vera Axelrod, and Jason Baldridge. 2018. Mind the GAP: A balanced corpus of gendered ambiguous pronouns. *Transactions of the Association for Computational Linguistics*, 6:605–617.

Ralph Weischedel, Eduard Hovy, Mitchell Marcus, Martha Palmer, Robert Belvin, Sameer Pradhan, Lance Ramshaw, and Nianwen Xue. 2011. Ontonotes: A large training corpus for enhanced processing. *Handbook of Natural Language Processing and Machine Translation. Springer*, 3(3):3–4.

Wei Wu, Fei Wang, Arianna Yuan, Fei Wu, and Jiwei Li. 2020. CorefQA: Coreference resolution as query-based span prediction. In *Proceedings of the 58th Annual Meeting of the Association for Computational Linguistics*, pages 6953–6963, Online. Association for Computational Linguistics.

Liyan Xu and Jinho D. Choi. 2020. Revealing the myth of higher-order inference in coreference resolution. In *Proceedings of the 2020 Conference on Empirical Methods in Natural Language Processing (EMNLP)*, pages 8527–8533, Online. Association for Computational Linguistics.

Amir Zeldes. 2017. The GUM corpus: Creating multilayer resources in the classroom. *Language Resources and Evaluation*, 51(3):581–612.

Voldemaras Žitkus and Rita Butkiene. 2018. Coreference annotation scheme and corpus for Lithuanian language. In *2018 Fifth International Conference on Social Networks Analysis, Management and Security (SNAMS)*, pages 243–250. IEEE.

Evaluating Coreference Resolvers on Community-based Question Answering: From Rule-based to State of the Art

Haixia Chai[†] **Nafise Sadat Moosavi**[Φ Ψ] **Iryna Gurevych**[Φ] **Michael Strube**[†]
[†] Heidelberg Institute for Theoretical Studies
[Φ] UKP Lab, Technische Universität Darmstadt
[Ψ] Department of Computer Science, The University of Sheffield
{haixia.chai, michael.strube}@h-its.org

Abstract

Coreference resolution is a key step in natural language understanding. Developments in coreference resolution are mainly focused on improving the performance on standard datasets annotated for coreference resolution. However, coreference resolution is an intermediate step for text understanding and it is not clear how these improvements translate into downstream task performance. In this paper, we perform a thorough investigation on the impact of coreference resolvers in multiple settings of a community-based question answering task, i.e., answer selection with long answers. Our settings cover multiple text domains and encompass several answer selection methods. We first inspect extrinsic evaluation of coreference resolvers on answer selection by using coreference relations to decontextualize individual sentences of candidate answers, and then annotate a subset of answers with coreference information for intrinsic evaluation. The results of our extrinsic evaluation show that while there is a significant difference between the performance of the rule-based system vs. state-of-the-art neural model on coreference resolution datasets, we do not observe a considerable difference on their impact on downstream models. Our intrinsic evaluation shows that (i) resolving coreference relations on less-formal text genres is more difficult even for trained annotators, and (ii) the values of linguistic-agnostic coreference evaluation metrics do not correlate with the impact on downstream data.[1]

1 Introduction

Coreference resolution is the task of determining the expressions of the text that refer to the same entity. Modeling coreference relations is a key step for understanding the meaning of the text that can benefit various tasks like machine reading comprehension (Huang et al., 2022), summarization (Huang and Kurohashi, 2021), and dialogue processing (Xu and Choi, 2022).

The progress in coreference resolution is tailored to improve the performance on available coreference resolution datasets (Lee et al., 2017, 2018; Joshi et al., 2019, 2020; Kirstain et al., 2021; Chai and Strube, 2022), but it is not clear how this progress translates to downstream applications.

In this paper, we take a new perspective to directly evaluate the impact of coreference resolvers on a downstream task. First, we implement the extrinsic evaluation of coreference resolvers on the task of community-based question answering (CQA), in which the task is to select the correct answer given a question and a set of candidate answers. Answers in CQA are often very long, and they contain multiple referring expressions in each answer. To do so, we use existing coreference resolvers for decontextualizing candidate answers — i.e., replacing less informative nouns and pronouns with their most informative antecedent — so that the containing information in each individual sentence would be more standalone. To ensure that the resulting effects are not specific to a single dataset, domain, or downstream model, our settings cover multiple text domains and encompass several CQA methods. Second, we provide coreference annotations on a subset of answers from two CQA domains to enable intrinsic evaluation of coreference resolvers on a downstream data.

We evaluate several coreference resolvers from the rule-based system (Lee et al., 2013) to the state-of-the-art coreference resolver (Joshi et al., 2020) using our extrinsic and intrinsic evaluation setups.

The results of our extrinsic evaluation show that (i) rule-based system has a more positive and less negative impact on CQA compared to neural coreference resolvers, (ii) while there is a significant difference between the performance of the rule-based system vs. state-of-the-art neural model on coreference resolution datasets, we do not observe

[1] Our code and coreference annotations on CQA datasets are publicly available at: https://github.com/HaixiaChai/Coref_CQA

Proceedings of the Fifth Workshop on Computational Models of Reference, Anaphora and Coreference (CRAC 2022), pages 61–73
Gyeongju, Republic of Korea, October 16–17, 2022.

a considerable difference on their impact on CQA models. This means that intrinsic evaluation has to be accompanied by extrinsic evaluation, (iii) the impact of coreference resolution is different on various CQA methods. Thus, we suggest to consider the overall impact on multiple CQA models in order to investigate the effect of a coreference resolver on CQA, and (iv) coreference resolvers are most beneficial when both training and test data are decontextualized, and the rule-based system has consistent impact on different domains of the data while the state-of-the-art neural models have a considerable different impact on different domains.

Our extrinsic evaluation results show that (i) resolving coreference relations on less-formal text genres — like ones in the Stack Exchange answers — is more difficult even for trained annotators, and (ii) the results of linguistic-agnostic coreference evaluation metrics do not correlate with the impact of coreference resolvers on downstream data.

2 Coreference for Answer Selection

Given a question, the task of answer selection is to find the correct answer among the set of candidate answers. We use answer selection datasets from community question answering (CQA). CQA questions are non-factoid and they often require answers with descriptions or explanations. Therefore, CQA answers are long multi-sentence texts.

With the length of answers, the use of less informative expressions like pronouns increases. This presents a challenge for answer selection methods that mainly rely on the lexical forms to compute the similarity of the candidate answers to the question. Especially, when CQA data is collected by using a search engine or the answers to the similar questions for candidates, incorrect answers also have high lexical similarity with questions.

Using coreference resolvers for decontextualizing individual sentences in answer selection datasets makes correct answers more similar to the question and incorrect ones more dissimilar. Table 1 shows a sample question and two candidate answers, in which mentions that refer to the same entity are specified by the same index in each of the answers. **A1** and **A2** address two different issues, i.e., the need for a visa from Ireland to UK vs. getting an Irish visa given that your UK visa has been rejected. Both candidate answers contain a similar text sequence that is relevant to the question, i.e., "need to acquire a visa to enter the country" in

Q: Do I need a UK visa to enter UK from Ireland?
A1: What is your nationality? According to the [UK]$_1$ government service information website (URL), people from the countries who are mentioned in URL would still need to acquire a visa to enter [the country]$_1$.
A2: Data sharing means only that they share data, so while [the officers in [Ireland]$_6$]$_3$ are able to see details of [your]$_4$ failed UK visa when [they]$_3$ process [[your]$_4$ Irish visa]$_5$, that doesn't mean [you]$_4$ will be refused to get [the visa]$_5$ to enter [the country]$_6$.

Table 1: An example of a question and a correct (**A1**) and an incorrect (**A2**) candidate answer.

A1 and "get the visa to enter the country" in **A2**. These two text sequences can be easily discriminated given coreference information, i.e., "need to acquire a visa to enter UK" in **A1** and "get your Irish visa to enter Ireland" in **A2**.

3 Extrinsic Evaluation on CQA

The following sections describe different components for the extrinsic evaluation of coreference resolvers using CQA. Figure 1 shows the flow chart.

3.1 Answer Selection Models

Sentence-BERT. We use Sentence-BERT (Reimers and Gurevych, 2019) as an unsupervised baseline for answer selection. Here, we use the pre-trained model, MPNet (Song et al., 2020), to compute sentence embeddings.[2] By computing the sentence embedding of each candidate answer and that of the question, we select the candidate answer with the highest cosine similarity to the question.[3]

CNN. We train a CNN network for computing the semantic representation of candidate answers and questions. Similar to Tan et al. (2016) and Rücklé et al. (2019), we use a max-pooling layer on top of a CNN to get fix-sized representations. The similarity of the candidate answer and question representations is computed by cosine similarity.

Attentive LSTM. Instead of computing independent representations for questions and candidate answers, Tan et al. (2016) propose to use the attentive LSTM model in which the representation of answers is computed based on the question representation.

[2]MPNet shows the best performance at `https://www.sbert.net/docs/pretrained_models.html`.

[3]This approach is the state of the art on the datasets (Rücklé et al., 2019) on which we study the extrinsic evaluation of coreference resolution systems.

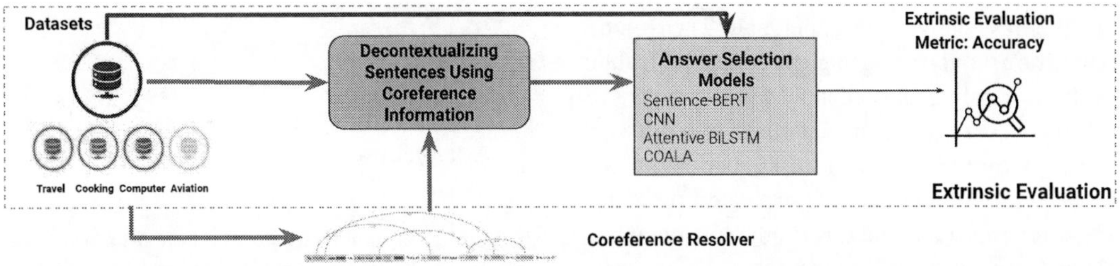

Figure 1: The figure shows our extrinsic evaluation of coreference resolvers on CQA. The red line indicates decontextualizing sentences using coreference information in the data, while the blue line shows the original data.

COALA. The COALA model (Rücklé et al., 2019) first uses a CNN to compute a representation for the local aspect (bi-grams) of both the question and each candidate answer. It selects the candidate answer that covers more aspects of the question.[4]

3.2 Datasets

The datasets (Rücklé et al., 2019) are in English from a diverse set of domains from StackExchange including Travel (Q&A for travelers), Cooking (Q&A for professional and amateur chefs), Computer (Q&A for the users of Apple hardware and software), and Aviation (Q&A for aircraft pilots, mechanics, etc.) communities. Table 2 provides the statistics of these datasets.

Dataset	Number of Questions			Answer
	Train	Valid	Test	Length
Travel	3 572	765	766	214
Cooking	3 692	791	792	189
Computer	5 831	1 249	1 250	114
Aviation	3 035	650	652	281

Table 2: The statistics of the answer selection datasets.

These datasets contain predefined train, validation, and test splits. We train each of the supervised answer selection models on the training split of each of the datasets.[5] For instance, we have four different CNN trained models for each of the datasets. Models that are trained on the travel training set are used for evaluating the effect of coreference resolution on the travel test set.

Note that existing supervised coreference resolvers are trained on the CoNLL-2012 data (Pradhan et al., 2012) that contains different domains including newswire, broadcast news, broadcast conversations, telephone conversations, weblogs, magazines, and Bible domains.

[4]It has two variants, from which we select the one with higher scores, i.e., COALA p-means.

[5]We use same hyper-parameters as Rücklé et al. (2019).

3.3 Incorporating Coreference Relations

To benefit from coreference information in downstream tasks, one can either incorporate coreference relations in the model, e.g., (Dhingra et al., 2018; Du and Cardie, 2018; De Cao et al., 2019; Dua et al., 2020), or in its input data, e.g., (Steinberger et al., 2007; Du and Cardie, 2018), from which we use the second approach. The approach is similar to decontextualization (Choi et al., 2021), in which the goal is to make the meaning of individual sentences standalone in an empty context. Coreference resolution is one of the main steps for decontextualization, and as shown by Choi et al. (2021), it is a valuable preprocessing step for tasks that require document understanding.[6] In addition, using coreference resolvers for decontextualizing input sentences has the following benefits: (1) a single coreference annotated dataset can be used for evaluating various answer selection models, and (2) it does not require developing specialized coreference-aware models for the application.

We first apply the coreference resolver on all candidate answers and get the resulting coreference chains. Then for each mention in the coreference chains, we determine the most representative antecedent[7] using the rules proposed by Lee et al. (2013): if two mentions are of different types, proper names are the most representative mentions and common nouns are more representative than pronouns, e.g., "the UK visa" vs. "it". Otherwise, the mention containing more words is more representative, "the UK visa" vs. "the visa".

In our experiments, we examine and report two different settings: (1) **coreference resolution**: replacing all types of referring expressions with their

[6]Note that the full decontextualization of sentences requires more than coreference resolution — e.g., bridging resolution. We aim to evaluate coreference resolvers, so we focus on using coreference resolution for decontextualization.

[7]All coreferring mentions that appear before the current mention are considered as antecedents.

most representative antecedent, and (2) **pronoun resolution**: only replacing pronouns with their most informative antecedent. Meanwhile, we incorporate coreference annotations in two different ways: (1) **only in the test data**: models trained on original training data are evaluated on different coreference annotations on the test data, and (2) **both in the training and test sets**: we train and test the supervised CQA models on the training and test sets that are decontextualized by using coreference relations.

3.4 Extrinsic Evaluation Metric

We use accuracy — i.e., the ratio of correctly selected answers — to measure the performance of answer selection models. The impact of each coreference resolver on answer selection is measured by computing the difference between the accuracy of answer selection models on the coreference annotated test sets vs. the original ones. Table 3 reports the performance of CQA models.

Model	Dataset			
	Travel	Cooking	Computer	Aviation
Sentence-BERT	81.98	77.65	64.32	80.06
CNN	34.46	26.01	20.24	26.22
Att.-BiLSTM	43.34	38.38	25.60	36.34
COALA	54.83	47.34	33.52	52.45

Table 3: Accuracy of answer selection models.

4 Intrinsic Evaluation on CQA data

We enable intrinsic evaluation of coreference resolvers on CQA data by annotating coreference relations on a subset of the CQA data.

We annotate a subset of examples from the Travel and Cooking test sets. We use *MMAX2* (Müller and Strube, 2006) for the annotations.[8] The annotations are done by six bachelor and master students with NLP background from the Departments of Computational Linguistics and Computer Science. They received a minimal training for coreference resolution and the *MMAX2* annotation tool. Table 4 presents the statistics of this annotated data. We annotate a subset of 100 answers by two of the annotators and perform an inter-annotator agreement study. The inter-annotator agreement is 0.71 using Krippendorff's α (Krippendorff, 1980) with MASI distance metric (Passonneau, 2006).[9]

[8] `http://mmax2.net/`

[9] Details are included in Appendix A.

	Travel	Cooking
answers	389	558
max words/answer	319	283
coreference chains/answer	4.2	3.4
mentions/answer	14.0	12.3

Table 4: Statistics of our human anotations based on the number of annotated answers, maximum number of words per answer, average number of coreference chains per answer, and average number of annotated mentions per answer in each of the domains.

While our agreement study shows a high inter-annotator agreement, we also perform a manual error analysis on the resulting annotations.[10] Based on our analysis, annotating coreference relations in less-formal genres is more difficult than in the common genres in existing NLP datasets, e.g., news, and their error-free annotations would require expert linguists.[11] In particular, human annotations in Travel contain more errors. This indicates that resolving coreference relations of the answers in the Travel domain, which contains more nominal expressions, is more difficult than Cooking.

5 Examined Coreference Resolvers

We evaluate four different coreference resolvers.

First, the Stanford **rule-based** system (Lee et al., 2013) that uses heuristic rules like string match for resolving coreference relations. There is a considerable gap between its performance and state-of-the-art coreference resolvers on the CoNLL-2012 test set. However, it has a reasonable performance across different domains (Moosavi and Strube, 2017).

Second, **deep-coref** (Clark and Manning, 2016), which is a neural coreference resolver. *deep-coref* is a neural model that first extracts candidate mentions using syntactic information. For each candidate mention, it scores all preceding mentions to select the best scoring one as the antecedent. It also includes a dummy antecedent to determine non-anaphoric mentions, i.e., if the dummy antecedent has the highest score, the mention is non-anaphoric.

Third, **e2e-coref** (Lee et al., 2018) that is an end-to-end neural coreference resolver and the base model for the majority of state-of-the-art coreference resolvers since 2018. Unlike *deep-coref* and

[10] For the error analysis of the human annotations, we refer to Appendix A.

[11] This is consistent with the previous observation of Chai et al. (2020) that resolving coreference relations in noisy user-generated texts is very challenging.

Coreference	Answer Selection	Travel	Cooking	Computer	Aviation
rule-based	Sentence-BERT	-1.57	-1.39	-0.96	-1.54
	CNN	**1.17**	**0.50**	**0.80**	0.00
	Att.-BiLSTM	***1.17***	***0.63***	***0.88***	***0.92***
	COALA	**0.78**	**0.13**	**1.44**	**0.46**
deep-coref	Sentence-BERT	-0.65	-0.63	-0.48	-1.54
	CNN	***0.52***	***0.75***	***0.40***	0.00
	Att.-BiLSTM	-0.13	**0.63**	**0.16**	**0.92**
	COALA	-0.40	**0.38**	**0.96**	**0.46**
e2e-coref	Sentence-BERT	**0.26**	-1.14	-0.48	-1.23
	CNN	***1.04***	***0.75***	***0.24***	***0.16***
	Att.-BiLSTM	-0.26	**0.50**	-0.24	-0.61
	COALA	**0.52**	-0.12	**0.24**	0.00
bert-coref	Sentence-BERT	-0.13	-1.01	0.00	-1.38
	CNN	**0.78**	-0.38	-0.40	**0.31**
	Att.-BiLSTM	**0.39**	**0.25**	**0.32**	**0.31**
	COALA	***0.39***	0.00	***0.56***	***0.61***

Table 5: Effect of the coreference resolvers on different answer selection models and datasets. Cell values indicate the difference between the accuracy when incorporating coreference annotations on test sets vs. the baseline results. The bold-faced values mean that the coreference resolver has a positive impact on the corresponding CQA models and domains. The values in italic and underline show the answer selection models on which each coreference system has the best impact.

rule-based systems, *e2e-coref* does not use syntactic information or a separate modules to determine candidate mentions. It jointly determines mention spans as well as their corresponding coreference relations by an end-to-end neural model.

Last, **bert-coref** (Joshi et al., 2020) that is one of the most recent state-of-the-art coreference resolvers on the CoNLL-2012 dataset. *bert-coref* is an extension of *e2e-coref* by replacing the bidirectional LSTM encoder with SpanBERT encodings. Concretely, we use the SpanBERT-large language model, which has a novel span masking pretraining objective that predicts the entire masked span instead of individual tokens.

For the reported extrinsic and intrinsic evaluations, the supervised coreference resolvers are trained on the English CoNLL-2012 dataset. Table 6 presents the scores of these coreference resolvers on the CoNLL-2012 test set based on the standard coreference evaluation metrics, i.e., MUC (Vilain et al., 1995), B^3 (Bagga and Baldwin, 1998), $CEAF_e$ (Luo, 2005), and LEA (Moosavi and Strube, 2016).

Metric	rule-based	deep-coref	e2e-coref	bert-coref
MUC	64.7	74.2	80.4	**85.3**
B^3	52.7	63.0	70.8	**78.1**
$CEAF_e$	49.3	58.7	67.6	**75.3**
LEA	47.3	59.5	67.7	**75.9**

Table 6: Performance of examined coreference resolvers on the English CoNLL-2012 test set based on coreference evaluation metrics.

6 Results

6.1 Extrinsic Evaluation

Evaluating CQA using coreference annotations in the test data. Table 5 shows the results of using the examined coreference resolvers on the CQA models and domains in the **coreference resolution** setting, i.e., replacing all referring expressions with their most representative antecedent.[12]

First, we observe that compared to state-of-the-art coreference resolvers, *rule-based* has a more positive impact and less negative impact on CQA.[13]

[12] Appendix C includes results of the **pronoun resolution**.

[13] We compute the statistical significance of *rule-based* and *bert-coref* by using Wilcoxon's Signed Rank test on all CQA models and two domains. For the travel domain the differences are statistically significant ($p \leq 0.05$), while in the cooking domain the results are not.

To further investigate this result, we report the total number of resolved mentions and pronouns by the examined resolvers across all CQA domains in Table 7. We observe that *rule-based* resolves the highest number of mentions (99k) and the lowest percentage of pronouns (64%), i.e., the ratio of pronouns in all resolved mentions, indicating that *rule-based* resolves more nominal mentions than the other coreference resolvers. Based on this observation, we hypothesize that resolving more nominal mentions and improving the precision of resolved pronouns will improve the effectiveness of state-of-the-art coreference resolvers on downstream applications.

Resolver	Mentions	Pronouns	% of Pronouns
rule-based	99k	63k	64%
deep-coref	70k	51k	73%
e2e-coref	72k	56k	77%
bert-coref	81k	57k	70%

Table 7: The statistics of total mentions and pronouns resolved by coreference resolvers on all domains.

Second, while there is a significant difference between performance of coreference resolvers on the CoNLL-2012 coreference dataset, e.g., ≈ 20 point difference between *rule-based* and *bert-coref* based on various coreference metrics in Table 6, we do not observe a considerable difference in their impact on CQA models. This suggests that intrinsic evaluation on CoNLL should be accompanied by extrinsic evaluation to approximate the utility of the coreference resolvers for end tasks.

Finally, we find that CNN and COALA that encode the text based on the local context have better performance with neural coreference resolvers, Attentive LSTM which encodes the context globally performs best with *rule-based*, and no coreference resolvers have a clear positive impact on SentenceBERT[14] in Table 5. In general, the impact of coreference resolvers varies for different CQA models. So, we suggest to consider the overall impact on multiple CQA models to investigate the effect of a coreference resolver on CQA.

Table 10 shows an example of replaced coreference relations in a candidate answer.

[14]It is shown that pretrained models, like SentenceBERT, capture linguistic structures like anaphoric coreference to some extent (Manning et al., 2020), that may be the reason that using the incorporating the noisy output of coreference resolvers does not improve the performance of such systems.

Evaluating CQA using coreference annotations in both training and test data. For the above experiments, we only evaluate the impact of coreference resolvers by incorporating coreference information only on the test data. However, this may results in disparity between the data that models are trained on vs. testing data. We also investigate the impact of incorporating coreference relations on both training and test CQA data. Table 8 presents the results of this experiment for the *rule-based* and *bert-coref* systems and for the two representative domains, Travel and Cooking. For each of the experiments, we train and test the CQA models on the training and test data in which referring expressions are replaced with their most representative detected antecedent.

Resolver	CQA	Travel	Cooking
rule-based	CNN	-0.78	1.26
	Att.-BiLSTM	2.35	0.13
	COALA	0.91	0.63
bert-coref	CNN	2.22	0.63
	Att.-BiLSTM	2.09	-2.27
	COALA	0.13	-2.14

Table 8: Evaluating the impact of coreference resolution on supervised CQA models when the coreference information is used both in training and test sets.

Based on the results, incorporating coreference relations in both training and test datasets results in higher improvements compared to only incorporating them in the test data since the models see similar data formats during training and evaluation. From both challenging domains, we observe that *bert-coref* performs better on the Travel domain, while *rule-based* shows most positive results on both domains, even on Cooking that has shorter texts and contains more disfluent and ungrammatical expressions compared to the Travel domain. Thus, we encourage people to research more on diverse domains or genres beyond well-structured narrative texts.

6.2 Intrinsic Evaluation

Table 9 shows the evaluation of the examined coreference resolvers on our CQA coreference data described in §4 based on standard coreference resolution evaluation metrics as well as Application Related Coreference Scores (ARCS). ARCS is proposed by Tuggener (2014) for evaluating coreference resolvers based on their potential impact on downstream applications.

As mentioned in §5, all systems are trained on

the CoNLL-2012 training data, which contains different genres that those in our CQA data.

Metric	rule-based	deep-coref	e2e-coref	bert-coref
		Travel		
MUC	28.07	**55.36**	34.90	39.53
B^3	28.81	**50.66**	34.28	39.31
$CEAF_e$	33.56	**45.83**	38.95	44.62
LEA	23.19	**46.86**	30.19	35.29
ARCS	18.24	23.99	29.47	**36.80**
		Cooking		
MUC	31.58	**59.43**	37.82	43.07
B^3	30.99	**54.85**	36.17	40.70
$CEAF_e$	34.77	**52.42**	41.36	45.11
LEA	24.47	**50.01**	30.88	36.04
ARCS	15.49	24.37	26.27	**34.17**

Table 9: Intrinsic evaluation of examined coreference resolvers on our CQA coreference data.

As we see from the results, all standard coreference evaluation metrics — including MUC, B^3, $CEAF_e$, and LEA — agree on the ranking of the examined resolvers on both domains, based on which *deep-coref* performs better than the other systems.[15] ARCS, on the other hand, ranks *bert-coref* higher than the rest of the systems on both domains. Interestingly, none of the above rankings is consistent with our extrinsic evaluations in Table 5, e.g., the *rule-based* system receives the lowest ranking based on all metrics in intrinsic evaluations while its overall impact on CQA models is better than that of *bert-coref*.

Note that existing coreference resolution evaluation metrics are linguistic-agnostic, i.e., they do not discriminate the resolution of different types of mentions. This can be a potential reason that existing metrics do not correlate with the performance on a downstream task. For instance, as shown by Agarwal et al. (2019) resolving the corresponding proper name of each entity is more important than the resolution of other relations for certain downstream tasks.

7 Related Work

Task-oriented evaluation of coreference resolution. Tuggener classifies the use of coreference resolution in higher-level applications into three classes and proposes a different evaluation metric for each usecase:

- *Modeling entity distributions* to determine the exact sequence of each entity occurrence, which is useful in applications like modeling local coherence (Barzilay and Lapata, 2008). For such use-cases, Tuggener proposes to evaluate the detection of the immediate antecedent of each mention.
- *Inferring local entities* to determine the closest nominal antecedent of each mention. This use-case can be useful in applications like machine translation and summarization in which resolving pronouns with a nominal antecedent reduces ambiguity of the text. The proposed evaluation for this category is to only evaluate the closest preceding nominal antecedent of each mention.[16]
- *Finding context for a specific entity* to determine all references to the entity. This is useful for finding parts of the context that are related to a given question. Tuggener proposes to evaluate this setting by first finding the most representative mention of each coreference chain, called the anchor mention. He then computes the number of correct and incorrect references for each anchor mention in order to measure the performance.

Evaluation metrics of Tuggener (2014) are applicable on coreference annotated datasets. However, (1) existing coreference resolvers do not generalize well to new datasets and the performance in in-domain vs. out-of-domain settings may be completely different, and (2) as we saw in §6.2, they do not necessarily correlate with the impact on downstream applications.

Coreference for question answering. The use of coreference resolution in answer selection has been explored by various work, e.g., (Morton, 1999, 2000; Vicedo and Ferrández, 2000, 2008; Wang, 2010).[17] Morton (1999) proposes to rank candidate answers based on their coreference relations with the question, so that answers having more common entities with the question would get a higher rank. Stuckhardt (2003) and Wang et al. (2010) use anaphora resolution to detect common entities between the question and the candidate document for improving QA.

Morton (2000) evaluates the use of coreference resolution for QA. In order to compute the relevance of each sentence to the given question, he

[15] Based on our analysis, *deep-coref* resolves fewer informative mentions and more repeated pronouns compared to other systems.

[16] ARCS used in §6.2 refers to this metric.

[17] For the use of coreference resolution for other NLP applications refer to Stuckardt (2016).

Original text: Short answer, you can't. However, you can at least make sure they have an official license, and any other accreditation which might lend some credence to their claims. Look for **ones that are licensed by the <URL>**, and consider **<URL>**, to see if anyone has mentioned **them$_1$** or complained about **them$_2$**. All you can do is research, and ask around when you get there as well. Or consider approaching **the companies** and ask **them$_3$** directly-I 'm sure you'd not be the first, even if **it** is rather brazen;)
rule-based: {them$_1$, them$_2$} ← ones that are licensed by the <URL>; {them$_3$} ← the companies; {it} ← <URL>
deep-coref: NIL
e2e-coref: {them$_1$, them$_2$} ← ones that are licensed by the <URL>; {them$_3$} ← the companies
bert-coref: {them$_1$, them$_2$} ← ones that are licensed by the <URL>; {them$_3$} ← the companies
human-annot: {them$_1$, them$_2$} ← ones that are licensed by the <URL>, <URL>; {them$_3$} ← the companies

Table 10: An example from the replacements made by each of the examined coreference resolvers.

considers all the other mentions beyond the boundary of the sentence itself, that are coreferent with any of the sentence mentions. Vicedo and Ferrández (2000) evaluate the use of pronoun resolution in QA, and more specifically answer selection in QA. They show that incorporating information regarding the antecedent of pronouns improves, and in some cases is essential, for QA.

Aforementioned works, which show that coreference is beneficial for QA, use small-scale evaluations and simple QA models, e.g., TF-IDF, and coreference resolvers, e.g., rule-based systems. In this work, we investigate the use of coreference using recent answer selection models and coreference resolvers as well as multiple large-scale datasets.

Du and Cardie (2018) incorporate coreference information both at the input- and model-level for QA. At the input-level, they add the most informative antecedent of the pronouns to the input. At the model-level, they add coreference position feature embeddings to the model that specify the position of pronouns and their corresponding antecedents. They incorporate a gating mechanism to refine position embeddings based on the corresponding coreference score of each antecedent-pronoun relation.

These methods are costly to train, and therefore, they are not suitable to facilitate an efficient evaluation of various coreference resolvers on different CQA models and domains, e.g., their experiments are based on a single coreference output.

Quoref (Dasigi et al., 2019) is a question answering dataset that is designed based on coreference relations, i.e., answering the question requires resolving the coreference relation between two mentions in the context. However, it is shown that answering questions in Quoref does not necessarily require coreference resolution and the questions may be answered by using simple shortcuts in the dataset (Wu et al., 2020). Dua et al. (2020) annotate the required coreference relations for answering questions in a subset of Quoref examples. They then propose a model that jointly predict coreference relations and the final answer. They show that this joint prediction improves the result of the question answering model. They use gold annotations in their study, and they only annotate the relations that are related to the question. This work does not explicitly use a coreference resolver to obtain coreference relations and does not aim to resolve all coreference relations.

8 Discussion

As mentioned in §7, there are many ways to incorporate coreference information in QA. In this work, we make it at the input-level by decontextualizing the input sentences. This makes the extrinsic evaluations efficient and enables evaluating any coreference resolvers on any downstream models and datasets. On the downside, the decontextualization results in unnatural sentences in some examples, which may negatively impact the downstream model. For instance, we observe that most coreference resolvers have a negative impact on Sentence-BERT in Table 5. Meanwhile, we find that the other three CQA models are more robust on the revised data especially for the *rule-based* system. Overall, evaluating coreference resolution systems in downstream tasks is a complicated task. Various evaluation methods could result in very different extrinsic evaluation results on different downstream models and datasets that could be similar or dissimilar with standard coreference datasets. In this paper, our method evaluates coreference resolvers more on the out-of-domain corpora with less-formal text in a downstream task, community-based question answering.

9 Conclusions

Coreference resolution is an important step for text understanding. The main shortcoming of recent developments in coreference resolution is that they mainly target improving the performance in standard coreference datasets. However, coreference resolution is not an end-application and it is not clear how the progress in in-domain evaluations translates into downstream tasks performance. In this work, we enable direct extrinsic and intrinsic evaluation of coreference resolvers on downstream models and data, respectively. For the extrinsic evaluations, we use coreference resolvers for decontextualizing the input sentences in community-based question answering (CQA) task. For intrinsic evaluation, we have annotated a subset of CQA data with coreference relations. Our extrinsic evaluations suggest that (1) while there is a significant gap on the performances of state-of-the-art coreference resolver and the rule-based system on coreference datasets, the rule-based system has a more consistent and positive impact on CQA while the impact of the state-of-the-art model can considerably vary based on the domain of the downstream data, and (2) using coreference resolvers for decontextualizing both training and test datasets is more beneficial than decontextualizing the test data. Our intrinsic evaluations suggest that there is a discrepancy between the rankings of existing coreference resolution evaluation metrics and the resulting rankings from the extrinsic evaluations. This suggests that intrinsic evaluation on CoNLL should be accompanied by extrinsic evaluation to approximate the utility of the coreference resolvers for downstream tasks.

Acknowledgements

The authors thank the anonymous reviewers for their constructive comments and suggestions. We also thank Friederike Lenke, Michael Tilli, Muhammad Usman and Fabian Dueker for coreference annotations on the CQA data. This work has been funded by the Klaus Tschira Foundation, Heidelberg, Germany. The first author has been supported by a Heidelberg Institute for Theoretical Studies PhD scholarship.

References

Oshin Agarwal, Sanjay Subramanian, Ani Nenkova, and Dan Roth. 2019. Evaluation of named entity coreference. In *Proceedings of the Second Workshop on Computational Models of Reference, Anaphora and Coreference*, pages 1–7, Minneapolis, USA. Association for Computational Linguistics.

Ron Artstein and Massimo Poesio. 2008. Inter-coder agreement for computational linguistics. *Computational Linguistics*, 34(4):555–596.

Amit Bagga and Breck Baldwin. 1998. Algorithms for scoring coreference chains. In *The First International Conference on Language Resources and Evaluation Workshop on Linguistics Coreference, Volume 1*, pages 563–566. Citeseer.

Regina Barzilay and Mirella Lapata. 2008. Modeling local coherence: An entity-based approach. *Computational Linguistics*, 34(1).

Haixia Chai and Michael Strube. 2022. Incorporating centering theory into neural coreference resolution. In *Proceedings of the 2022 Conference of the North American Chapter of the Association for Computational Linguistics: Human Language Technologies*, pages 2996–3002, Seattle, United States. Association for Computational Linguistics.

Haixia Chai, Wei Zhao, Steffen Eger, and Michael Strube. 2020. Evaluation of coreference resolution systems under adversarial attacks. In *Proceedings of the First Workshop on Computational Approaches to Discourse*, pages 154–159, Online. Association for Computational Linguistics.

Eunsol Choi, Jennimaria Palomaki, Matthew Lamm, Tom Kwiatkowski, Dipanjan Das, and Michael Collins. 2021. Decontextualization: Making sentences stand-alone. *Transactions of the Association for Computational Linguistics*, 9:447–461.

Kevin Clark and Christopher D. Manning. 2016. Improving coreference resolution by learning entity-level distributed representations. In *Proceedings of the 54th Annual Meeting of the Association for Computational Linguistics (Volume 1: Long Papers)*, pages 643–653, Berlin, Germany. Association for Computational Linguistics.

Michael Collins. 2003. Head-driven statistical models for natural language parsing. *Computational linguistics*, 29(4):589–637.

Pradeep Dasigi, Nelson F. Liu, Ana Marasović, Noah A. Smith, and Matt Gardner. 2019. Quoref: A reading comprehension dataset with questions requiring coreferential reasoning. In *Proceedings of the 2019 Conference on Empirical Methods in Natural Language Processing and the 9th International Joint Conference on Natural Language Processing (EMNLP-IJCNLP)*, pages 5925–5932, Hong Kong, China. Association for Computational Linguistics.

Nicola De Cao, Wilker Aziz, and Ivan Titov. 2019. Question answering by reasoning across documents with graph convolutional networks. In *Proceedings of the 2019 Conference of the North American Chapter of the Association for Computational Linguistics: Human Language Technologies, Volume 1 (Long and Short Papers)*, pages 2306–2317, Minneapolis, Minnesota. Association for Computational Linguistics.

Bhuwan Dhingra, Qiao Jin, Zhilin Yang, William Cohen, and Ruslan Salakhutdinov. 2018. Neural models for reasoning over multiple mentions using coreference. In *Proceedings of the 2018 Conference of the North American Chapter of the Association for Computational Linguistics: Human Language Technologies, Volume 2 (Short Papers)*, pages 42–48, New Orleans, Louisiana. Association for Computational Linguistics.

Lee R Dice. 1945. Measures of the amount of ecologic association between species. *Ecology*, 26(3):297–302.

Xinya Du and Claire Cardie. 2018. Harvesting paragraph-level question-answer pairs from Wikipedia. In *Proceedings of the 56th Annual Meeting of the Association for Computational Linguistics (Volume 1: Long Papers)*, pages 1907–1917, Melbourne, Australia. Association for Computational Linguistics.

Dheeru Dua, Sameer Singh, and Matt Gardner. 2020. Benefits of intermediate annotations in reading comprehension. In *Proceedings of the 58th Annual Meeting of the Association for Computational Linguistics*, pages 5627–5634, Online. Association for Computational Linguistics.

Baorong Huang, Zhuosheng Zhang, and Hai Zhao. 2022. Tracing origins: Coreference-aware machine reading comprehension. In *Proceedings of the 60th Annual Meeting of the Association for Computational Linguistics (Volume 1: Long Papers)*, pages 1281–1292, Dublin, Ireland. Association for Computational Linguistics.

Yin Jou Huang and Sadao Kurohashi. 2021. Extractive summarization considering discourse and coreference relations based on heterogeneous graph. In *Proceedings of the 16th Conference of the European Chapter of the Association for Computational Linguistics: Main Volume*, pages 3046–3052, Online. Association for Computational Linguistics.

Paul Jaccard. 1912. The distribution of the flora in the alpine zone. 1. *New phytologist*, 11(2):37–50.

Mandar Joshi, Danqi Chen, Yinhan Liu, Daniel S. Weld, Luke Zettlemoyer, and Omer Levy. 2020. SpanBERT: Improving pre-training by representing and predicting spans. *Transactions of the Association for Computational Linguistics*, 8:64–77.

Mandar Joshi, Omer Levy, Luke Zettlemoyer, and Daniel Weld. 2019. BERT for coreference resolution: Baselines and analysis. In *Proceedings of the 2019 Conference on Empirical Methods in Natural Language Processing and the 9th International Joint Conference on Natural Language Processing (EMNLP-IJCNLP)*, pages 5803–5808, Hong Kong, China. Association for Computational Linguistics.

Yuval Kirstain, Ori Ram, and Omer Levy. 2021. Coreference resolution without span representations. In *Proceedings of the 59th Annual Meeting of the Association for Computational Linguistics and the 11th International Joint Conference on Natural Language Processing (Volume 2: Short Papers)*, pages 14–19, Online. Association for Computational Linguistics.

Klaus Krippendorff. 1980. *Content Analysis: An Introduction to its Methodology*. CA: Sage Publications, Beverly Hills.

Klaus Krippendorff. 2004. Content analysis: An introduction to its methodology (2nd edition).

Heeyoung Lee, Angel Chang, Yves Peirsman, Nathanael Chambers, Mihai Surdeanu, and Dan Jurafsky. 2013. Deterministic coreference resolution based on entity-centric, precision-ranked rules. *Computational Linguistics*, 39(4):885–916.

Kenton Lee, Luheng He, Mike Lewis, and Luke Zettlemoyer. 2017. End-to-end neural coreference resolution. In *Proceedings of the 2017 Conference on Empirical Methods in Natural Language Processing*, pages 188–197, Copenhagen, Denmark. Association for Computational Linguistics.

Kenton Lee, Luheng He, and Luke Zettlemoyer. 2018. Higher-order coreference resolution with coarse-to-fine inference. In *Proceedings of the 2018 Conference of the North American Chapter of the Association for Computational Linguistics: Human Language Technologies, Volume 2 (Short Papers)*, pages 687–692, New Orleans, Louisiana. Association for Computational Linguistics.

Xiaoqiang Luo. 2005. On coreference resolution performance metrics. In *Proceedings of Human Language Technology Conference and Conference on Empirical Methods in Natural Language Processing*, pages 25–32.

Christopher D. Manning, Kevin Clark, John Hewitt, Urvashi Khandelwal, and Omer Levy. 2020. Emergent linguistic structure in artificial neural networks trained by self-supervision. volume 117, pages 30046–30054.

Nafise Sadat Moosavi and Michael Strube. 2016. Which coreference evaluation metric do you trust? a proposal for a link-based entity aware metric. In *Proceedings of the 54th Annual Meeting of the Association for Computational Linguistics (Volume 1: Long Papers)*, pages 632–642, Berlin, Germany. Association for Computational Linguistics.

Nafise Sadat Moosavi and Michael Strube. 2017. Lexical features in coreference resolution: To be used with caution. In *Proceedings of the 55th Annual Meeting of the Association for Computational Linguistics (Volume 2: Short Papers)*, pages 14–19, Vancouver, Canada. Association for Computational Linguistics.

Thomas S. Morton. 1999. Using coreference for question answering. In *Coreference and Its Applications*.

Thomas S. Morton. 2000. Coreference for NLP applications. In *Proceedings of the 38th Annual Meeting of the Association for Computational Linguistics*, pages 173–180, Hong Kong. Association for Computational Linguistics.

C. Müller and M. Strube. 2006. Multi-level annotation of linguistic data with MMAX 2.

Rebecca Passonneau. 2006. Measuring agreement on set-valued items (MASI) for semantic and pragmatic annotation.

Sameer Pradhan, Alessandro Moschitti, Nianwen Xue, Olga Uryupina, and Yuchen Zhang. 2012. CoNLL-2012 shared task: Modeling multilingual unrestricted coreference in OntoNotes. In *Joint Conference on EMNLP and CoNLL - Shared Task*, pages 1–40, Jeju Island, Korea. Association for Computational Linguistics.

Nils Reimers and Iryna Gurevych. 2019. Sentence-bert: Sentence embeddings using siamese bert-networks. In *Proceedings of the 2019 Conference on Empirical Methods in Natural Language Processing*. Association for Computational Linguistics.

Andreas Rücklé, Nafise Sadat Moosavi, and Iryna Gurevych. 2019. COALA: A neural coverage-based approach for long answer selection with small data. In *Proc. of AAAI-19*.

Kaitao Song, Xu Tan, Tao Qin, Jianfeng Lu, and Tie-Yan Liu. 2020. Mpnet: Masked and permuted pre-training for language understanding. *arXiv preprint arXiv:2004.09297*.

Josef Steinberger, Massimo Poesio, Mijail A Kabadjov, and Karel Ježek. 2007. Two uses of anaphora resolution in summarization. *Information Processing & Management*, 43(6):1663–1680.

Roland Stuckardt. 2016. Towards a procedure model for developing anaphora processing applications. In *Anaphora Resolution, Massimo Poesio, Roland Stuckardt and Yannick Versley*, pages 457–484. Springer.

Roland Stuckhardt. 2003. Coreference-based summarization and question answering: A case for high precision anaphor resolution. In *Proc. of the 2003 International Symposium on Reference Resolution and Its Applications to Question Answering and Summarization*, pages 33–42.

Ming Tan, Cicero dos Santos, Bing Xiang, and Bowen Zhou. 2016. Improved representation learning for question answer matching. In *Proceedings of the 54th Annual Meeting of the Association for Computational Linguistics (Volume 1: Long Papers)*, pages 464–473, Berlin, Germany. Association for Computational Linguistics.

Don Tuggener. 2014. Coreference resolution evaluation for higher level applications. In *Proceedings of the 14th Conference of the European Chapter of the Association for Computational Linguistics, volume 2: Short Papers*, pages 231–235, Gothenburg, Sweden. Association for Computational Linguistics.

José L. Vicedo and Antonio Ferrández. 2000. Importance of pronominal anaphora resolution in question answering systems. In *Proceedings of the 38th Annual Meeting of the Association for Computational Linguistics*, pages 555–562, Hong Kong. Association for Computational Linguistics.

José L. Vicedo and Antonio Ferrández. 2008. Coreference in Q&A. In *Advances in Open Domain Question Answering*, pages 71–96.

Marc Vilain, John Burger, John Aberdeen, Dennis Connolly, and Lynette Hirschman. 1995. A model-theoretic coreference scoring scheme. In *Sixth Message Understanding Conference (MUC-6): Proceedings of a Conference Held in Columbia, Maryland, November 6-8, 1995*.

Kai Wang. 2010. *Retrieving questions and answers in community-based question answering services*. Ph.D. thesis.

Kai Wang, Zhao-Yan Ming, Xia Hu, and Tat-Seng Chua. 2010. Segmentation of multi-sentence questions: towards effective question retrieval in cqa services. In *Proc. of ACM-SIGIR-10*, pages 387–394.

Mingzhu Wu, Nafise Sadat Moosavi, Dan Roth, and Iryna Gurevych. 2020. Coreference reasoning in machine reading comprehension. *arXiv preprint arXiv:2012.15573*.

Liyan Xu and Jinho D. Choi. 2022. Online coreference resolution for dialogue processing: Improving mention-linking on real-time conversations. In *Proceedings of the 11th Joint Conference on Lexical and Computational Semantics*, pages 341–347, Seattle, Washington. Association for Computational Linguistics.

A Human Annotation Study

Annotation guidelines. Annotators were required to detect all noun phrase markables, except pronouns which were highlighted in advance through a chunker. Since the replacement for incorporating coreference information applies to coreferent mentions, non-referring markables (singletons) are not requested to be annotated.

Annotation procedure. The annotation process was run in three stages. First, we gave a training to the annotators to show the annotation guidelines and how to use the *MMAX2*. Then, home exercises containing 5 candidate answers from Travel domain were assigned to the annotators, so that we can point out problems they made promptly.

Finally, all annotators independently labeled annotations on their assigned work.

A.1 Inter-Annotator Agreement

To evaluate the reliability of the human annotations, we use Krippendorff's α (Krippendorff, 1980) to measure inter-annotator agreement, which allows for partial agreement among coreference chains by using distance metrics as weights. The alpha value can be affected by 'too strict' or 'too generous' distance metrics applied (Artstein and Poesio, 2008), so we report three different distance metrics, MASI (Passonneau, 2006), Jaccard (Jaccard, 1912) and Dice (Dice, 1945) for references. Since annotators can freely decide the boundary of markables, we use head-finding algorithm (Collins, 2003) for the overlapped markables identified by annotators to verify if they agree the markables are identical.

We randomly select two annotators to annotate the same 100 candidate answers from Travel domain. The final inter-annotator agreement was computed by the average of Krippendorff's α value of all answers. As showing in Table 11, our results are greater than 0.66 which was suggested as acceptable by Krippendorff (2004).

	MASI	Jaccard	Dice
Krippendorff's α	0.71	0.78	0.82

Table 11: Inter-Annotator agreement.

A.2 Error Analysis

In Table 12, we show three annotations from two annotators and one expert linguist on one answer from Travel domain. While two human annotators have similar coreference resolution results, the expert linguist resolves one more cluster that the annotators do not recognize. In addition, without the questions context, the annotation is sometimes harder for annotators.

H1: [I]$_1$ am from croatia and [I]$_1$ find their site confusing as well. Maybe [<url>]$_2$ can help [you]$_3$. imho, on [this link]$_2$ [you]$_3$ have very clear timetable for selected date if that is what [you]$_3$ want to find.
H2: [I]$_1$ am from croatia and [I]$_1$ find their site confusing as well. Maybe [<url>]$_2$ can help [you]$_3$. imho, on this [link]$_2$ [you]$_3$ have very clear timetable for selected date if that is what [you]$_3$ want to find.
L: [I]$_1$ am from croatia and [I]$_1$ find their site confusing as well. Maybe [<url>]$_2$ can help [you]$_3$. imho, on [this link]$_2$ [you]$_3$ have [very clear timetable for selected date]$_4$ if [that]$_4$ is what [you]$_3$ want to find.

Table 12: An example of human annotations on Travel domain by two annotators (**H1**) and (**H2**) and one expert linguist (**L**).

B Why applying coreference resolvers on candidate answers?

To incorporate coreference resolution, we can apply the coreference resolver on (1) the question, (2) the candidate answer, or (3) the concatenation of the question and each candidate answer. We examined all the above settings in our preliminary experiments, and we find out that the second one, i.e., resolving coreference relations of the candidate answers, is the most beneficial one. Questions are usually too short and do not contain coreference relations, so it is not useful to apply coreference resolvers on them.

To examine the third setting, we concatenate the question in the beginning of each candidate answer so that the model would be able to resolve intra-coreference relations among mentions of the candidate answer as well as inter-relations among the answer and the question. However, based on our experiments, the use of this setting results in lower performance in answer selection compared to the second one. The reason is that resolving coreference relations between candidate answers and the question makes many incorrect candidate answers more similar to the question by resolving the pronouns of the incorrect answer to the named entities of the question.[18] In addition, the question and answer have different speakers, which makes the resolution of first- and second-person pronouns more difficult across question-answer. Therefore, we only apply coreference resolvers to resolve the coreference relations of candidate answers.

C Results

Table 13 below shows the impact of pronoun resolution of the examined coreference resolvers on the answer selection models and domains. In this setting, we only replace pronouns with their most informative antecedent.

[18]For instance, the pronoun "it" from the incorrect candidate answer "You can get it by going to the closest grocery store", which is the answer of the question "where can I buy tomatoes?", can be resolved to "UK visa" from the other question, and makes the candidate answer more similar to this question.

Coreference	Answer Selection	Travel	Cooking	Computer	Aviation
rule-based	Sentence-BERT	-0.39	-1.14	-0.56	-0.77
	CNN	1.31	0.75	0.80	-0.61
	Att.-BiLSTM	1.17	1.14	0.80	0.92
	COALA	0.26	0.51	0.56	-0.15
deep-coref	Sentence-BERT	-0.39	-0.63	-0.40	-0.77
	CNN	0.39	0.37	0.40	-0.61
	Att.-BiLSTM	-0.66	0.76	0.16	0.92
	COALA	0.00	0.13	0.80	-0.15
e2e-coref	Sentence-BERT	0.13	-0.89	-0.16	-0.62
	CNN	0.78	0.88	0.16	0.46
	Att.-BiLSTM	-0.79	0.50	-0.16	0.46
	COALA	0.52	-0.38	0.00	0.46
bert-coref	Sentence-BERT	0.13	-1.01	-0.08	-0.31
	CNN	1.04	-0.26	-0.48	0.46
	Att.-BiLSTM	-0.53	0.13	-0.16	0.31
	COALA	0.13	-0.25	0.08	0.15

Table 13: Effect of the examined pronoun resolution on the answer selection models and datasets. Cell values indicate the difference in accuracy when incorporating pronoun resolution on test sets compared to the baseline results.

Improving Bridging Reference Resolution using Continuous Essentiality from Crowdsourcing

Nobuhiro Ueda and **Sadao Kurohashi**
Graduate School of Informatics, Kyoto University
{ueda, kuro}@nlp.ist.i.kyoto-u.ac.jp

Abstract

Bridging reference resolution is the task of finding nouns that complement essential information of another noun. The essentiality varies depending on noun combination and context and has a continuous distribution. Despite the continuous nature of essentiality, existing datasets of bridging reference have only a few coarse labels to represent the essentiality (Poesio and Artstein, 2008; Hangyo et al., 2012). In this work, we propose a crowdsourcing-based annotation method that considers continuous essentiality. In the crowdsourcing task, we asked workers to select both all nouns with a bridging reference relation and a noun with the highest essentiality among them. Combining these annotations, we can obtain continuous essentiality. Experimental results demonstrated that the constructed dataset improves bridging reference resolution performance. The code is available at https://github.com/nobu-g/bridging-resolution.

1 Introduction

The meaning of natural language texts is supported by cohesion among various linguistic units such as words, sentences, and paragraphs (Halliday and Hasan, 2014). Analyzing cohesion is indispensable for capturing the semantic structure of natural language texts.

Among cohesion analysis tasks, predicate-argument structure (PAS) analysis and semantic role labeling (SRL) have been actively studied (Shibata and Kurohashi, 2018; Omori and Komachi, 2019; He et al., 2018). These tasks aim to find nouns that complement a predicate's essential meaning, such as *who* does/did *what* to *whom*.

On the other hand, bridging reference resolution is the task of finding nouns that complement a noun's essential meaning. It is a special case of an anaphora resolution in which the anaphor and its antecedent have non-identical yet associated relations (Kobayashi and Ng, 2020).

(1) I can see a house over there. **The roof** is covered with snow.

In the above example, *the roof* is semantically insufficient by itself, and *a house* plays an essential role in complementing the meaning of *the roof*. Here, *the roof* is called an anaphor, and *a house* is called an antecedent. The performance of bridging reference resolution is only 40-60%, while PAS analysis and SRL have reached 70-90% (Ueda et al., 2020; Konno et al., 2021; Umakoshi et al., 2021; Zhang et al., 2021).

One challenge of bridging reference resolution is the continuous distribution of the strength of the relation between nouns (We call the strength **essentiality**, hereafter). In the example (2), *he*, *world swimming championships*, and *100m breaststroke* all modify *record* semantically but have different essentiality.

(2) He won the world swimming championships with a world **record** in 100m breaststroke.

The most essential information for *record* is what kind of event the *record* was set in, i.e., *100m breaststroke*. Although other phrases, *he* and *world swimming championships*, also complement the meaning of *record*, their essentiality is lower than that of *100m breaststroke*. Therefore, essentiality varies depending on noun combination and context and has a continuous distribution.

Although predicates and their modifiers also have essentiality, their continuity is less than that of nouns. Predicates have syntactically required highly essential modifiers called arguments. For example, intransitive verbs always have their subject, and transitive verbs always have their subject and object. In contrast to arguments, less essential modifiers are called adjuncts. The argument/adjunct distinction is ambiguous, especially in prepositional phrases. Thus the essentiality distributes continuously, like nouns. However, many of the modifiers

Proceedings of the Fifth Workshop on Computational Models of Reference, Anaphora and Coreference (CRAC 2022), pages 74–87
Gyeongju, Republic of Korea, October 16–17, 2022.

are syntactically linked to the predicate. On the other hand, few nouns have such syntactic links, making it more difficult to distinguish between essential and non-essential due to many implicit modifiers.

Despite their continuous nature, existing datasets of bridging references have only a few coarse labels, such as *essential*, *ambiguous*, and *optional* (Poesio and Artstein, 2008; Hangyo et al., 2012). This fact suggests that there is a gap between the phenomenon of bridging reference and the annotations in existing datasets. This gap leads to performance degradation in bridging reference resolution.

In this work, we utilize crowdsourcing to obtain annotations in which continuous essentiality is considered. Crowdsourcing makes it possible to obtain multiple annotations for each example at a low cost. We asked crowd workers to select all nouns that have a bridging reference relation with a given noun. We also asked them to select the most essential one from the selected nouns. We assigned eight workers per example. Considering the number of votes as essentiality between nouns, we collected annotations of essentiality on a 16-point scale.

We used this method to create a corpus (**Crowd** hereafter) consisting of about 3,900 documents. Each document in **Crowd** consists of three sentences, which add up to 11,700 sentences. We compared **Crowd** with an existing corpus annotated with coarse labels by experts (**Expert** hereafter). In the experiment, we trained bridging reference resolution models on **Crowd**, **Expert**, and the combination of them. The models trained on **Crowd** or the combination always outperformed models trained only on **Expert**, which demonstrated the effectiveness of using **Crowd** as a training dataset. Our general-purpose crowdsourcing interface is publicly available for further research.[1] Our constructed dataset and training code are also publicly available.[2]

2 Existing Corpora for Bridging Reference

This section compares our dataset with existing corpora for bridging reference resolution. First, we introduce corpora for English bridging reference resolution, which is most actively studied, and then we describe Japanese corpora, which we compare in this work, in detail.

2.1 English Corpora

Some of the most widely used corpora in English are ARRAU (Poesio and Artstein, 2008), ISNotes (Markert et al., 2012), BASHI (Rösiger, 2018), and SciCorp (Roesiger, 2016). Most of these corpora contain only a few thousand bridging anaphors. Even the largest ARRAU contains 5,512 bridging anaphors, which is insufficient to apply neural network-based methods. Some works proposed data augmentation methods to address the issue. Hou (2020) converted examples into QA format and augmented the examples with existing QA datasets, and Yu and Poesio (2020) performed multi-task learning with coreference resolution. However, even with these methods, the accuracy is around 40–60%.[3] On the other hand, our corpus consists of 3,933 documents, including 25,217 bridging anaphors[4], which is large enough to train a neural network model. In addition, while all the four corpora have coarse labels to distinguish bridging reference relations, our corpus has more continuous annotations.

Recently, Elazar et al. (2022) created a corpus annotated with a wide range of noun phrase relations, including bridging reference. They annotated all noun phrase pairs whose relation type can be expressed by an English preposition. Their corpus comprises 5.5k documents covering over 1 million noun phrase relations. However, they do not deal with the strength of the relations. In addition, their annotation method relies heavily on English prepositions and does not apply to languages that do not have prepositions, such as Japanese (Masuoka and Takubo, 1992).

2.2 Japanese Corpora

There are two large corpora with bridging reference annotations in Japanese, KWDLC (Hangyo et al., 2012) and Kyoto Corpus (Kurohashi and Nagao, 2003; Kawahara et al., 2002). KWDLC consists of 5,124 documents containing 16,038 sentences annotated with various linguistic information, including bridging reference relations. Each

[1] https://github.com/nobu-g/bridging-annotation

[2] https://github.com/nobu-g/bridging-resolution

[3] This is the result in the setting of gold anaphors are given. The score would be even lower when anaphor detection is also performed.

[4] This is calculated for anaphors that at least half of the workers considered to be bridging.

label	example
essential	<u>*Amerika*</u> *no* ***shuto*** **the capital** of <u>the US</u>
ambiguous	<u>*watashi*</u> *no* ***megane*** **glasses** of <u>mine</u>
optional	<u>*50 sento*</u> *no* ***ame*** A <u>50 cent</u> **candy**

Table 1: Labels of bridging reference relations defined in KWDLC (Hangyo et al., 2012).

document in KWDLC consists of the leading three sentences of web pages. Kyoto Corpus is also a corpus with various linguistic annotation but originated from newspaper articles. Kyoto Corpus has the same types of annotations as KWDLC, and bridging reference relations are annotated to 1,909 documents containing 15,872 sentences. This work focuses on KWDLC because of the diversity of texts it contains.

Both KWDLC and Kyoto Corpus have three types of labels for bridging reference relations: *essential*, *ambiguous*, and *optional*. These labels distinguish the strength of bridging reference relations (i.e., essentiality). Table 1 shows some examples. In the top example, the anaphor "the capital" is semantically insufficient by itself, and the antecedent "the US" makes up the insufficiency, which means "the US" has an *essential* relation for "the capital." *Optional* indicates the anaphor is already semantically sufficient by itself, or even if it is semantically insufficient, the antecedent does not make up the insufficiency. In the bottom example, "candy" is already semantically sufficient and the price is supplementary information. These two examples are typical, and there are many examples where it is hard to distinguish between *essential* and *optional*, and they are labeled as *ambiguous*.

3 Data Construction with Crowdsourcing

In Japanese, a noun pair which has a bridging reference relation can typically be connected by a genitive case "*no*."[5] In other words, when an anaphor *noun B* has a bridging reference relation with an antecedent *noun A*, "*A no B*" is a semantically valid noun phrase.

Although it is difficult for non-experts to judge whether two nouns have a bridging reference relation, they can judge whether "*A no B*" is a valid noun phrase. We showed crowd workers a text in which one word (i.e., *noun B*) was underlined. We asked them to select all words (i.e., *noun A*) where "*A no B*" is semantically valid, based on the contexts.

The *noun A*s selected by the workers have continuous latent values of essentiality for the *noun B*. In order to obtain the continuous essentiality values, we adopt the following strategies: (1) we asked workers to select the most essential noun for the *noun B*; (2) for each sample, we assigned eight workers to obtain multiple annotations.

We constructed the new corpus based on KWDLC (Hangyo et al., 2012) (i.e., **Expert**) in order to evaluate the quality of crowd workers' annotations. As shown in Table 2, we collected crowd workers' annotations (i.e., **Crowd**) for a subset of **Expert**, which correspond to approximately 77% of **Expert**.

We plan to make the annotations publicly available in the future. Workers agreed that the annotations will be used for academic research purposes in a non-personally identifiable manner.

3.1 Filtering Nouns to Annotate

In crowdsourcing, reducing the burden on workers leads to improved data quality. A possible burden in this task is the number of candidate noun pairs. **Expert** has an approximately 250 noun pairs per document, while only a few of them have bridging reference relations. So we used the following conditions to reduce the number of candidates of *noun B* and *noun A*.

The conditions of selecting *noun B*

- *noun B* is not a nominal predicate
- *noun B* is the tail noun if *noun B* is a part of a noun phrase
- *noun B* is not a numeral

The condition of selecting *noun A*

- *noun A* appears in the same or preceding sentence as *noun B*

Applying the above conditions reduced the number of candidate noun pairs by about 56%. Meanwhile, only 28% of the noun pairs in **Expert** with the relations of *essential*, *ambiguous*, or *optional* were excluded.

The conditions require linguistic features for each noun. We used the Japanese morphological

[5] "*no*" roughly corresponds to "of" in English, but has a broader usage than "of."

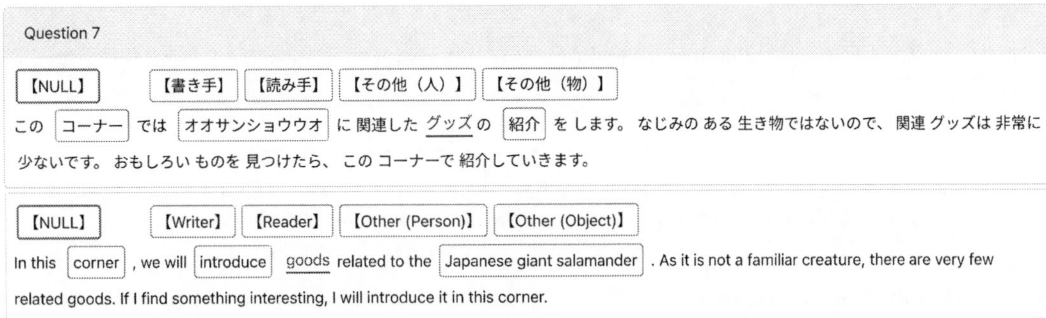

Figure 1: A sample question in our crowdsourcing interface. The upper one is from the original interface, and the lower one is the English translation. Workers select *noun A*s from framed words so that the *noun A*s have a relation of "*A no B*" ("*B of A*" in English) for the *noun B* (red underlined word). Workers can select *noun A*s easily by clicking the framed words.

corpus	train	dev	test
Expert	3,912	512	700
Crowd	2,721	512	700

Table 2: The number of documents contained in each corpus. **Expert** provides an official split and we split **Crowd** following **Expert**.

analyzer Juman++ (Morita et al., 2015; Tolmachev et al., 2018) and the Japanese syntactic analyzer KNP (Kurohashi and Nagao, 1994) to obtain the features. Juman++ performs morphological segmentation and assigns linguistic features such as parts of speech to morphemes. Based on the features from Juman++, KNP identifies noun phrases and assigns linguistic features to them.

3.2 Special Targets

Following the setting in **Expert** corpus (Hangyo et al., 2012), we introduce five special targets. Workers can select the special targets in addition to the nouns in a text. The first is the `[NULL]`, which is selected when none of the nouns in a text is related to the *noun B*. Introducing the `[NULL]` target enables us to require workers to answer all questions, which is expected to prevent workers from skipping questions.

The others are used for collecting annotations for exophora. Exophora is a reference to entities that do not appear in the text. In Japanese, exophora occurs 13% of all the bridging references. As exophora has no definite textual antecedents, we introduce the following four typical types of exophora.

- `[Writer]`:
  The one who wrote the text
- `[Reader]`:
  Someone who would read the text
- `[Other:Person]`:
  Someone except for the above
- `[Other:Object]`:
  Some entity external to text

Hereafter, we refer to the reference targets, including these special targets, as *noun A*s.

3.3 Crowdsourcing Interface

An annotation interface also plays an essential role in reducing the burden on crowd workers. However, existing crowdsourcing platforms of Japanese[6] do not provide an interface flexible enough to conduct this task. Therefore, we developed our own interface and directed workers to the interface from the existing platform.

Figure 1 shows one question sample of our interface. In this sample, the underlined red word corresponds to *noun B*, and the words with blue frames correspond to *noun A* candidates. For the given *noun B*, workers click to select *noun A*s from the framed words. By clicking on one of the selected words twice, the workers can select it as the most essential noun. If they select `[NULL]`, they can select none of the other words, and there is no need to select the most essential noun.

In addition to the question part, our interface consists of task instructions and practice questions. Workers first read the task instructions, solve the practice questions, and then start annotation. Appendix A.2 shows the interface of the task instructions and the practice questions.

[6] `https://crowdsourcing.yahoo.co.jp/` `https://crowdworks.jp/`

	Multi				Single			
	Multi-Prec.	Multi-Rec.	Multi-F1	mAP	Single-Prec.	Single-Rec.	Single-F1	Acc.
Endophora	38.4	40.1	39.2	30.0	29.9	71.6	42.2	58.4
Exophora	12.2	20.7	15.4	7.3	6.7	48.9	11.8	52.9

Table 3: The evaluation result of **Crowd**, considering **Expert** as the gold. Endophora is a reference to words that appears in the text. Exophora is a reference to entities that do not appear in the text.

3.4 Cost of the Data Construction

We used Yahoo! Crowdsourcing[7] as our crowdsourcing platform. It charges 17.7 yen per task, including the commission fee. Overall, the cost of the data construction was approximately 580,000 yen for 31,200 tasks. In contrast, the cost of constructing **Expert** was over 6,000,000 yen. Although the cost is not directly comparable because **Expert** has other types of linguistic annotations besides bridging reference relations, the cost for **Crowd** would be less than half of that for **Expert**.

4 Corpus Evaluation

In order to verify the quality of the constructed corpus (i.e., **Crowd**), we compared it with the corpus with expert annotations (i.e., **Expert**). For the quantitative evaluation, we define **essentiality score** for a *noun A* in **Crowd** as follows.

$$\begin{cases} n(A) \times 2 & \text{if } \textit{noun A} \text{ is } \texttt{[NULL]}, \\ n(A) + N(A) & \text{otherwise,} \end{cases} \tag{1}$$

where $n(A)$ denotes the number of workers who selected *noun A*, and $N(A)$ denotes the number of workers who selected *noun A* as the most essential noun. In this work, since eight workers annotated each noun pair, essentiality score takes values from 0 to 16. Since workers cannot select `[NULL]` as the most essential noun, we double $n(\texttt{[NULL]})$ for normalization.

4.1 Evaluation Metrics

We want to evaluate whether essentiality score reflects the essentiality for the *noun B*. To evaluate **Crowd** in this criteria, we assumed **Expert** as the ground truth and calculated Multi-F1, Single-F1, mean average precision (mAP), and accuracy.

Multi-F1 is an F measure to evaluate how well all the *noun A*s with bridging reference relations are selected. Multi-F1 measures the ability of a model to find *noun A*s with less essential relations as well as the most essential relation. We defined a threshold and selected *noun A*s that many workers selected. And then, we calculated precision and recall for the selected *noun A*s, regarding *noun A*s annotated as *essential* or *ambiguous* in **Expert** as positive. Multi-F1 is the harmonic mean of the precision and recall. We varied the threshold from 0 to 16 and picked the one with the highest Multi-F1 value. The threshold obtained was 7.

Single-F1 is an F measure to evaluate how well the most essential *noun A* is selected. In Single-F1, we consider one *noun A* for each *noun B*. For *noun A*s in **Crowd**, we select the one with the highest essentiality score. For *noun A*s in **Expert**, we select the one annotated as *essential*.[8] If none of the nouns are annotated as *essential*, we select the one annotated as *ambiguous*. In Single-F1, we ignored `[NULL]`, that is, we did not count `[NULL]` as a true positive or false positive.

Mean average precision (mAP) is the mean of average precision (AP) over all *noun B*s. AP is the average of precision at each recall value varying the threshold. The precision and the recall are defined in the same way as Multi-F1, but without a need to set a threshold. Accuracy is calculated, including `[NULL]`.

4.2 Evaluation Results

First, we evaluate **Crowd** in comparison to **Expert**. Table 3 shows the scores of each evaluation metric. In general, recall tends to be higher than precision, demonstrating that our method enabled us to collect a broader range of examples than the experts' annotation.

However, the precision, especially the Single-Precision of exophora, was considerably low. This result is partly due to the nature of `[Other:Person]` and `[Other:Object]`. Since, in most cases, an entity is owned by someone or is part of something, we can say that the entity has a bridging relation with `[Other:Person]`

[7] `https://crowdsourcing.yahoo.co.jp/`

[8] When multiple nouns are annotated as *essential*, we prioritize the one that most crowd workers selected.

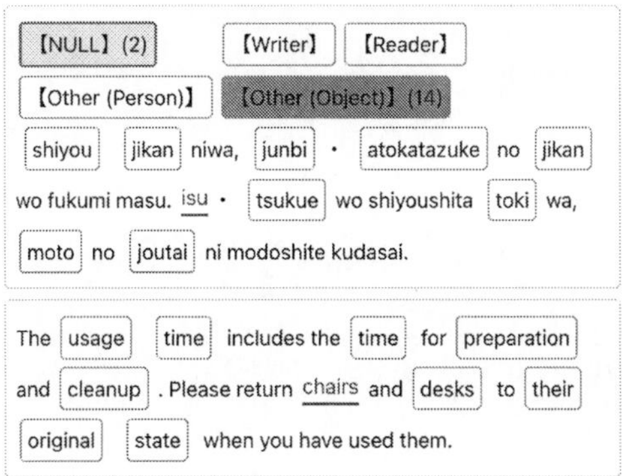

Figure 2: An example of collected annotations in Japanese (upper) and its English translation (lower). The numbers in parentheses and the color intensity indicates essentiality score.

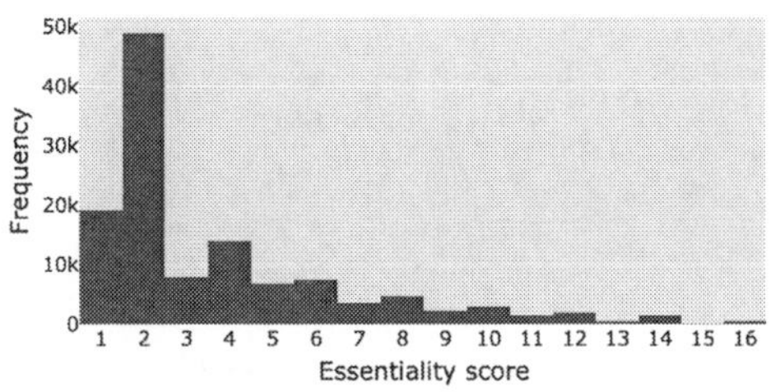

Figure 3: The distribution of essentiality score in **Crowd**.

or `[Other:Object]`. Although experts did not annotate such general modifiers because they are too obvious, many crowd workers did. In the example in Figure 2, many workers selected `[Other:Object]` because "chairs" are considered to be chairs of some facility, while experts annotated nothing.

Next, we evaluate **Crowd** itself. For each noun pair, we can formulate this task as a three-class classification: *select*, *select as the most essential noun*, and *do not select*. This formulation enables us to calculate Krippendorff's alpha (Krippendorff, 2018) to measure the inter-worker agreement. We found it to be about 0.28. For a more intuitive agreement measure, 57% of all workers selected *noun A* with the highest number of votes, and 52% selected such *noun A* as the most essential noun. Although this value is relatively low for an inter-annotator agreement, this is a minor problem because our purpose is to obtain diverse annotations for this inherently subjective task.

We can see the diversity of annotations in Figure 3. It shows the distribution of essentiality score

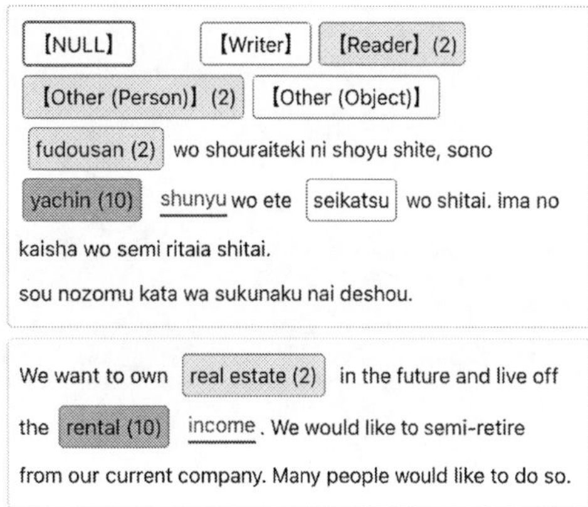

Figure 4: An example of collected annotations. The format is the same as Figure 2.

for *noun A*s except for `[NULL]`. *Noun A*s whose essentiality score is 0 are excluded because they are too frequent (449k). The figure shows high frequency of *noun A*s with low essentiality score. This means that the continuous nature of essentiality is reflected as the diversity of essentiality score in **Crowd**. We can also see the characteristic that even essentiality score is more frequent than odd one. This is because many workers selected only one *noun A*. When a worker selects only one *noun A*, it is necessarily the most essential noun, and the essentiality score increases by 2.

Figure 4 shows another collected example. The selected *noun* As, *Reader*, *Other (Person)*, *real estate*, and *rental*, are all related to the *noun B*, *income*. In addition, the *noun A* with the highest essentiality score is *rental*, which is considered to be the most essential information for *income*. This example shows that in our corpus, the essentiality of nouns is represented as the number of crowd workers' votes.

5 Evaluation with Bridging Reference Resolution

In this section, we examine the effectiveness of **Crowd** for improving bridging reference resolution performance through evaluation experiments. In the experiments, we use three kinds of corpora, **Expert**, **Crowd**, and the combination of **Expert** and **Crowd**, as the training data. We compare the performance of the models trained on each corpus.

5.1 Task Definition

In Japanese, the formulation of bridging reference resolution is different from the one in English.

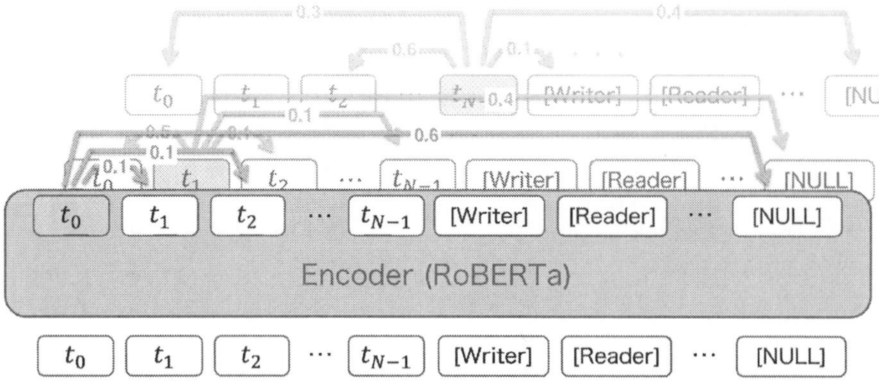

Figure 5: An overview of our model. For an input sequence of length N, the model outputs $N \times N$ values. Note that five special targets, `[Writer]`, `[Reader]`, `[Other:Person]`, `[Other:Object]`, and `[NULL]`, are appended to the input text.

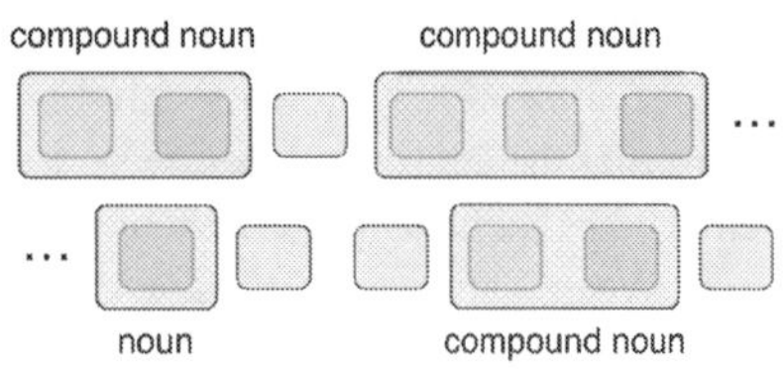

Figure 6: A simplified illustration of how we select *noun A*s and *noun B*s. Each cell denotes a word. The cells colored with light red and bordered with light blue are selected as *noun B*s and *noun A*s, respectively.

In English, the task is formulated as a span prediction problem, similar to coreference resolution. In Japanese, on the other hand, it is formulated as a word prediction problem. Therefore, we can solve the task by performing binary classification for each noun pair in a text. Figure 6 shows an illustration of how we select target nouns.

Bridging reference resolution consists of two sub tasks: bridging anaphor recognition and antecedent selection. Many studies refer to bridging reference resolution (or bridging anaphora resolution) as a task of antecedent selection, that is, the gold anaphors are given (Kobayashi and Ng, 2020; Hou, 2020, 2018). In this work, we tackle full bridging resolution, in which we perform bridging anaphor recognition as well as antecedent selection.[9] Instead of performing bridging anaphor recognition, we use `[NULL]` as a special antecedent and perform antecedent selection for all *noun B*s. Reference to `[NULL]` means that the *noun B* is not an anaphor, similar to the data construction stage.

[9]Because we limit anaphors and antecedents by the rule described in section 3.1, our task is a little easier than full bridging resolution.

label	value
essential	1.0
ambiguous	0.5
optional	0.25

Table 4: The label conversion table in **Expert**.

Furthermore, we also consider bridging exophora resolution. In a similar manner to full bridging resolution described above, we use additional special targets, `[Writer]`, `[Reader]`, `[Other:Person]`, `[Other:Object]`, and `[NULL]`.

5.2 Label Conversion

For the comparison between **Crowd** and **Expert**, we need to treat both corpora in a common framework. For this purpose, we convert the relation between each noun in both corpora into a value between 0 and 1, called **normalized essentiality score**. For **Crowd**, we just normalize essentiality score by dividing it by its maximum value, 16. For **Expert**, since the relation is defined as a label rather than a value, we define the label to value mapping heuristically as shown in Table 4.

5.3 Resolution Method

We train a model that outputs normalized essentiality scores for each token pair as shown in Figure 5. $s(t_a, t_b)$, the normalized essentiality score

Training Corpus	Evaluated on Crowd Multi-F1 (Prec. / Rec.)	Single-F1 (Prec. / Rec.)	mAP	Spearman
Expert	34.2 ± 7.0 (30.4 / 39.2)	30.3 ± 1.3 (63.2 / 19.9)	24.9 ± 5.1	36.5 ± 1.6
Crowd	**57.6 ± 1.3** (58.7 / 56.5)	**61.5 ± 1.0** (62.3 / 60.8)	**60.8 ± 1.0**	**53.3 ± 0.4**
Crowd+Expert (MR)	38.7 ± 4.3 (36.8 / 41.5)	42.8 ± 0.7 (74.7 / 30.0)	34.8 ± 5.2	46.9 ± 4.4
Crowd+Expert (MSE)	42.1 ± 3.9 (40.7 / 44.1)	37.8 ± 0.9 (69.5 / 26.0)	41.7 ± 1.7	49.2 ± 0.6

Table 5: Results of bridging reference resolution evaluated on **Crowd** corpora (%). The scores are the mean and 95% confidence interval over three training runs with different random seeds. MR and MSE represent the model is trained using MR loss and MSE loss, respectively.

Training Corpus	Evaluated on Expert Multi-F1 (Prec. / Rec.)	Single-F1 (Prec. / Rec.)	mAP	Spearman
Expert	47.7 ± 1.1 (50.6 / 45.3)	63.6 ± 1.4 (66.7 / 60.8)	43.2 ± 2.3	43.7 ± 0.3
Crowd	32.7 ± 0.7 (33.0 / 32.3)	35.4 ± 1.2 (24.6 / 63.3)	27.3 ± 0.1	36.8 ± 0.5
Crowd+Expert (MR)	48.3 ± 2.5 (52.1 / 45.0)	62.8 ± 0.5 (59.8 / 66.1)	45.4 ± 3.1	42.4 ± 0.9
Crowd+Expert (MSE)	**53.0 ± 1.8** (57.5 / 49.3)	**64.5 ± 1.8** (63.6 / 65.5)	**52.2 ± 2.0**	**43.8 ± 0.3**

Table 6: Results of bridging reference resolution evaluated on **Expert** corpora (%). The representations are the same as in Table 5.

of token t_a for token t_b, is calculated as follows:

$$s(t_b, t_a) = \boldsymbol{v}^{\mathrm{T}} \tanh(W_1 \boldsymbol{t}_b + W_2 \boldsymbol{t}_a), \quad (2)$$

where W_1 and W_2 denote weight matrices. $\boldsymbol{v}$ is a weight vector. $\boldsymbol{t}_b$ and $\boldsymbol{t}_a$ denote hidden vectors of the encoder's final layer corresponding to the tokens t_b and t_a. The encoder was RoBERTa (Liu et al., 2019) model that has been pre-trained with Japanese web texts.[10]

In addition to a tokenized text, the encoder's input sequence contains special tokens at the end of the sequence, similar to Ueda et al. (2020). The special tokens are `[Reader]`, `[Writer]`, `[Other:Person]`, `[Other:Object]`, and `[NULL]`.

5.4 Training Objective

When training on **Crowd**, we employed mean squared error loss (MSE loss) as the loss function. As shown in the following equation, for each t_b and t_a, MSE loss optimizes the system output $s(t_b, t_a)$ to be close to the normalized essentiality score $e(t_b, t_a)$.

$$\mathcal{L}_{MSE} = \frac{1}{Z} \sum_{a,b} \Big(s(t_b, t_a) - e(t_b, t_a) \Big)^2, \quad (3)$$

where t_b and t_a are tokens in a input sequence. $s(t_b, t_a)$ and $e(t_b, t_a)$ are the system output and normalized essentiality score, respectively. Z is the normalization term.

When training on **Expert**, we employed margin ranking loss (MR loss) because we expected that using ranking-based loss mitigates the bias of arbitrarily defined values in the label conversion stage.[11] MR loss is calculated as follows:

$$\mathcal{L}_{MR} = \frac{1}{Z} \sum_{a,b,c<a} \max(0, d_{abc}),$$

$$d_{abc} = \mathrm{sign}(\Delta e_{abc}) \cdot (-\Delta s_{abc} + \Delta e_{abc}),$$
$$\Delta s_{abc} = s(t_b, t_a) - s(t_b, t_c),$$
$$\Delta e_{abc} = e(t_b, t_a) - e(t_b, t_c).$$

MR loss optimizes the difference of the system outputs and normalized essentiality scores (Δs and Δe, respectively) rather than the values themselves. This way of optimization avoids forcing the model to output arbitrarily defined discrete values. See Appendix A.1 for more details on the implementation.

5.5 Experimental Results

Table 5,6 shows the results of the experiments when **Crowd**, **Expert**, and both are used for the training. For the evaluation metrics, in addition to Multi-F1, Single-F1, and mAP described in section 4, we used Spearman's rank correlation coefficient to measure the ranking-based agreement.

[10] `https://huggingface.co/nlp-waseda/roberta-base-japanese`

[11] Using MR loss showed better performances than using MSE loss in our preliminary experiments.

For Multi-F1, Single-F1, and mAP, we ignored `[NULL]`. Table 5 shows adding **Crowd** to the training data improved the performance by 8–15 points in all the evaluation metrics. Furthermore, when training with only **Crowd**, the performance was even higher. It makes sense that the model shows the higher performance when the evaluation set's data distribution matches the training set's distribution.

Moreover, we also confirmed the effectiveness of **Crowd** when evaluated on **Expert** (Table 6). Although training with only **Crowd** did not improve the performance, training with both **Crowd** and **Expert** improved the performance compared to only using **Expert**. Especially, the performance of Multi-F1 and mAP improved by 5.3 and 9.0 points, respectively.

The performance improvements in Multi-F1 are due to the high coverage of the relations annotated in **Crowd**. This high coverage is an advantage of crowdsourcing, which enables us to obtain diverse annotations by many people at a reasonable cost. The performance improvements in mAP and Spearman's rank correlation coefficient are due to annotations in **Crowd**, in which the continuous nature of essentiality are represented precisely.

6 Conclusion

In the existing datasets of bridging reference resolution, the strength of relations between nouns was unnaturally represented by coarse-grained labels despite the continuous distribution of the strength. We focused on this gap and proposed a crowdsourcing-based annotation method to construct a dataset with more continuous annotations. We have developed a general-purpose interface for the data collection with crowdsourcing. This interface can be applied to crowdsourcing not only for bridging reference resolution but also for any relational analysis tasks.

By training with our newly constructed dataset, we improved the performance of bridging reference resolution on a Japanese standard benchmark dataset. Moreover, the performance improvement was over 16 points, evaluated on the constructed dataset.

References

Lukas Biewald. 2020. Experiment tracking with weights and biases. Software available from wandb.com.

Yanai Elazar, Victoria Basmov*, Yoav Goldberg, and Reut Tsarfaty. 2022. Text-based NP enrichment. *Transactions of the Association for Computational Linguistics*, 10:764–784.

Michael Alexander Kirkwood Halliday and Ruqaiya Hasan. 2014. *Cohesion in English*. 9. Routledge.

Masatsugu Hangyo, Daisuke Kawahara, and Sadao Kurohashi. 2012. Building a diverse document leads corpus annotated with semantic relations. In *Proceedings of PACLIC*, pages 535–544.

Shexia He, Zuchao Li, Hai Zhao, and Hongxiao Bai. 2018. Syntax for semantic role labeling, to be, or not to be. In *Proceedings of the 56th Annual Meeting of the Association for Computational Linguistics (Volume 1: Long Papers)*, pages 2061–2071, Melbourne, Australia. Association for Computational Linguistics.

Yufang Hou. 2018. Enhanced word representations for bridging anaphora resolution. In *Proceedings of the 2018 Conference of the North American Chapter of the Association for Computational Linguistics: Human Language Technologies, Volume 2 (Short Papers)*, pages 1–7, New Orleans, Louisiana. Association for Computational Linguistics.

Yufang Hou. 2020. Bridging anaphora resolution as question answering. In *Proceedings of the 58th Annual Meeting of the Association for Computational Linguistics*, pages 1428–1438, Online. Association for Computational Linguistics.

Daisuke Kawahara, Sadao Kurohashi, and Kôiti Hasida. 2002. Construction of a Japanese relevance-tagged corpus. In *Proceedings of the Third International Conference on Language Resources and Evaluation (LREC'02)*. European Language Resources Association (ELRA).

Hideo Kobayashi and Vincent Ng. 2020. Bridging resolution: A survey of the state of the art. In *Proceedings of the 28th International Conference on Computational Linguistics*, pages 3708–3721, Barcelona, Spain (Online). International Committee on Computational Linguistics.

Ryuto Konno, Shun Kiyono, Yuichiroh Matsubayashi, Hiroki Ouchi, and Kentaro Inui. 2021. Pseudo zero pronoun resolution improves zero anaphora resolution. In *Proceedings of the 2021 Conference on Empirical Methods in Natural Language Processing*, pages 3790–3806. Association for Computational Linguistics.

Klaus Krippendorff. 2018. *Content analysis: An introduction to its methodology*. Sage publications.

Sadao Kurohashi and Makoto Nagao. 1994. A syntactic analysis method of long Japanese sentences based on the detection of conjunctive structures. *Computational Linguistics*, 20(4).

Sadao Kurohashi and Makoto Nagao. 2003. Building a Japanese parsed corpus. In *Treebanks*, pages 249–260. Springer.

Yinhan Liu, Myle Ott, Naman Goyal, Jingfei Du, Mandar Joshi, Danqi Chen, Omer Levy, Mike Lewis, Luke Zettlemoyer, and Veselin Stoyanov. 2019. RoBERTa: A robustly optimized BERT pretraining approach. *CoRR*, abs/1907.11692.

Katja Markert, Yufang Hou, and Michael Strube. 2012. Collective classification for fine-grained information status. In *Proceedings of the 50th Annual Meeting of the Association for Computational Linguistics (Volume 1: Long Papers)*, pages 795–804, Jeju Island, Korea. Association for Computational Linguistics.

Takashi Masuoka and Yukinori Takubo. 1992. *Kiso Nihongo bunpō: kaiteiban.* Kuroshio shuppan.

Hajime Morita, Daisuke Kawahara, and Sadao Kurohashi. 2015. Morphological analysis for unsegmented languages using recurrent neural network language model. In *Proceedings of the 2015 Conference on Empirical Methods in Natural Language Processing*, pages 2292–2297, Lisbon, Portugal. Association for Computational Linguistics.

Hikaru Omori and Mamoru Komachi. 2019. Multi-task learning for Japanese predicate argument structure analysis. In *Proceedings of NAACL*, pages 3404–3414.

Massimo Poesio and Ron Artstein. 2008. Anaphoric annotation in the ARRAU corpus. In *Proceedings of the Sixth International Conference on Language Resources and Evaluation (LREC'08)*, Marrakech, Morocco. European Language Resources Association (ELRA).

Ina Roesiger. 2016. SciCorp: A corpus of English scientific articles annotated for information status analysis. In *Proceedings of the Tenth International Conference on Language Resources and Evaluation (LREC'16)*, pages 1743–1749, Portorož, Slovenia. European Language Resources Association (ELRA).

Ina Rösiger. 2018. BASHI: A corpus of Wall Street Journal articles annotated with bridging links. In *Proceedings of the Eleventh International Conference on Language Resources and Evaluation (LREC 2018)*, Miyazaki, Japan. European Language Resources Association (ELRA).

Tomohide Shibata and Sadao Kurohashi. 2018. Entity-centric joint modeling of Japanese coreference resolution and predicate argument structure analysis. In *Proceedings of ACL*, pages 579–589.

Arseny Tolmachev, Daisuke Kawahara, and Sadao Kurohashi. 2018. Juman++: A morphological analysis toolkit for scriptio continua. In *Proceedings of the 2018 Conference on Empirical Methods in Natural Language Processing: System Demonstrations*, pages 54–59, Brussels, Belgium.

Nobuhiro Ueda, Daisuke Kawahara, and Sadao Kurohashi. 2020. BERT-based cohesion analysis of Japanese texts. In *Proceedings of the 28th International Conference on Computational Linguistics*, pages 1323–1333, Barcelona, Spain (Online). International Committee on Computational Linguistics.

Masato Umakoshi, Yugo Murawaki, and Sadao Kurohashi. 2021. Japanese zero anaphora resolution can benefit from parallel texts through neural transfer learning. In *Findings of the Association for Computational Linguistics: EMNLP 2021*, pages 1920–1934, Punta Cana, Dominican Republic. Association for Computational Linguistics.

Thomas Wolf, Lysandre Debut, Victor Sanh, Julien Chaumond, Clement Delangue, Anthony Moi, Pierric Cistac, Tim Rault, Rémi Louf, Morgan Funtowicz, Joe Davison, Sam Shleifer, Patrick von Platen, Clara Ma, Yacine Jernite, Julien Plu, Canwen Xu, Teven Le Scao, Sylvain Gugger, Mariama Drame, Quentin Lhoest, and Alexander M. Rush. 2019. Huggingface's transformers: State-of-the-art natural language processing. *ArXiv*, abs/1910.03771.

Juntao Yu and Massimo Poesio. 2020. Multi-task learning based neural bridging reference resolution. *ArXiv*, abs/2003.03666.

Yu Zhang, Qingrong Xia, Shilin Zhou, Yong Jiang, Zhenghua Li, Guohong Fu, and Min Zhang. 2021. Semantic role labeling as dependency parsing: Exploring latent tree structures inside arguments.

A Appendix

A.1 Implementation Details

Table 7–10 show the hyperparameters used in our experiments. We tuned training epochs, learning rate, and scheduler warmup steps based on the mAP score on the validation set. Learning rate was selected from {0.00001, 0.00005, 0.0001, 0.0002} in all the experiments. Training epochs was selected from {12, 16, 20, 24} when training on **Expert**, {16, 20, 24, 28} when training on **Crowd**, and {12, 16, 20} when training on the combination of **Expert** and **Crowd**. Scheduler warmup steps was selected from {160, 200, 240, 280} when training on **Expert**, {100, 140, 180, 220} when training on **Crowd**, and {200, 240, 280, 320} when training on **Expert** and **Crowd**. We used Weights and Biases (Biewald, 2020) for the hyperparameter tuning.

The computation was performed on NVIDIA TITAN X (Pascal) or NVIDIA GeForce RTX 2080 Ti GPUs. Each training run took about 0.5–2 hours on two GPUs.

[12]This scheduler is implemented in Transformers (Wolf et al., 2019) and we used it.

Parameter name	Parameter value
Optimizer	AdamW
Training epochs	20
Learning rate	2×10^{-4}
Optimizer eps	1×10^{-8}
Weight decay	0.01
Dropout rate (RoBERTa layer)	0.1
Dropout rate (output layer)	0.0
LR scheduler	linear_schedule_with_warmup[12]
Scheduler warmup steps	160
Batch size	32

Table 7: Hyperparameters used for training on **Expert**.

Parameter name	Parameter value
Optimizer	AdamW
Training epochs	28
Learning rate	1×10^{-4}
Optimizer eps	1×10^{-8}
Weight decay	0.01
Dropout rate (RoBERTa layer)	0.1
Dropout rate (output layer)	0.0
LR scheduler	linear_schedule_with_warmup
Scheduler warmup steps	180
Batch size	32

Table 8: Hyperparameters used for training on **Crowd**.

Parameter name	Parameter value
Optimizer	AdamW
Training epochs	16
Learning rate	1×10^{-4}
Optimizer eps	1×10^{-8}
Weight decay	0.01
Dropout rate (RoBERTa layer)	0.1
Dropout rate (output layer)	0.0
LR scheduler	linear_schedule_with_warmup
Scheduler warmup steps	240
Batch size	32

Table 9: Hyperparameters used for training on the combination of **Expert** and **Crowd** with margin ranking loss.

Parameter name	Parameter value
Optimizer	AdamW
Training epochs	20
Learning rate	5×10^{-5}
Optimizer eps	1×10^{-8}
Weight decay	0.01
Dropout rate (RoBERTa layer)	0.1
Dropout rate (output layer)	0.0
LR scheduler	linear_schedule_with_warmup
Scheduler warmup steps	280
Batch size	32

Table 10: Hyperparameters used for training on the combination of **Expert** and **Crowd** with mean squared error loss.

A.2 Crowdsourcing Instructions and Practice Questions

Figure 7,8 show the task instructions, and Figure 9 shows the practice questions. After reading the task instructions, workers need to answer the practice questions which they can answer as many times as they want until they answer correctly.

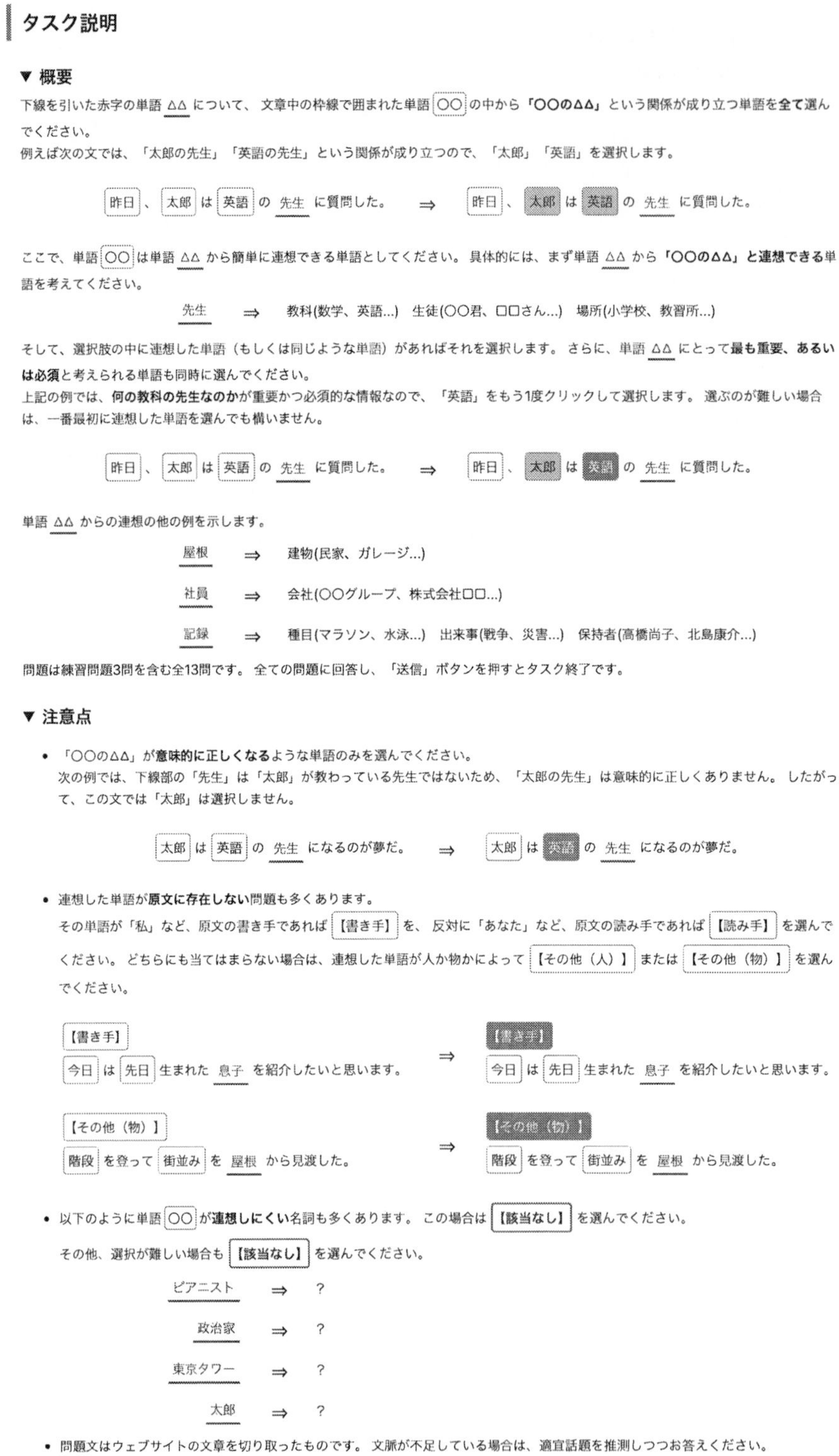

タスク説明

▼ 概要

下線を引いた赤字の単語 ΔΔ について、文章中の枠線で囲まれた単語 OO の中から**「OOのΔΔ」**という関係が成り立つ単語を**全て**選んでください。
例えば次の文では、「太郎の先生」「英語の先生」という関係が成り立つので、「太郎」「英語」を選択します。

昨日、太郎は英語の先生に質問した。 ⇒ 昨日、太郎は英語の先生に質問した。

ここで、単語 OO は単語 ΔΔ から簡単に連想できる単語としてください。具体的には、まず単語 ΔΔ から**「OOのΔΔ」と連想できる**単語を考えてください。

先生 ⇒ 教科(数学、英語...) 生徒(OO君、□□さん...) 場所(小学校、教習所...)

そして、選択肢の中に連想した単語（もしくは同じような単語）があればそれを選択します。さらに、単語 ΔΔ にとって**最も重要、あるいは必須**と考えられる単語も同時に選んでください。
上記の例では、**何の教科の先生なのか**が重要かつ必須的な情報なので、「英語」をもう1度クリックして選択します。選ぶのが難しい場合は、一番最初に連想した単語を選んでも構いません。

昨日、太郎は英語の先生に質問した。 ⇒ 昨日、太郎は英語の先生に質問した。

単語 ΔΔ からの連想の他の例を示します。

屋根 ⇒ 建物(民家、ガレージ...)

社員 ⇒ 会社(OOグループ、株式会社□□...)

記録 ⇒ 種目(マラソン、水泳...) 出来事(戦争、災害...) 保持者(高橋尚子、北島康介...)

問題は練習問題3問を含む全13問です。全ての問題に回答し、「送信」ボタンを押すとタスク終了です。

▼ 注意点

- 「OOのΔΔ」が**意味的に正しくなる**ような単語のみを選んでください。
  次の例では、下線部の「先生」は「太郎」が教わっている先生ではないため、「太郎の先生」は意味的に正しくありません。したがって、この文では「太郎」は選択しません。

  太郎は英語の先生になるのが夢だ。 ⇒ 太郎は英語の先生になるのが夢だ。

- 連想した単語が**原文に存在しない**問題も多くあります。
  その単語が「私」など、原文の書き手であれば【書き手】を、反対に「あなた」など、原文の読み手であれば【読み手】を選んでください。どちらにも当てはまらない場合は、連想した単語が人か物かによって【その他（人）】または【その他（物）】を選んでください。

  【書き手】
  今日は先日生まれた息子を紹介したいと思います。 ⇒ 【書き手】
  今日は先日生まれた息子を紹介したいと思います。

  【その他（物）】
  階段を登って街並みを屋根から見渡した。 ⇒ 【その他（物）】
  階段を登って街並みを屋根から見渡した。

- 以下のように単語 OO が**連想しにくい**名詞も多くあります。この場合は【該当なし】を選んでください。
  その他、選択が難しい場合も【該当なし】を選んでください。

  ピアニスト ⇒ ?

  政治家 ⇒ ?

  東京タワー ⇒ ?

  太郎 ⇒ ?

- 問題文はウェブサイトの文章を切り取ったものです。文脈が不足している場合は、適宜話題を推測しつつお答えください。

Figure 7: A screen capture of the instruction page of our crowdsourcing task (1/2).

Figure 8: A screen capture of the instruction page of our crowdsourcing task (2/2).

Figure 9: A screen capture of the practice questions page of our crowdsourcing task.

Investigating Cross-Document Event Coreference for Dutch

Loic De Langhe, Orphée De Clercq, Veronique Hoste
LT3, Language and Translation Technology Team, Ghent University, Belgium
Groot-Brittanniëlaan 45, 9000 Ghent, Belgium
firstname.lastname@ugent.be

Abstract

In this paper we present baseline results for Event Coreference Resolution (ECR) in Dutch using gold-standard (i.e non-predicted) event mentions. A newly developed benchmark dataset allows us to properly investigate the possibility of creating ECR systems for both within and cross-document coreference. We give an overview of the state of the art for ECR in other languages, as well as a detailed overview of existing ECR resources. Afterwards, we provide a comparative report on our own dataset. We apply a significant number of approaches that have been shown to attain good results for English ECR including feature-based models, monolingual transformer language models and multilingual language models. The best results were obtained using the monolingual BERTje model. Finally, results for all models are thoroughly analysed and visualised, as to provide insight into the inner workings of ECR and long-distance semantic NLP tasks in general.

1 Introduction

With the focus of Natural Language Processing (NLP) applications shifting more towards large-scale discourse-oriented tasks, there is a growing need for systems that can model language not only at the word level, but which can also capture long-distance semantic dependencies. Event coreference resolution (ECR) has been one of the domains within NLP that has been at the forefront of this transition. The ambition in ECR is to determine whether or not two textual events refer to the same real-life or fictional event. For this to be true, two candidate event mentions should have the same event trigger, which denotes the action performed, and non-contradicting event arguments, which include spatio-temporal information and possible participants to the event. Consider the examples below that were taken from two different Dutch (Flemish) newspaper articles:

1. Frankrijk Verslaat België in de halve finales van de FIFA wereldbeker voetbal *EN: France beats Belgium in the semi-final of the FIFA world cup.*

2. België verliest halve finale *EN: Belgium loses semi-final.*

For a human reader, it is perfectly obvious that these two events refer to the same real-world occurrence, even though the event pair has different triggers and the second event mention has no additional argument information. For algorithms, however, this is no trivial task because event mentions are often spread throughout a text, which requires insight into the general discourse structure rather than the local context alone. In addition to this, it is also paramount that coreference can be performed not only at a within-document level, but also across different documents, dramatically increasing the search space of potential event antecedents. In the latter case, the task is possibly further complicated by the fact that the context, target audience and register can inevitably vary between documents. Other than the inherent complexity of creating a (language) model that can accurately resolve long-distance semantic dependencies, ECR research is hindered by the lack of available resources, especially for traditionally lower-resourced languages. In addition to this, data is generally sparse and creating new fully-annotated resources takes considerable time and effort. Despite the challenges, it is important to thoroughly investigate the potential of event coreference resolution because it is a key component of many practical applications such as content-based news recommendation, question answering and contradiction detection. Moreover, researching the links between individual entities and events in texts is paramount to a good understanding of natural language in general.

In this paper, we present baseline results for the task of event coreference resolution on the first

Proceedings of the Fifth Workshop on Computational Models of Reference, Anaphora and Coreference (CRAC 2022), pages 88–98
Gyeongju, Republic of Korea, October 16–17, 2022.

large-scale Dutch cross-document ECR corpus using gold-standard event mentions. This new resource allows us to investigate the possibility of performing ECR on languages other than English and to potentially create an effective end-to-end event coreference resolution system for Dutch in the future. As previous research has exclusively focused on English, Chinese and Spanish, we aim to adapt existing methodologies for those languages and apply them to this Dutch dataset. We hope that this paper, combined with the first large-scale Dutch corpus can be an incentive for future research into event coreference resolution and discourse-oriented tasks for both Dutch and lower-resourced languages in general.

2 Related work

2.1 Resources

Existing annotated datasets for event coreference resolution are scarce even for languages that are generally well-resourced. In this section, we briefly discuss the most widely used corpora for event coreference resolution, detailing strengths and weaknesses for each of them.

Among the most popular of event coreference corpora is the EventCorefBank+ (ECB+) dataset (Cybulska and Vossen, 2014b) which is itself an extension of the earlier EventCorefBank (ECB) (Bejan and Harabagiu, 2010) corpus. ECB+ includes both within and cross-document event coreference annotations, as well as extensive annotation of event arguments and linguistic properties. In addition to this, this dataset contains events belonging to a variety of topics, such as financial news, geopolitical events and local news stories, making it particularly fit for simulation of real-word practical scenarios. Another large-scale resource which is often used as a benchmark dataset for ECR is the OntoNotes corpus (Pradhan et al., 2007). In this corpus both entity and event coreference has been annotated in a within-document fashion. However, a notable caveat for this corpus is that no distinction has been made between entities and events in the annotation. Another group of datasets often used to train and evaluate ECR systems are the TAC KBP corpora (Mitamura et al., 2015). This resource is strictly limited to within-document coreference and events are only annotated when belonging to a more strict event typology. In addition to its English component, the corpus includes a more limited set of Chinese and Spanish documents for event coreference resolution. The last large-scale cross-document corpus for English that should be mentioned is the more recently created WEC-Eng dataset (Eirew et al., 2021), which adopts a novel method of leveraging data where both event mentions and coreference links between events are not restricted to pre-defined topics. A final ECR corpus that should be mentioned is the Newsreader Meantime dataset (Minard et al., 2016). While this corpus is very limited in size, it has extensive event annotations and includes both within and cross-document coreference. Moreover, it includes documents in English, Italian, Dutch and Spanish. However, the articles in Dutch, Spanish and Italian were machine-translated from the original English news articles which is arguably a non-optimal way of collecting data. Table 1 presents an overview of the relative size and most important characteristics of the aforementioned corpora.

Corpus	#Documents	Coref	Languages
OntoNotes	600	CD	EN
TAC KBP	1000, 800, 400	WD	EN, SP, CH
ECB	480	CD	EN
ECB+	982	CD	EN
Newsreader Meantime	120	CD	EN, DU, IT, SP

Table 1: Overview of the most popular corpora annotated with event coreference, both within-document (WD) and cross-document (CD).

2.2 Methodology

Following standards set by research in entity coreference resolution (Rahman and Ng, 2009), event coreference resolvers often take the form of mention-pair models. The mention-pair approach reduces the task to a binary decision problem in which two candidate events are presented to a classification algorithm. The task is then to determine whether or not the two candidates refer to the same event, where the event can be either a fictitious or real-world event. The classification algorithms selected for mention-pair models are often traditional feature-based machine-learning approaches such as support vector machines (Chen and Ng, 2014), decision trees (Cybulska and Vossen, 2015) and, more recently, deep neural networks (Nguyen et al., 2016) and transformer architectures. Note that after this pairwise task, an additional step is needed to construct coreference clusters.

A shortcoming of the mention-pair models is their inability to consider an event coreference chain consisting of more than two events collectively, as the algorithm boils down to pairwise decisions and not to a decision based on the document as a whole. A possible solution to this conundrum can be found in the mention-ranking models. In these systems, all possible candidate antecedents are considered simultaneously and a probability distribution over the most likely partition within a given document is generated (Lu and Ng, 2017b).

Note that the algorithms discussed above strictly require events as input. While this is not an issue in optimal settings where all gold-standard events are known to us, it does raise some problems when trying to apply event coreference resolution in real-life practical applications on unseen data. In this case, events first need to be extracted and analyzed in order to make an accurate prediction regarding a possible coreferential relation. To this purpose, recent work in ECR research has primarily focused on end-to-end systems (Lu and Ng, 2018a). These systems often include a mention detection component, which extracts the events from raw text, a component that identifies spatio-temporal information of the event and finally a component that identifies coreference relationships between entities partaking in the event, as logically, knowing which entities participate in the events is a huge step towards resolving the coreference of the events themselves. Until recently, this was primarily done through pipeline architectures, where one component feeds directly into the next one (Choubey and Huang, 2017). While effective, pipelines are inherently prone to error propagation, which complicates matters enormously. In order to circumvent this problem, interest in joint-modelling techniques for end-to-end coreference resolution has been steadily growing (Lu and Ng, 2018a). Joint models have typically focused on performing joint inference over the output of the various tasks contained within the pipeline through the use of integer linear programming (Chen and Ng, 2016) and Markov Logic Networks (Lu and Ng, 2016), where manually defined constraints are used in order for the individual components to improve one another. Alternatively, joint-learning techniques in which interactions between upstream tasks are modelled have also been applied successfully using both traditional probabilistic methods (Lu and Ng, 2017a) and deep learning (Lu et al., 2022).

Finally and perhaps most importantly, advancements in transformer-based language architectures (Vaswani et al., 2017) have had a major impact on both entity and event coreference alike. Transformer-based language embeddings are often used to extend and improve existing ECR systems for both within -and cross-document settings (Cattan et al., 2021a). Additionally, span-based models have been shown to provide massive improvements when integrated in earlier entity pipelines (Joshi et al., 2020). Similarly, span-based architectures attain state-of-the-art results on the benchmark KBP2017 for event coreference resolution, both in pipeline (46,2 F1) and in joint settings (48,0 F1) (Lu and Ng, 2021).

3 The ENCORE Corpus

The recently developed ENCORE corpus (De Langhe et al., 2022) provides us with the opportunity to lay the groundwork for cross-document event coreference in Dutch. As far as we know, the ENCORE corpus is the largest annotated cross-document event coreference corpus in existence, not only for the Dutch language, but also compared to existing English language corpora.

Data for the ENCORE corpus was sourced from a large collection of unannotated Dutch (Flemish) news texts (De Clercq, Orphée and De Bruyne, Luna and Hoste, Veronique, 2020) collected from a variety of online sources during a one-year period. As event coreference data is notoriously sparse, additional measures were taken in order to maximise the total number of coreference links i.e events referring to one another in the corpus. First, named entities were extracted from each of the documents in the aforementioned larger collection. Second, articles containing a given number (>5) of unique overlapping entities were grouped together in so-called "event clusters", as it was hypothesized that news texts containing a high number of overlapping named entities are much more likely to contain overlapping events as well. Finally, the resulting event clusters were (manually) pruned in order to avoid duplicate and irrelevant news texts. After this process, the corpus totalled 91 event clusters, each containing on average 13 - 14 unique documents.

Table 2 provides a side-by-side view of the ENCORE corpus and comparable event coreference corpora. As the ECB+ corpus was considered to be the largest ECR corpus in existence, the newly created corpus is larger than the corpora presented in Table 1, both in terms of actual size (number of documents) and in terms of the total number of event clusters.

Corpus	Doc.	Topics	Events
ECB (ENG)	482	43	1744
ECB+ (ENG)	982	43	14884
MeanTime (DU)	120	4	1510
ENCORE (DU)	**1115**	**91**	**15407**

Table 2: Comparison of various event coreference corpora at the level of the number of annotated documents, topics and events.

3.1 Event annotation

Annotating event data can be a complicated task in itself. There exists a multitude of annotation schemes ranging from concise, in which the main verb alone is considered to be representative of the entire event (NIST, 2005), to extensive fine-grained annotation where participant information, (extra-) linguistic properties and spatio-temporal cues of the events are all annotated. Since the explicit goal of the corpus is to perform event coreference resolution, a rich annotation style was employed based on the aforementioned ECB+ corpus (Cybulska and Vossen, 2014a). Concretely, the ECB+ guidelines specify four types of event arguments: EVENT-PARTICIPANT, EVENT-TIME, EVENT-LOCATION and EVENT-ACTION that are (if present) annotated for each event. The example below illustrates how an event is typically annotated in the ENCORE corpus.

3. [[Het vliegtuig van vlucht MH17]$^{Non-humanParticipant}$ werd [op 17 juli 2014]^{Time} boven [Oost-Oekraïne]^{Location} uit de lucht [geschoten]^{Action} door [een Buk-raket, een wapen van Russische makelij]$^{Non-humanParticipant}$]^{Event} *EN: The airplane of flight MH17 was shot down on July 17th 2014 above eastern Ukraine by a Russian-made BUK-missile.*

3.2 Coreference annotation

Coreference between events was annotated, both on the within and cross-document level. Events were considered to be coreferent when three criteria were fulfilled: events should occur at the same time (i), in the same place (ii) and the same participants should be involved (iii). Note that the cross-document annotation of event coreference was limited to documents within one event cluster, as manual coreference annotation over the entire corpus would be an almost insurmountable task. Subtypes of coreference were also annotated for events. A distinction was made here between identity relations and part-whole relations. Traditionally, studies in event coreference resolution have exclusively focused on the identity relation between events, even though a solid case can be made that other relationships exist between textual events. For instance, one can argue that, given the proper context, an event such as *the opening speech* is a part of *the Oscars ceremony*, a nuance that is currently overlooked in, to the best of our knowledge, virtually all ECR research.

4 Experimental Setup

We present baseline results using gold event mentions on the Dutch ENCORE corpus. The goal is to correctly reconstruct coreference chains for the events in the documents based on the gold mentions and any spatio-temporal, participant and (meta) linguistic information that was annotated. We report experimental results for both a within and a cross-document coreference resolution task using a variety of algorithms that have shown to perform well throughout the years. The algorithms used for this set of baseline experiments includes both traditional feature-based mention-pair and mention-ranking systems, as well as newer monolingual and multilingual transformer models.

4.1 Feature-based approaches

As there is no earlier work regarding Dutch event coreference resolution, we use a combination of traditional Dutch entity coreference features as well as a set of well-performing language-independent features that have been used previously for English and Chinese ECR. For both the mention-pair and mention-ranking approach, features are identical and have been generated for each possible pair of events.

Lexical-semantic features mostly compare events based on outward similarity. Both string-matching and string-similarity features are known to be important for event coreference resolution, despite their apparent simplicity (Lu and Ng, 2018b). Among the lexical features we apply the exact string match of both event action and span for each pair, as well as POS matching of the event actions. In addition, we add a hoist of string similarity features for both spans and actions in event pairs including Levenshtein distance, Dice coefficient, Jaro-Winkler coefficient and cosine distance based on FastText embeddings (Bojanowski et al.,

2017). Finally, synonym-hypernym relations of the event actions are also extracted.

Discourse features are another category of regularly used characteristics for event coreference resolution. These features include sentence distance between two events, event distance and encoded token distance. In addition, we include matching of (meta) linguistic event aspects that have been specifically annotated in the corpus such as the events' prominence, realis and sentiment.

Logical and constraining features are entirely reliant on successful completion of upstream tasks in the ECR pipeline. Among others, possible conflict of event times and locations are modelled through these features, as well as the possible coreference between event participants. Finally, following earlier success with applying distance-based features for event arguments (Lu and Ng, 2018b), we also include the use of Dice coefficient and FastText-based cosine distance between event locations, times and participant head words.

4.1.1 Feature-based Mention-Pair

We use the popular XGBoost algorithm (Chen et al., 2015) for the pairwise classification of event pairs and then reconstruct the event coreference chains from those pairs using agglomerative clustering. The model is trained using 10-fold cross-validation and extensive hyperparameter tuning for both the within and cross-document setting.

4.1.2 Feature-based Mention-Ranking

We use an adapted implementation of the mention-ranking algorithm used in Lu and Ng (2017c). The base algorithm first generates all possible partitions for the events in a given document. In the partition, each event slot can either be the start of a new coreference chain, or can designate the possible anaphora of said event. Concretely, this means that a document with three events (*event 1*, *event 2*, *event 3*) has 6 possible partitions, as shown in Figure 1. In this setting, each event can either be the start of a new coreference chain (i.e *NEW*) or refer to each of its possible antecedents, which would indicate that these events corefer. Logically, some partitions will, in practice, result in the same output coreference chain e.g. [NEW, E1, E1] and [NEW, E1, E2], where *event 1* starts a new coreference chain and both *event 2* and *event 3* refer to that real-life event.

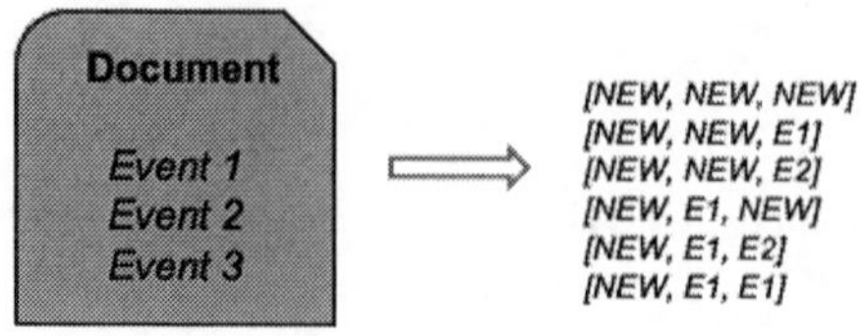

Figure 1: Generated partitions for the mention-ranking model

The original log-linear model defines a distribution over all possible partition vectors a given document d, weights w and feature vector f.

$$p(a|d;w) \propto exp(\sum_{i=1}^{n} w \cdot f(i, a_i, d)) \quad (1)$$

The authors include a task-specific loss function in their original implementation where the weighted sum of three different error types is taken into account.

$$p(a|d;w)' \propto p(a|d;w)l(a, C_d^*) \quad (2)$$

The augmentation for the task-specific loss function $l(a, C_d^*)$ includes the number of non-anaphoric mentions misclassified as anaphoric, anaphoric mentions misclassified as non-anaphoric and incorrectly resolved anaphora based on the gold-standard document partitions C_d^*. Each error type is individually weighed by a floating point parameter, optimized during the training process. For this set of baseline experiments, we test the system using both a general and task-specific loss function and learn the weights that maximise the conditional likelihood of our training data:

$$L(\Theta) = \sum_{d=1}^{t} log \sum_{a \in A(C_d^*)} p(a|d;w)' + \lambda||\Theta||_1 \quad (3)$$

In addition to the two base algorithms described above, we make a series of modifications, as described in the paragraphs below.

For the within-document version, instead of selecting the most likely document partition for each of the documents, we implement a k-majority voting system. We found that in many cases some of the top predicted partitions would result in the correct output chain. By issuing a hard majority vote over the top k predictions we can use this to our advantage and optimally use the probability mass assigned to the resulting output chain.

Additionally, we present two versions of the cross-document algorithm. The original algorithm did not account for the possibility of cross-document coreference and while one can simply concatenate all documents in a given event cluster and generate all cluster partitions similarly to the document partitions, this does pose some scaling issues. First, generating the number of total possible partitions increases almost exponentially when the number of events within a cluster increases, potentially causing memory issues. Second, generating all possible event cluster partitions creates an artificial sparsity problem since, as stated before, the number of total partitions is large. Despite this, the number of correct partitions remains relatively low. While generating all cluster partitions is still feasible with this dataset, we believe that this would be a significant problem in end-to-end settings. We therefore propose an alternative way of performing cross-document coreference using pairwise chain classification. We first determine and extract the coreference chains using the within-document algorithm, then we generate word2vec embeddings for each of the event mentions and average them. Finally, we apply a simple feedforward neural network to determine pairwise coreference between chain representations and reconstruct the final chains using the same clustering algorithm mentioned in section 4.1.1. For the final evaluation, we present cross-document scores using both concatenated cluster partitions (MR) and pairwise document coreference chains (MR Embedding).

4.2 Transformer-based approaches

Fine-tuned transformer language models attain state-of-the-art performance on a multitude of NLP tasks and event coreference resolution is no exception in this regard. The best results are obtained using span-based transformers such as modified versions of SpanBERT-base and SpanBERT-large (Lu and Ng, 2021). It should be noted, however, that results for ECR are still comparatively low (SOTA F1 is 58 on KBP2017).

As no span-based models are available for Dutch, we opt for a series of transformer-based mention-pair models based on the Dutch language models BERTje (de Vries et al., 2019) and RobBERT (Delobelle et al., 2020). These models are monolingual Dutch versions of the BERT-base and RoBERTa-base models respectively. BERTje was pre-trained on a total of around 2.4B tokens of high-quality Dutch texts which include the Dutch Sonar-500 (Oostdijk et al., 2013) and TwNC (Ordelman et al., 2007) corpora, Wikipedia data, historical fiction and a large collection of Dutch online newspaper articles collected over a 4 year period. As a significant portion of the BERTje pretraining data is made out of newspaper articles, we believe this model is particularly fit for event-related tasks on this dataset. RobBERT on the other hand was pre-trained on 6.6B tokens of Commoncrawl webdata (Suárez et al., 2019). However, since the Commoncrawl data consists of individual lines and not every line contains more than one sentence, we anticipate that this model might be less effective on our dataset.

Finally, we also finetune the monolingual RobBERTje model for this task. The RobBERTje models include a series of distilled languague models (Sanh et al., 2019), employing both the aforementioned BERTje and RobBERT as teacher models. The distillation model has previously been shown to outperform the two previous language models on coreference-based tasks such as die-dat disambiguation (Allein et al., 2020) and pronoun prediction (Delobelle et al., 2022). In addition to these three monolingual models, we finetune the multilingual models XLM-ROBERTa (Lample and Conneau, 2019) and multilingual BERT (mBERT) (Devlin et al., 2018), as they both contain a substantial amount of Dutch data and have been shown to be quite effective at a number of Dutch NLP tasks (Bouma, 2021).

5 Evaluation

5.1 Evaluation metrics for coreference

Evaluating coreference, much like any cluster-based task, can be a complex affair. Many different evaluation metrics have been proposed throughout the years with some being more robust, while others provide counter-intuitive results in certain situations. Common practice is to evaluate coreference systems by computing the average F1-score of 3 metrics in particular: MUC (Vilain et al., 1995), B3 (Bagga and Baldwin, 1998) and CEAF (Luo, 2005). In addition to this, we also report evaluation using the recently developed LEA metric, a link-based evaluation method that has shown to often produce reliable and highly interpretable results (Moosavi and Strube, 2016). It must be noted that in our evaluation we exclude any singleton event mention, i.e. events that are predicted to form a coreference

	CONLL	LEA
MP XGBoost	0.36	0.21
MR_{base}	0.39	0.25
$MR_{task-specific}$	0.42	0.26
MR $Embedding_{base}$	/	/
MR $Embedding_{task-specific}$	/	/
MP BERTje	**0.52**	**0.33**
MP RobBERT	0.49	0.29
MP RobBERTje	0.48	0.29
MP XLM-RoBERTa	0.17	0.11
MP mBERT	0.14	0.08

(a) Results for within-document ECR

	CONLL	LEA
MP XGBOOST	0.37	0.23
MR_{base}	0.35	0.22
$MR_{task-specific}$	0.38	0.25
MR $Embedding_{base}$	0.36	0.24
MR $Embedding_{task-specific}$	0.40	0.28
MP BERTje	**0.59**	**0.39**
MP RobBERT	0.56	0.38
MP RobBERTje	0.54	0.35
MP XLM-RoBERTa	0.23	0.14
MP mBERT	0.19	0.10

(b) Results for cross-document ECR

Table 3: Results of the baseline ECR experiments in the within (a) and cross-document (b) setting for both the Mention-Pair (MP) and Mention-Ranking (MR) paradigms. Naturally, the Mention-ranking algorithm using chain embeddings is not applicable to the within-document setting.

chain of size one. While the inclusion of singleton clusters can be useful for the evaluation of joint and pipeline systems, it has been shown that singletons can artificially inflate certain metrics. B3 and CEAF are particularly prone to this, but recent work has revealed that also the LEA metric can be distorted by it to some extent (Poot and van Cranenburgh, 2020; Cattan et al., 2021b).

5.2 Results

Tables 3a and 3b show results for the within and cross-document respectively. These are fully in line and proportional to similar research for English and Chinese ECR (Lu and Ng, 2018b). Monolingual transformer language models such as BERTje (0.59 F1) and RobBERT (0.56 F1) produce by far the best results, followed by feature-based mention-ranking (0.40 F1) and mention-pair (0.37 F1) models respectively. Somewhat surprisingly, multilingual transformer models such as XLM-RoBERTa (0.23 F1) and mBERT (0.19 F1) perform rather poorly, especially when considering their potential when it came to other multilingual NLP problems (Li et al., 2021). Finally, we also notice a slight increase in performance for almost all models when comparing the within-document trial to the cross-document setting.

5.3 Analysis and discussion

5.3.1 Feature-based models

Despite the discrepancy in performance between transformer models and more traditional approaches, the inclusion of feature-based models can still be useful going forward, as hybrid models combining transformer-based embeddings with traditional features and encoding feature information within transformer architectures have shown to provide promising results for many NLP applications (van Cranenburgh et al., 2021). In order for such an approach to be explored in closer detail it is important to know which features can exactly be useful.

We explore feature importance for the XGBoost algorithm by calculating the amount that each feature improves the overall performance for each decision tree weighted by the number of observations the feature node is responsible for. The final score for each individual feature is then determined by averaging the aforementioned per-tree score over all trees in the model. For the log-linear mention ranking algorithm we study which feature coefficients it employed in order to determine the weight of each feature in the classification decision. Figures 2a and 2b report feature importance for the 10 most important features in the used mention-pair and mention-ranking models, respectively. The most important features were fairly consistent for the mention-pair and mention-ranking approaches respectively. Our observations generally confirm earlier research in the sense that outward (Dice coefficient) and lexical similarity (cosine similarity) between the two events are paramount when it comes to resolving coreference between them. For the cross-document setting specifically, argument-constraining features also seem to have an (minimal) impact on the task, while discourse-based features seem to have no real contribution.

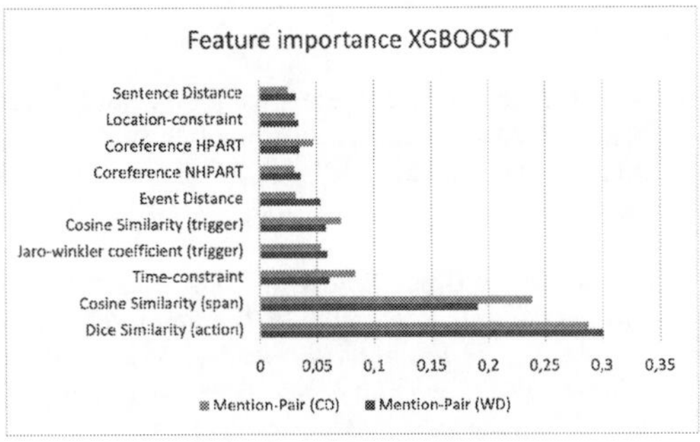

(a) Top 10 features Mention-Pair

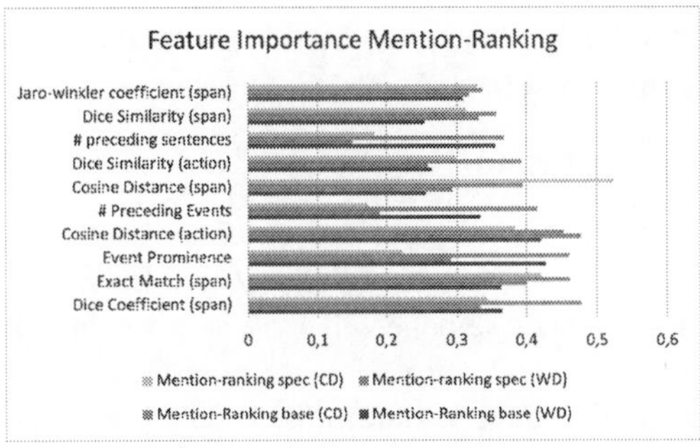

(b) Top 10 features Mention-Ranking

Figure 2: Feature Importances for the Mention-pair and Mention-ranking algorithms

5.3.2 Transformer-based models

As could be observed in Table 3, BERTje performs best. This is most likely due to the thematic overlap of the training corpus (news) and the ENCORE dataset, as well as the fact that the data tends to be less fragmented than RobBERT's. As stated before, successful event coreference resolution is mainly dependent on successfully modelling long-distance semantic dependencies and RobBERT's training data might not be sufficient. Nonetheless, both models perform well, especially when compared to multilingual models XLM-RoBERTa and mBERT. Intuitively, we assumed the task of cross-document coreference to be more difficult than within-document coreference, however, when looking at the results the opposite seems to be true. We assume this is because for the cross-document setting the models had access to significantly increasing training data (1M event pairs compared to 100k for within-document).

Recently, interpretation of transformer-based models has been a hot topic. Vig (2019) and Vig and Belinkov (2019) have revealed that insights regarding syntactic and semantic relations important to a given task can be gained from transformer architectures by visualizing attention heads. We use the Bertviz tool (Vig, 2019) to visualize attention between mention-pairs. We observe that our best performing model (Cross-document BERTje) can consistently model action-to-action relationships for both semantically similar events (figure 3a) and, to a lesser degree, between semantically more distant events (Figure 3b). In addition to this, these aforementioned relationships were absent in the

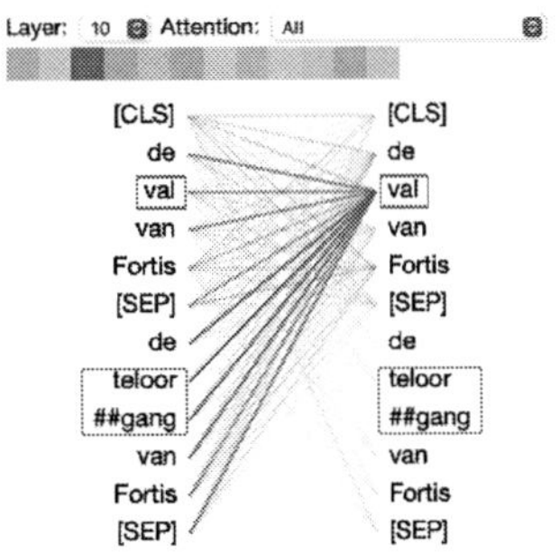

(a) *The [downfall] of Fortis vs. The [decline] of Fortis*

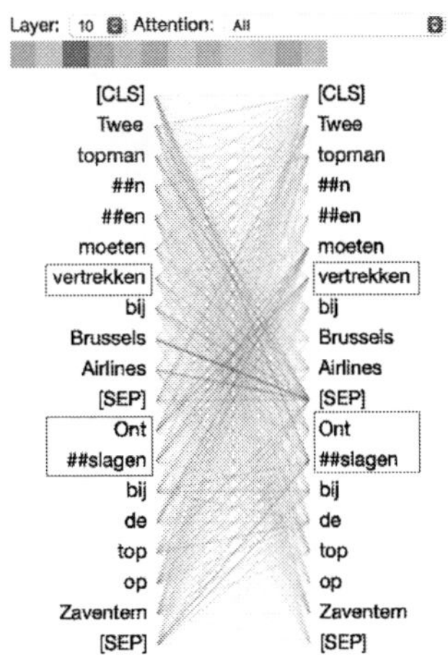

(b) *Two executives have to [leave] at Brussels Airlines vs. [Dismissals] at the top of Zaventem*

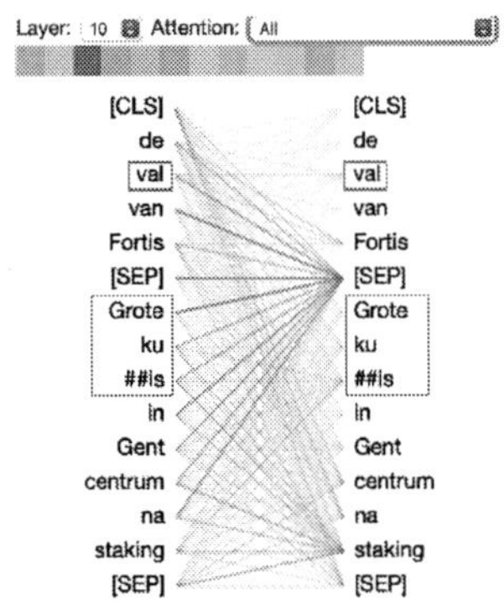

(c) *The [downfall] of Fortis vs. [Large cleanup] in Gent city center after strikes*

Figure 3: Visualisation of the CD BERTje attention heads

same layer and attention head for events that did corefer (Figure 3c).

6 Conclusion

In this paper, we presented baseline results for Dutch ECR on the recently developed ENCORE dataset, which we hope will serve as a benchmark for future investigations into the possibility of developing ECR applications for Dutch. We use a selection of both feature-based and transformer-based models that have shown to work well for English ECR and evaluate these for within-document and cross-document coreference. Our experiments show that monolingual Dutch language models perform best. It should also be noted that multilingual language models perform poorly. This has implications for future work not only in Dutch, but possibly for ECR research in other lower-resourced languages. We also present an analysis of our models, confirming earlier observations that semantic similarity features have a large impact on the task of ECR, while discourse features are less effective. Additionally, by visualising the attention heads we reveal that transformer architectures can specifically model syntactic and semantic relationships that are important in event coreference. In future work we will progress to the development of an end-to-end Dutch ECR system. We will also focus on systems that can accurately model long-distance semantic dependencies, both in context of ECR and language understanding in general.

7 Acknowledgements

This research is part of the ENCORE project which is funded by the Research Foundation–Flanders, Project No. G013820N

References

Liesbeth Allein, Artuur Leeuwenberg, and Marie-Francine Moens. 2020. Automatically correcting dutch pronouns" die" and" dat". *Computational Linguistics in the Netherlands Journal*, 10:19–36.

Amit Bagga and Breck Baldwin. 1998. Algorithms for scoring coreference chains. In *The first international conference on language resources and evaluation workshop on linguistics coreference*, volume 1, pages 563–566. Citeseer.

Cosmin Bejan and Sanda Harabagiu. 2010. Unsupervised Event Coreference Resolution with Rich Linguistic Features. *Proceedings of the 48th Annual Meeting of the Association for Computational Linguistics*, (July):1412–1422.

Piotr Bojanowski, Edouard Grave, Armand Joulin, and Tomas Mikolov. 2017. Enriching word vectors with subword information. *Transactions of the association for computational linguistics*, 5:135–146.

Gosse Bouma. 2021. Probing for dutch relative pronoun choice. *Computational Linguistics in the Netherlands Journal*, 11:59–70.

Arie Cattan, Alon Eirew, Gabriel Stanovsky, Mandar Joshi, and Ido Dagan. 2021a. Cross-document coreference resolution over predicted mentions. *arXiv preprint arXiv:2106.01210*.

Arie Cattan, Alon Eirew, Gabriel Stanovsky, Mandar Joshi, and Ido Dagan. 2021b. Realistic evaluation principles for cross-document coreference resolution. *arXiv preprint arXiv:2106.04192*.

Chen Chen and Vincent Ng. 2014. SinoCoreferencer : An End-to-End Chinese Event Coreference Resolver. *Lrec 2014*, pages 4532–4538.

Chen Chen and Vincent Ng. 2016. Joint Inference over a Lightly Supervised Information Extraction Pipeline: Towards Event Coreference Resolution for Resource-Scarce Languages. In *Proceedings of the Thirtieth AAAI Conference on Artificial Intelligence, February 12-17, 2016, Phoenix, Arizona, USA.*, pages 2913–2920.

Tianqi Chen, Tong He, Michael Benesty, Vadim Khotilovich, Yuan Tang, Hyunsu Cho, et al. 2015. Xgboost: extreme gradient boosting. *R package version 0.4-2*, 1(4).

Prafulla Kumar Choubey and Ruihong Huang. 2017. Event Coreference Resolution by Iteratively Unfolding Inter-dependencies among Events. pages 2124–2133. Association for Computational Linguistics.

Agata Cybulska and Piek Vossen. 2014a. Guidelines for ecb+ annotation of events and their coreference. In *Technical Report*. Technical Report NWR-2014-1, VU University Amsterdam.

Agata Cybulska and Piek Vossen. 2014b. Using a sledgehammer to crack a nut? Lexical diversity and event coreference resolution. *Proceedings of the Ninth International Conference on Language Resources and Evaluation (LREC'14)*, pages 4545–4552.

Agata Cybulska and Piek Vossen. 2015. Translating Granularity of Event Slots into Features for Event Coreference Resolution. In *Proceedings of the The 3rd Workshop on EVENTS: Definition, Detection, Coreference, and Representation*, pages 1–10, Denver, Colorado. Association for Computational Linguistics.

De Clercq, Orphée and De Bruyne, Luna and Hoste, Veronique. 2020. News topic classification as a first step towards diverse news recommendation. *COMPUTATIONAL LINGUISTICS IN THE NETHERLANDS JOURNAL*, 10:37–55.

Loic De Langhe, Orphee De Clercq, and Veronique Hoste. 2022. Constructing a cross-document event coreference corpus for dutch. *Language Recources and Evaluation*, page Accepted for publication.

Wietse de Vries, Andreas van Cranenburgh, Arianna Bisazza, Tommaso Caselli, Gertjan van Noord, and Malvina Nissim. 2019. Bertje: A dutch bert model. *arXiv preprint arXiv:1912.09582*.

Pieter Delobelle, Thomas Winters, and Bettina Berendt. 2020. Robbert: a dutch roberta-based language model. *arXiv preprint arXiv:2001.06286*.

Pieter Delobelle, Thomas Winters, and Bettina Berendt. 2022. Robbertje: A distilled dutch bert model. *arXiv preprint arXiv:2204.13511*.

Jacob Devlin, Ming-Wei Chang, Kenton Lee, and Kristina Toutanova. 2018. Bert: Pre-training of deep bidirectional transformers for language understanding. *arXiv preprint arXiv:1810.04805*.

Alon Eirew, Arie Cattan, and Ido Dagan. 2021. Wec: Deriving a large-scale cross-document event coreference dataset from wikipedia. *arXiv preprint arXiv:2104.05022*.

Mandar Joshi, Danqi Chen, Yinhan Liu, Daniel S Weld, Luke Zettlemoyer, and Omer Levy. 2020. Spanbert: Improving pre-training by representing and predicting spans. *Transactions of the Association for Computational Linguistics*, 8:64–77.

Guillaume Lample and Alexis Conneau. 2019. Cross-lingual language model pretraining. *arXiv preprint arXiv:1901.07291*.

Bing Li, Yujie He, and Wenjin Xu. 2021. Cross-lingual named entity recognition using parallel corpus: A new approach using xlm-roberta alignment. *arXiv preprint arXiv:2101.11112*.

Jing Lu and Vincent Ng. 2016. Event Coreference Resolution with Multi-Pass Sieves. page 8.

Jing Lu and Vincent Ng. 2017a. Joint Learning for Event Coreference Resolution. pages 90–101. Association for Computational Linguistics.

Jing Lu and Vincent Ng. 2017b. Learning antecedent structures for event coreference resolution. In *2017 16th IEEE International Conference on Machine Learning and Applications (ICMLA)*, pages 113–118. IEEE.

Jing Lu and Vincent Ng. 2017c. Learning Antecedent Structures for Event Coreference Resolution. In *Machine Learning and Applications (ICMLA), 2017 16th IEEE International Conference on*, pages 113–118. IEEE.

Jing Lu and Vincent Ng. 2018a. Event coreference resolution: A survey of two decades of research. In *IJCAI*, pages 5479–5486.

Jing Lu and Vincent Ng. 2018b. Event Coreference Resolution: A Survey of Two Decades of Research. In *Proceedings of the Twenty-Seventh International Joint Conference on Artificial Intelligence*, pages 5479–5486, Stockholm, Sweden. International Joint Conferences on Artificial Intelligence Organization.

Jing Lu and Vincent Ng. 2021. Conundrums in event coreference resolution: Making sense of the state of the art. In *Proceedings of the 2021 Conference on Empirical Methods in Natural Language Processing*, pages 1368–1380.

Yaojie Lu, Hongyu Lin, Jialong Tang, Xianpei Han, and Le Sun. 2022. End-to-end neural event coreference resolution. *Artificial Intelligence*, 303:103632.

Xiaoqiang Luo. 2005. On coreference resolution performance metrics. In *Proceedings of Human Language Technology Conference and Conference on Empirical Methods in Natural Language Processing*, pages 25–32.

Anne-Lyse Minard, Manuela Speranza, Ruben Urizar, Marieke van Erp, Anneleen Schoen, and Chantal van Son. 2016. MEANTIME, the NewsReader Multilingual Event and Time Corpus. In *Proceedings of the 10th language resources and evaluation conference (LREC 2016)*, page 6, Portorož, Slovenia. European Language Resources Association (ELRA).

Teruko Mitamura, Zhengzhong Liu, and Eduard Hovy. 2015. Overview of TAC KBP 2015 Event Nugget Track. *Kbp Tac 2015*, pages 1–31.

Nafise Sadat Moosavi and Michael Strube. 2016. Which coreference evaluation metric do you trust? a proposal for a link-based entity aware metric. In *Proceedings of the 54th Annual Meeting of the Association for Computational Linguistics (Volume 1: Long Papers)*, pages 632–642.

Thien Huu Nguyen, Adam Meyers, and Ralph Grishman. 2016. New York University 2016 System for KBP Event Nugget: A Deep Learning Approach. *Text Analysis Conference*, page 7.

NIST. 2005. The ACE 2005 (ACE 05) Evaluation Plan.

Nelleke Oostdijk, Martin Reynaert, Véronique Hoste, and Ineke Schuurman. 2013. The Construction of a 500-Million-Word Reference Corpus of Contemporary Written Dutch. pages 219–247.

Roeland J.F. Ordelman, Franciska M.G. de Jong, Adrianus J. van Hessen, and G.H.W. Hondorp. 2007. Twnc: a multifaceted dutch news corpus. *ELRA Newsletter*, 12(3-4).

Corbèn Poot and Andreas van Cranenburgh. 2020. A benchmark of rule-based and neural coreference resolution in dutch novels and news. *arXiv preprint arXiv:2011.01615*.

Sameer S. Pradhan, Lance Ramshaw, Ralph Weischedel, Jessica MacBride, and Linnea Micciulla. 2007. Unrestricted coreference: Identifying entities and events in ontonotes. *ICSC 2007 International Conference on Semantic Computing*, pages 446–453.

Altaf Rahman and Vincent Ng. 2009. Supervised models for coreference resolution. In *Proceedings of the 2009 conference on empirical methods in natural language processing*, pages 968–977.

Victor Sanh, Lysandre Debut, Julien Chaumond, and Thomas Wolf. 2019. Distilbert, a distilled version of bert: smaller, faster, cheaper and lighter. *arXiv preprint arXiv:1910.01108*.

Pedro Javier Ortiz Suárez, Benoît Sagot, and Laurent Romary. 2019. Asynchronous pipeline for processing huge corpora on medium to low resource infrastructures. In *7th Workshop on the Challenges in the Management of Large Corpora (CMLC-7)*. Leibniz-Institut für Deutsche Sprache.

Andreas van Cranenburgh, Esther Ploeger, Frank van den Berg, and Remi Thüss. 2021. A hybrid rule-based and neural coreference resolution system with an evaluation on dutch literature. In *Proceedings of the Fourth Workshop on Computational Models of Reference, Anaphora and Coreference*, pages 47–56.

Ashish Vaswani, Noam Shazeer, Niki Parmar, Jakob Uszkoreit, Llion Jones, Aidan N. Gomez, Lukasz Kaiser, and Illia Polosukhin. 2017. Attention is all you need.

Jesse Vig. 2019. A multiscale visualization of attention in the transformer model. *arXiv preprint arXiv:1906.05714*.

Jesse Vig and Yonatan Belinkov. 2019. Analyzing the structure of attention in a transformer language model. *arXiv preprint arXiv:1906.04284*.

Marc Vilain, John D Burger, John Aberdeen, Dennis Connolly, and Lynette Hirschman. 1995. A model-theoretic coreference scoring scheme. In *Sixth Message Understanding Conference (MUC-6): Proceedings of a Conference Held in Columbia, Maryland, November 6-8, 1995*.

The Role of Common Ground for Referential Expressions in Social Dialogues

Jaap Kruijt
Vrije Universiteit Amsterdam
j.m.kruijt@vu.nl

Piek Vossen
Vrije Universiteit Amsterdam
p.t.j.m.vossen@vu.nl

Abstract

In this paper, we frame the problem of co-reference resolution in dialogue as a dynamic social process in which mentions to people previously known and newly introduced are mixed when people know each other well. We restructured an existing data set for the Friends sitcom as a coreference task that evolves over time, where close friends make reference to other people either part of their common ground (inner circle) or not (outer circle). We expect that awareness of common ground is key in social dialogue in order to resolve references to the inner social circle, whereas local contextual information plays a more important role for outer circle mentions. Our analysis of these references confirms that there are differences in naming and introducing these people. We also experimented with the SpanBERT coreference system with and without fine-tuning to measure whether preceding discourse contexts matter for resolving inner and outer circle mentions. Our results show that more inner circle mentions lead to a decrease in model performance, and that fine-tuning on preceding contexts reduces false negatives for both inner and outer circle mentions but increases the false positives as well, showing that the models overfit on these contexts[1].

1 Introduction

People that have a long-term relationship develop an effective way of communication which also targets the relationship as such. We call such conversations "social dialogues" and we expect that common ground plays an important role and has an impact in the way reference is made. As two conversation partners develop a closer bond, they form conventions in how they refer to individuals that are often part of their shared experiences, and these references may become vague and ambiguous to others (Hawkins et al., 2021). How present and important a particular individual is within the common ground not only influences the ambiguity of the references used, it also influences how readily they can be introduced into the conversation. While less popular or newly introduced individuals (outer circle) need a more elaborate and explicit reference, well-known individuals (inner circle) can be referenced with their name or a short and vague description, which may be difficult to infer for outsiders. For instance, someone's grandmother could be brought up with the reference 'Nana'. We would thus expect to see a difference between less important or unknown individuals on the one hand and important individuals on the other hand with respect to their *co-reference chains*.

When agents become more and more part of our lives, we can expect that they also build up long-term relationships with us, just like people do. An agent that needs to engage in social conversation with a human should therefore be sensitive to these changes in the way reference is made as the common ground grows. Some parts of this common ground, such as observations within the visual scene, can be established based on the context of the shared environment (Gergle et al., 2013). However, references to individuals in their shared experience (i.e. individuals that have been mentioned before) belong to the common ground that is based on the more long-term shared world context that needs to be retained across interactions, and which can also change over time.

In this paper, we report on a first analysis of how inner and outer circle people are referred to in social dialogues in which common ground plays a role and we test how sensitive existing co-reference resolution models are to this. To test this, we use a data set consisting of episodes of the *Friends* TV series that has been annotated with mentions of individuals (Choi and Chen, 2018). This data set contains both social dialogue and long-term connections between mentions that go above the level

[1]Our code is available at: https://github.com/cltl/inner-outer-coreference

Proceedings of the Fifth Workshop on Computational Models of Reference, Anaphora and Coreference (CRAC 2022), pages 99–110
Gyeongju, Republic of Korea, October 16–17, 2022.

of a single document, and therefore it could serve as a useful simulation of the buildup of common ground over time.

Our main contributions are: 1) we frame the problem of resolving co-reference in dialogues as a dynamic process in which common ground plays a role, introducing the concepts of inner and outer circle references, 2) we provide new insight into the way inner and outer circle references are made by "friends" with a lot of common ground, 3) we test the sensitivity of machine learning models to (long-term) common ground in dialogue, 4) we restructure an existing data set of social dialogue in such a way that the existing temporal and topical relations between the conversations are maintained, which can be used for investigating the buildup of common ground and the development of conventions in referencing.

This paper is structured as follows: in section 2 we discuss related work, and present our motivation and problem statement. In section 3 we analyze the data on the difference in mention patterns for well-known and lesser-known individuals, and we discuss our approach to testing model performance with respect to references with common ground, and in section 4 we present the results of our tests and perform some error analysis. Finally, in section 5 we interpret our results and link them to the broader question of achieving common ground in human-agent communication.

2 Related Work

Common ground is what we call the established shared information that speakers rely on within a conversation (Stalnaker, 2002). It is essential to successful communication. Consequently, an agent that communicates with a human also needs to establish common ground to overcome mismatched representations of the world (Chai et al., 2014). In a process called *grounding*, this common ground also needs to be continually updated (Clark and Brennan, 1991).

Various research has been done on grounding in human agent-interaction, for instance on grounding in the visual scene in relation to tasks (Brawer et al., 2018; Roesler and Nowé, 2019; Shridhar and Hsu, 2018; Chai et al., 2014). Agents which develop this common ground have been shown to perform better on well-known tasks and also adapt better to new tasks (Brawer et al., 2018). However, in these task-oriented dialogues, the references tend to be explicit and refer to objects in the shared environment. In social dialogues, which are open, not task-oriented and between people that established a long social relationship, references become more vague quickly, and also refer to objects or individuals which are not present, but part of past (shared) experiences. This makes the references harder to latch on to, and means the agent must relate them to background knowledge rather than to what it sees in front of him.

The more interactions the agent has had with a particular human, the more shared experiences and background knowledge it can potentially rely on. However, in natural dialogue, as the number of shared experiences increases, the references become also more conventionalized, and as a result, more ambiguous to outsiders. Researchers have shown in simulations and experiments in human-human communication how this conventionalization occurs, and how it leads to more efficient but also more vague expressions over time that nonetheless remain understandable for the conversation partners who share the common ground (Hawkins et al., 2021; Shih et al., 2021; Haber et al., 2019). However, these simulations have been limited to task-oriented dialogue. We add to this research an analysis of social dialogues between humans.

Existing end-to-end coreference resolution models can achieve high scores on well-established datasets such as Ontonotes (Pradhan et al., 2012). However, these datasets do not relate well to our use-case of social dialogue. They consist of snippets of text from news articles, telephone conversations or talkshows, often more formal in nature, which likely makes the references more explicit. Most importantly, though, since the data does not contain a temporal aspect in which the various documents relate to each other, it cannot be used to examine how common ground builds up over time and how a model could utilise that common ground. The CODI-CRAC shared task (Khosla et al., 2021) is aimed at improving coreference resolution performance in dialogue. They also provide a selection of data sets consisting of dialogue, such as the Switchboard corpus (Holliman et al., 1992) and the Persuasion for Good dataset (Wang et al., 2019). However, these data sets are not ideal for our case either. Although they do consist of (social) dialogue, the conversations are between speakers who were previously unacquainted, and who do not share a common background which can be built upon in the conversation. This is a crucial part of the phenomenon that we aim to investigate. Therefore, we take an existing dataset containing social dialogue and temporal relations between documents (Choi and Chen, 2018) and adapt it to analyze the differences in referencing of inner-circle mentions, which are part of the common ground, and outer circle mentions, which are only relevant within the surrounding context. We also test to what extent a state-of-the-art end-to-end coreference resolution model utilizes background knowledge and how it resolves complex third-person references. We hypothesize that the model will perform worse on references that require common ground. A model failing to detect a vague introduction for an otherwise well-known individual could also have problems further on in the conversation, as third-person pronouns referring to this individual are instead linked to a different individual. Concretely, this means that the higher the amount of inner circle references in the test set, the lower the overall model performance will be for that set. We further investigate whether this performance can be improved by increasing the background knowledge by training on preceding interactions.

We believe that it is valuable to examine common ground buildup over time in the context of coreference resolution. To the best of our knowledge, this is a new approach to the problem of coreference resolution. In the next section, we describe how we created the dataset and how we tested the model.

3 Method

For our experiment, we take the current state-of-the-art model in co-reference resolution, SpanBERT (Joshi et al., 2019, 2020). We use an implementation of this model by Xu and Choi (2020). This model predicts co-reference chains by calculating scores for pairs of mention and antecedent span representations which have been contextualized using BERT. We test this model in two ways. First, we run the pre-trained model on the new data set without fine-tuning. We do this to examine what performance the model can already achieve without knowing anything about the background knowledge except for what may have been learned from public sources such as Wikipedia during pretraining. Next, we fine-tune the model on data of previous conversations that likely contain common ground information and discourse contexts specific to sitcom characters. We fine-tune three models, one on a small, one on a medium and on a large portion of the previous conversations (see Table 3). We then examine the impact of the level of conversational context knowledge on performance. Specifically, we analyze the performance for inner- and outer circle mentions separately. Crucially, the fine-tuning is only done on data which precedes the test set chronologically, since we want to investigate the effect of simulated buildup of conversational context over time, which may also represent common ground.

3.1 Data analysis

We use the data set from SemEval 2018 task 4 (Choi and Chen, 2018) which consists of transcripts from the first two seasons of *FRIENDS*. This show contains social multi-party and dyadic dialogue. The data set is formatted according to the CONLL-2012 standards (Pradhan et al., 2012) and contains gold mentions. The original task was described as 'character identification', which combined features from entity linking and co-reference resolution in one task (Choi and Chen, 2018). However, the format of the data set works just as well for a pure co-reference resolution task. Since the original task was aimed at the identification of characters though, the gold mentions only contain references to people, and not objects or other types of named entities such as companies or countries. For our task this is ideal, since we are only interested in references to individuals.

In the show, the main characters know each other well, and as such have developed certain ways to refer to the people that are in their common ground. These people are also referenced more often throughout the show, requiring less introduction. For instance, *Judy Geller*, mother of two of the main characters, is referenced with *mom, ... (your) mother , ... (my) mother* (among others), over the course of several episodes. Meanwhile, a minor character called *Debra* is only mentioned in one single scene, and is referenced with the references *(a) woman - her - Debra - she - she*, in succession while she is the topic of the conversation.

The original character identification task contained a list of all the characters mentioned for the entity linking part of the task, 401 in total. We use this list to categorize all of the characters into 'inner circle' and 'outer circle'. We took the following approach to selecting which characters belong to the inner circle: first, all of the six main characters of the show belong to the inner circle. Secondly, all of the family members of the six main characters also belong to the inner circle, since they can be mentioned by vague and ambiguous kinship terms which need background knowledge to be resolved (Kemp et al., 2018). All of the real-life famous persons which are mentioned in the show also belong to the inner circle, since they are well-known to all of the main characters in the show. However, they are mostly referred to by name. Lastly, we selected a few characters which have an entry on the Wikidata page for *FRIENDS* [2] relating them to the main characters. Since only the most important characters in the show have entries on Wikidata, this serves as a good indication that they are characters which belong to the shared common ground within the show. In total, we end up with 50 characters in the inner circle. The remaining 351 characters belong to the outer circle.

Inner circle characters are referenced a bit more in total than outer circle people even though there are more than 7 times more outer circle characters in the data set: on average inner circle characters are referenced 91.8 times and outer circle characters 6.6 times. The average number of variants (unique tokens) used to make reference is 16.4 for inner circle entities and 1 for outer circle entities. Furthermore, 112 outer circle characters are only mentioned once, whereas the lowest number of mentions for inner circle entities is 3 ('dad':2, 'he':1).

In Table 1, we show the distribution of the part-of-speech of the mentions of the inner and outer circle people. Proportionally, inner circle characters are more often referenced by name (NNP) than by pronoun (PR) as compared to outer circle references, whereas both are referenced equally by noun phrase (NN).[3] Apparently, the inner circle references by name seem to preempt the use of pronouns: less than 30% of the references to the inner circle is made using a pronoun, while almost 45% of the outer circle references is a pronoun.

In order to get insight in the discourse sequences of the references, we counted the part-of-speech sequence pairs as shown in Table 2. The rows represent the first mention in a pair and the columns the next mention, where NULL marks the cases of a first introduction of the referent in a scene. The table shows trivial dependencies such as pronouns are often followed by other pronominal references and hardly used as the first reference. Use of a pronoun as the first reference still makes sense however because we are dealing with a multimodal setting in which people can be introduced visually and referenced with deictic pronouns. This happens twice more often proportionally for the outer circle (20.19%) than for the inner circle (11.19%). Further comparing inner and outer circle references, we indeed see more NNP-NNP sequences for inner circle people and NN-PR sequences for outer circle people. Inner circles are introduced by name in 58.56% of the cases, which is followed by a name again in 52.98% of the cases, compared to 42.72% and 46.34% for outer respectively. We can expect that NNP-NNP sequences are easier to resolve for systems, which is advantageous for inner circle references. NN introductions happen more often for outer (37.09%) than for inner circles (30.25%), which are mostly followed by pronouns for outer (53.57%) and another NN for inner (44.5%).

These statistics suggest that for inner circle references it would be better for the model to focus on NNP-NNP patterns whereas for outer circle references NN-PR patterns are more important. We expect the former to be less and the latter to be more discourse structure dependent.

3.2 Experiment

The aim of our experiment is to measure differences in performance of coreference models resolving inner and outer circle co-reference relations, given the different ways of making reference, the degree they rely on background knowledge and the potential of the preceding discourse to learn patterns for resolving coreference relations. We expect that inner circle references by pronouns and noun phrases are more difficult to resolve than their counter parts for outer circle references. On the other hand, the more frequent use of names referring to inner circle entities could make it easier to resolve inner circle co-references. We expect to measure the impact of these differences in the performance on test sets with different ratios of inner and outer circle references. Furthermore, we want to measure the effect of using the preceding conversational context on the performance as well. To what extent does this context contain knowledge and information to resolve either inner or outer cir-

[2] https://www.wikidata.org/wiki/Q79784

[3] Other parts-of-speech mostly result from annotation errors

	NNP		NN		PR		OTHER		Total	Avg ment. per ref.
Inner (50)	1075	0,384	674	0,241	838	0,299	212	0,076	2799	55.98
Outer (351)	530	0,261	493	0,243	908	0,447	100	0,049	2031	5.78

Table 1: Distribution of part of speech for inner and outer circle mentions and the average number of mentions per referent. The parts-of-speech listed are names/proper nouns (NNP), common nouns (NN), pronouns (PR) and an OTHER category for parts-of-speech not belonging to one of the previous.

Inner circle	NNP	NN	PR
NULL	58.56	30.25	11.19
NNP	52.98	19.04	27.98
NN	24.35	44.50	31.15
PR	16.99	13.89	69.12
Outer circle	NNP	NN	PR
NULL	42.72	37.09	20.19
NNP	46.34	14.33	39.33
NN	11.07	35.36	53.57
PR	10.79	15.25	73.96

Table 2: Overview of proportion of part-of-speech coreference pairs for inner and outer circle mentions. Rows represent the first mention and the columns the following mention part-of-speech. NULL signifies there was no preceding mention.

Set	Small	Medium	Large
Train	S1E1...E7	S1E1...E17	S1E1...2E12
N° tokens	22211	54138	110074
Dev	S1E08	S1E18	S2E13
N° tokens	2876	2356	2118

Table 3: Size of each of the train sets and their respective development set

cle co-reference relations? Does this knowledge represent discourse structures, background knowledge or simply frequency of names?

For our experiment, we adapted the data set by removing all first-person and second-person pronoun mentions. We are only interested in the resolution of third-person references, which can become part of the common ground (inner) and thus require background knowledge to resolve or are introduced in the discourse itself (outer). First-person and second-person pronouns can be resolved within the discourse by linking them to the speaker or hearer, and are therefore not relevant to our experiment.

In the original data set, the train, development and test set were randomly distributed. However, we want to maintain the temporal structure within the data. Therefore, we made new train/development sets and selected two new test sets, where the latter are chosen to follow the training data in time.

To investigate the effect of varying the prominence of inner circle mentions in the test data on the model performance, we calculated the amount of mentions in the gold data to inner circle and outer circle characters per episode. We use episodes as a base length, because we find that in the TV show minor characters belonging to the outer circle are usually only mentioned in at most one episode, while major characters belonging to the inner circle are mentioned throughout the show, in multiple episodes or even seasons. After categorizing the mentions into inner and outer circle, we calculated the ratio of inner circle/outer circle mentions per episode.

For the test set, we selected one episode which contains roughly 4 times as many mentions to the inner circle as to the outer circle (S2E14), and one with a roughly equal amount of inner and outer circle mentions (S2E24). In the Appendix, we show details for both test sets in Tables 7 and 8, respectively. Both tables list the identifiers for the different characters sorted for the number of mentions. They show that S2E14 is dominated by inner circle mentions (top 5) and S2E24 has mixed mentions for inner and outer circles. On the other hand, the non-coreferential mentions (mentioned once) in S2E24 are all outer circle entities, while they are mixed in SE14. Next, we made three different sizes of train sets: one small, one medium-size, and one large, to vary the degree of background in the model representations. Table 3 shows the sizes of the three train sets.

We test four models on the two sets: the SpanBERT-large co-reference resolution model (Joshi et al., 2020) pre-trained by Xu and Choi (2020) without any higher-order inferencing, which has not been fine-tuned on the new data, and three fine-tuned SpanBERT-large models trained on the small, medium and large train sets respectively. For testing and fine-tuning, we follow the procedure as described by Xu and Choi (2020)[4].

[4] https://github.com/lxucs/coref-hoi

Metric	Pretrained			Finetuned-small			Finetuned-medium			Finetuned-large		
	R	*P*	*F1*	*R*	*P*	*F1*	*R*	*P*	*F1*	*R*	*P*	*F1*
MUC	37.28	95.65	53.65	27.11	88.88	41.55	38.98	88.46	54.11	44.06	70.27	**54.16**
B^3	31.79	95.48	**47.70**	17.59	90.00	29.42	28.26	88.90	42.88	37.06	56.70	44.82
CEAFM	38.04	92.10	**53.84**	27.17	83.33	40.98	35.86	86.84	50.76	33.69	64.58	44.28
CEAFE	32.56	71.64	**44.77**	19.81	54.49	29.06	25.16	69.20	36.90	22.34	67.02	33.51
BLANC	26.40	93.14	**41.03**	12.28	82.72	21.35	22.86	86.60	35.97	22.86	62.56	30.84
- Coref	28.57	88.88	**42.24**	13.09	78.57	22.44	25.59	81.13	38.91	27.97	37.90	32.19
- Non-coref	23.23	97.39	**38.82**	11.47	86.88	20.26	20.12	92.07	33.03	17.74	87.23	29.49

Table 4: Performance for S2E14 (4/1 ratio). Recall *R*, precision *P* and F1 score are reported for each model and for each metric. BLANC coreference and non-coreference scores are provided separately.

Metric	Pretrained			Finetuned-small			Finetuned-medium			Finetuned-large		
	R	*P*	*F1*	*R*	*P*	*F1*	*R*	*P*	*F1*	*R*	*P*	*F1*
MUC	50.00	88.67	63.94	41.48	90.69	56.93	62.76	86.76	72.83	72.34	80.95	**76.40**
B^3	43.53	86.56	57.93	26.53	88.10	40.78	48.22	76.67	59.20	58.76	71.52	**64.52**
CEAFM	49.64	83.33	62.22	32.62	83.63	46.93	49.64	76.92	60.34	56.02	75.96	**64.48**
CEAFE	42.95	65.12	**51.76**	17.91	70.17	28.54	32.95	67.34	44.25	31.10	73.08	43.63
BLANC	37.44	86.64	51.57	18.96	75.50	29.38	43.06	72.03	50.37	47.82	73.30	**56.52**
- Coref	43.50	78.46	55.97	29.70	86.15	44.18	60.21	62.70	61.43	57.29	64.86	**60.84**
- Non-coref	31.39	94.82	47.16	8.21	64.86	14.58	25.91	81.36	39.30	38.35	81.75	**52.21**

Table 5: Performance for S2E24 (1/1 ratio). Recall *R*, precision *P* and F1 score are reported for each model and for each metric. BLANC coreference and non-coreference scores are provided separately.

4 Results

4.1 Preprocessing

Before analyzing, we converted the .jsonlines output into CONLL format using a third-party script[5]. However, we adapted this script to accommodate for the fact that the models ignore the gold mentions, leading to very low precision. To accurately compare the model performance on inner and outer circle mentions, we need to only analyze the mentions that the model found that are also a gold mention.

4.2 Model performance

We evaluated the models using the official CONLL-2012 scorer (Pradhan et al., 2012)[6]. Performance for the four models on S2E14 (4/1 ratio of inner/outer circle mentions) is shown in Table 4 and their performance on S2E24 (1/1 ratio) in Table 5.

Our prediction for this experiment was the models would perform worse on S2E14, which has a higher ratio of inner circle mentions compared to outer circle mentions, than on S2E24. The difference between S1E14 (Table 4) and S1E24 (Table 5) confirms our hypothesis both without and after fine-tuning, with especially recall being higher for S2E24. The only outlier is the non-coref recall of 8.21 on S2E24 using the fine-tuned model with least training data.

Another prediction was that the pre-trained model would have more trouble with resolving references than the fine-tuned model due to lack of background knowledge and relevant discourse information. The results show that this not the case for S2E14 (4/1), where the pretrained model outperforms all other models on almost all metrics. For S2E24 (1/1) however, we see that best results (on most metrics) are obtained for the model fine-tuned with most data. Fine-tuning with more data shows a trend of increasing scores for S2E24 as the training data grows, with the highest scores for large. However, this is not the case for S2E14 (4/1), as the medium model outperforms the large model for e.g. BLANC. Apparently, what the model learns by fine-tuning is more relevant for the outer circle cases (S2E24) than for the inner circle cases (S2E14).

4.3 Error analysis

To find out whether the models had more difficulty with inner- or outer circle mentions, we need to break down the model performances to each of

[5] https://github.com/boberle/corefconversion

[6] https://github.com/conll/reference-coreference-scorers

these circles separately. This means we have to use an entity-based analysis of the clusters. We cannot use a link-based approach, because we would then have to evaluate on a subset of the data which corresponds to only the mentions for one of the circles. This would change the problem, since this excludes errors which link inner circle mentions to outer circle clusters and vice versa. Our entity-based analysis, which is based on false and true positives and false negatives for each gold entity cluster, is most similar to the CEAFE metric in approach. Furthermore, we want to investigate to what extent errors are made by mentions of different part-of-speech, especially names, noun phrases and pronouns.

Table 6 shows proportions of false positives and false negatives for all the mentions of inner and outer circle entities for the different models on the two test sets. We divided the error counts by the total number of inner or outer circle mentions, respectively, per test set. We also split the error proportion by part-of-speech for the inner and outer circle references. Note that S2E14 has 77 mentions of inner circle characters and 21 mentions of outer circle characters, and S2E24 has 67 mentions of inner circle characters and 83 mentions of outer circle characters[7].

4.3.1 S2E14 VS. S2E24

We first consider the errors averaged over all models and compare the performance across S2E14 and S2E24 to examine the effect of the test set on the model behaviour. For this we look at the Average subtotals, which show the proportions of false positives and false negatives averaged over all four models. Remember that S2E14 has a 4/1 ratio of inner to outer mentions, while S2E24 has a 1/1 ratio. The proportion of false positives is higher in S2E24 for both for the inner and outer mentions, while the proportion of false negatives is higher in S2E14. The differences in proportion are larger for the outer circle than for the inner circle. If we compare the best-scoring model for S2E14, Pretrained (PreT), with the best-scoring model for S2E24, Finetuned-large (FTlarge), we observe that most of the errors for Pre in S2E14 are false negatives, while for FTlarge in S2E24 most errors are false positives. Again, these differences are bigger for the outer circle than for the inner circle. This suggests that for S2E14, the main challenge for the model was to detect the references to the outer circle in between the more abundant inner circle mentions. This could cause it to miss more of the outer mentions, increasing the false negative rate. For S2E24, where inner and outer circle mentions were more evenly distributed, the challenge might have been not to mix up more vague references to outer circle mentions with the inner circle mentions in between, causing the model to add the mention to the wrong entity cluster. This hypothesis is strengthened by the fact that most false positive errors are made with pronoun mentions (in bold), which are inherently ambiguous and easy to misinterpret. Of course, there is also a potential influence of finetuning for FTlarge which is not present for the pretrained model. We will look at this later.

4.3.2 Inner circle VS. outer circle

The Average subtotals show for S2E14 that more errors are made for inner circle mentions compared to outer circle mentions. This holds for both false positives and false negatives, although the difference is larger for the false positives. For S2E24, the proportion of false negatives is roughly equal for the inner and outer mentions, and here the proportion of false negatives for the inner mentions is quite large compared to the outer mentions. In general then, the models seem to have more difficulty with the inner circle mentions.

As for the errors for each part of speech, there is no strong difference between the inner and outer circle in terms of which part of speech error is most prominent for each. We see that most false negative errors (in bold) are made for names (NNPs) for all models for S2E14, both for the inner and outer circle. S2E24 shows a pattern where most false negatives occur in names (NNPs) for the inner circle, whereas common nouns (NN) make up most errors for the outer circle. Pronouns (PR) make up most of the false positive errors for all models, both for S2E14 and S2E24 and both for inner and outer circle mentions. This last point makes intuitive sense, since pronouns are highly ambiguous. However, we don't see a difference between the inner and outer mentions, despite the higher relative amount of pronouns for outer mentions. It makes less sense that most false negatives occur for names. Despite the fact that associating names to characters should be relatively easy, they are apparently

[7]Note that the subtotals for Fpos and Fneg may add up to over 100%. This is because a single mention can be a false positive for one cluster and a false negative for another, meaning that this mention appears twice.

		S2E14										S2E24									
		PreT		**FTsmall**		**FTmedium**		**FTlarge**		**Average**		**PreT**		**FTsmall**		**FTmedium**		**FTlarge**		**Average**	
	PoS	In	Out	In	Out	In	Out	In	Out	In	Out	In	Out	In	Out	In	Out	In	Out	In	Out
Fpos	NNP	4%				4%		19%	5%	7%	1%	3%	**7%**	1%	2%		6%	7%	14%	3%	8%
	NN	**5%**		1%	5%	3%		16%	5%	6%	2%	1%		1%	1%	10%	11%	**28%**	23%	10%	9%
	PR			**8%**		**10%**		**35%**	**33%**	**13%**	**8%**	**25%**	4%	**6%**	**7%**	**33%**	**27%**	16%	**36%**	**20%**	**18%**
	Other							1%	0%	0%	0%									0%	0%
	Subtot.	9%		9%	5%	17%		71%	43%	27%	12%	30%	11%	9%	11%	43%	43%	52%	73%	34%	35%
Fneg	NNP	17%	29%	**30%**	**29%**	**21%**	**29%**	17%	**29%**	**21%**	**29%**	24%	12%	**43%**	16%	**34%**	13%	**33%**	5%	**34%**	11%
	NN	**22%**	29%	19%	19%	19%	19%	17%	14%	19%	20%	25%	**23%**	19%	**24%**	13%	**16%**	9%	**10%**	17%	**18%**
	PR	3%		5%	10%	6%	5%	3%	0%	4%	4%	9%	2%	7%	16%	1%	1%	3%	2%	5%	5%
	Other	16%		14%		14%		14%	0%	15%	0%	1%		1%		1%		1%		1%	0%
	Subtot.	57%	57%	69%	57%	61%	52%	51%	43%	59%	52%	60%	37%	72%	55%	51%	30%	46%	17%	57%	35%

Table 6: Breakdown of proportions of false positives (Fpos) and false negative (Fneg) differentiated per part-of-speech for S2E14 and S2E24 and for the different models (PreT = pretrained, FT = finetuned) and averaged over all models. 'In' refers to the errors for the inner circle mentions, whereas 'out' refers to those for the outer circle mentions.

still missed to a large extent in establishing coreference relations. Finally, S2E14 shows a remarkable proportion of false negative errors for inner circle entities with part-of-speech **Other**. As these are mostly annotation errors in this specific episode, none of the models seems to detect these cases as they are non-representative. These annotation errors were originally found mostly in the training data, but some of them ended up in our test set due to our re-organization of the sets.

4.3.3 Effect of finetuning

We now investigate to what extent fine-tuning on previous conversations can learn to detect the correct coreference relations and whether there is a difference for inner and outer circle references. Figures 1 to 6 in the Appendix contain bar plots showing the effect of finetuning on more data on the proportion of false positives and negatives for both the inner and outer circle, per test set and per part of speech. Overall, it looks like with more finetuning data, false negatives decrease both for the inner and outer circle, with the notable exceptions of outer circle NNP's in S2E14 (Figure 1) and inner circle NNP's in S2E24 (Figure 4). For the outer circle in S2E14, this could mean that the model over-fitted on inner circle names, and together with the relatively high amount of inner circle mentions this causes the model to ignore most names referring to the outer circle. However, this does not explain the high proportion of false negatives for the inner circle in S2E24. In general, we also see false positives increase with more finetuning data, especially for the inner circle. Together with the general decrease in false negatives, this indeed seems to suggest that the model is over-fitting on a part of the training data. In Table 1, we showed that most inner mentions are names, whereas most outer mentions are pronoun mentions. As mentioned above, it looks like the model tends to prefer inner circle names, which are more present in the training data. However, for pronouns we see a remarkable increase in false positives both for the inner and outer circle. For pronoun mentions, the models might learn a different preference than for NNP mentions which is more based on discourse features rather than individual characters. In general we believe the model tends more towards learning discourse features, because the graphs do not show a much stronger effect of over-fitting for the inner or outer circle. Note that the fine-tuned models generate more errors than the pretrained model on S2E24 in entity-based evaluation, which correspond to the CEAFE scores given earlier in Table 5 but not with the other metrics.

4.3.4 Error examples

An example of a false negative for a common noun (NN) referring to the inner circle is *actor* in S2E24. It occurs in the sentence *Mr. Beatty comes up to me and says 'good **actor**'...* and refers to the inner circle character Joey, who utters the sentence. It could be that the model mis-identified this reference because it is uttered in direct speech, which makes it unclear that the speaker is the intended referent. Another curious case for a name (NNP) referring to the inner circle concerns *Rachel* and her nickname *Rach* in S2E24, where the first three occurrences of *Rachel* / *Rach* in the scene are not added to the same cluster as the latter three occurrences of *Rach* by the large model. Between these two sets of occurrences, another person is referenced, which could explain why they were assumed to be disjoint by the model. Possibly, this an effect of window size, which makes the earlier references unavailable to the system. While the sliding window is in principle a good method to constrain the context that the model takes into account, in this case it leads to errors which could have been avoided. Some false positives for pronouns are the result of an introduction in the visual scene (such as a speaker pointing at a character).

5 Discussion

Our results showed differences between models and across test sets with different ratios. All models perform lower on S2E14 with more inner circle references than on S2E24 with less. For most metrics, the pretrained model performed best on S2E14 (4/1) and the largest fine-tuned model on S2E24 (1/1) ratio, except for entity-based evaluations in which pretrained performed best on both. When breaking down the errors per part-of-speech and across inner and outer references, we found some patterns but it remains difficult to relate these to the different part-of-speech statistics observed. Many errors are made for outer circle names and in the case of S2E24 also for inner circle name mentions. Remarkable are the false positive (and to some extent false negative) errors in pronominal inner and outer circle mentions in S2E24. Since the false positives tend to increase with fine-tuning, we suspect that the fine-tuned models are over-fitting. Our experiments do not allow us to draw conclusions towards the potential of more knowledge-rich approaches that incorporate built-up common ground. This is partly because fine-tuned language models are not transparent to what knowledge is picked up from the preceding conversations.

Clearly, more research on the role of common ground in referencing in social dialogue is necessary. Most co-reference resolution models continue to be trained and tested on well-established data sets which are not useful for exploring this phenomenon. Although the data set of episodes of *FRIENDS* that we used in this paper has the necessary properties, it too has its drawbacks. Most of the dialogues are multi-party dialogues, whereas dyadic dialogue would be a more controlled setting in which to explore the buildup of common ground. The dialogues also partly rely on visual cues, which the model cannot rely on and for which the necessary metadata is not provided in the data set. Furthermore, the show is a sitcom, and the many quips might have a detrimental effect on the naturalness of the conversations. Therefore, we encourage the further development of more data sets of social dialogue with multiple interactions over time, based on a more natural setting or with fewer speakers involved in the conversation.

In this work, we have made a distinction between well-known 'inner circle' and lesser known 'outer circle' referents. We believe it is relevant to be aware of such a distinction in referencing, since people rely on the established references to the inner circle to create a bond and distinguish their shared social circle from the outside world. If we want systems to become a part of this shared social circle and develop their own bond with humans, they too need to learn this way of referencing, and in long-term interaction it could help them reinforce this bond and improve communicative efficiency and enjoyment on the part of the human.

In future work, we will further explore how the buildup of common ground influences referential expressions to well-known individuals over time in dyadic social dialogue. This will be done in an interactive setting, where an artificial agent engages in conversation with a human and can use visual cues and human feedback to improve its representation of the common ground. Due to the interactive nature of the dialogue, the model will not be a pure co-reference resolution model, but it will build upon properties of both co-reference resolution and entity linking models. In addition, we will use a more explicit modeling of common ground, and include more knowledge-rich features in our model.

6 Conclusion

In this paper, we framed the problem of resolving third-person references in social dialogues as a dynamic process in which common ground plays a role. We made a difference between inner and outer circle references and hypothesized that the former are more difficult to resolve, which was partially confirmed by the model performances on data with more and less inner circle references. Training models on preceding data did not show a corresponding increase in performance on inner circle references, indicating that such models do not acquire common ground knowledge, but did improve the performance for outer circle mentions. We propose that co-reference resolution models for social dialogue could benefit from a more knowledge-rich approach in order to better adjust to the common ground, which in turn facilitates the resolution of complex third-person references.

References

Jake Brawer, Olivier Mangin, Alessandro Roncone, Sarah Widder, and Brian Scassellati. 2018. Situated human–robot collaboration: predicting intent from grounded natural language. In *2018 IEEE/RSJ International Conference on Intelligent Robots and Systems (IROS)*, pages 827–833. IEEE.

Joyce Y. Chai, Lanbo She, Rui Fang, Spencer Ottarson, Cody Littley, Changsong Liu, and Kenneth Hanson. 2014. Collaborative effort towards common ground in situated human-robot dialogue. In *Proceedings of the 2014 ACM/IEEE International Conference on Human-Robot Interaction*, HRI '14, page 33–40, New York, NY, USA. Association for Computing Machinery.

Jinho D. Choi and Henry Y. Chen. 2018. SemEval 2018 task 4: Character identification on multiparty dialogues. In *Proceedings of The 12th International Workshop on Semantic Evaluation*, pages 57–64, New Orleans, Louisiana. Association for Computational Linguistics.

Herbert H Clark and Susan E Brennan. 1991. Grounding in communication. *Perspectives on Socially Shared Cognition*, pages 127–149.

Darren Gergle, Robert E. Kraut, and Susan R. Fussell. 2013. Using visual information for grounding and awareness in collaborative tasks. *Human–Computer Interaction*, 28(1):1–39.

Janosch Haber, Tim Baumgärtner, Ece Takmaz, Lieke Gelderloos, Elia Bruni, and Raquel Fernández. 2019. The photobook dataset: Building common ground through visually-grounded dialogue. *arXiv preprint arXiv:1906.01530*.

Robert D. Hawkins, Michael Franke, Michael C. Frank, Adele E. Goldberg, Kenny Smith, Thomas L. Griffiths, and Noah D. Goodman. 2021. From partners to populations: A hierarchical bayesian account of coordination and convention.

E. Holliman, J. Godfrey, and J. McDaniel. 1992. Switchboard: telephone speech corpus for research and development. In *Acoustics, Speech, and Signal Processing, IEEE International Conference on*, volume 1, pages 517–520, Los Alamitos, CA, USA. IEEE Computer Society.

Mandar Joshi, Danqi Chen, Yinhan Liu, Daniel S. Weld, Luke Zettlemoyer, and Omer Levy. 2020. SpanBERT: Improving Pre-training by Representing and Predicting Spans. *Transactions of the Association for Computational Linguistics*, 8:64–77.

Mandar Joshi, Omer Levy, Daniel S. Weld, and Luke Zettlemoyer. 2019. BERT for coreference resolution: Baselines and analysis. In *Empirical Methods in Natural Language Processing (EMNLP)*.

Charles Kemp, Yang Xu, and Terry Regier. 2018. Semantic typology and efficient communication. *Annual Review of Linguistics*, 4(1):109–128.

Sopan Khosla, Juntao Yu, Ramesh Manuvinakurike, Vincent Ng, Massimo Poesio, Michael Strube, and Carolyn Rosé. 2021. The CODI-CRAC 2021 shared task on anaphora, bridging, and discourse deixis in dialogue. In *Proceedings of the CODI-CRAC 2021 Shared Task on Anaphora, Bridging, and Discourse Deixis in Dialogue*, pages 1–15, Punta Cana, Dominican Republic. Association for Computational Linguistics.

Sameer Pradhan, Alessandro Moschitti, Nianwen Xue, Olga Uryupina, and Yuchen Zhang. 2012. Conll-2012 shared task: Modeling multilingual unrestricted coreference in ontonotes. In *Joint Conference on EMNLP and CoNLL-Shared Task*, pages 1–40.

Oliver Roesler and Ann Nowé. 2019. Action learning and grounding in simulated human–robot interactions. *The Knowledge Engineering Review*, 34.

Andy Shih, Arjun Sawhney, Jovana Kondic, Stefano Ermon, and Dorsa Sadigh. 2021. On the critical role of conventions in adaptive human-ai collaboration. *arXiv preprint arXiv:2104.02871*.

Mohit Shridhar and David Hsu. 2018. Interactive visual grounding of referring expressions for human-robot interaction. *arXiv preprint arXiv:1806.03831*.

Robert Stalnaker. 2002. Common ground. *Linguistics and philosophy*, 25(5/6):701–721.

Xuewei Wang, Weiyan Shi, Richard Kim, Yoojung Oh, Sijia Yang, Jingwen Zhang, and Zhou Yu. 2019. Persuasion for good: Towards a personalized persuasive dialogue system for social good.

Liyan Xu and Jinho D. Choi. 2020. Revealing the myth of higher-order inference in coreference resolution. In *Proceedings of the 2020 Conference on Empirical Methods in Natural Language Processing (EMNLP)*, pages 8527–8533. Association for Computational Linguistics.

7 Appendix

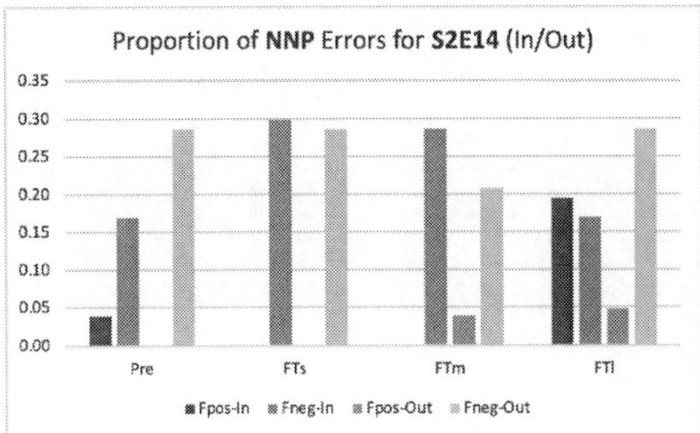

Figure 1

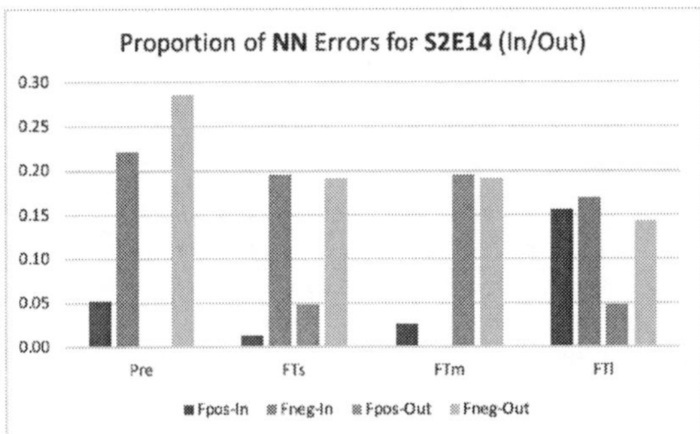

Figure 2

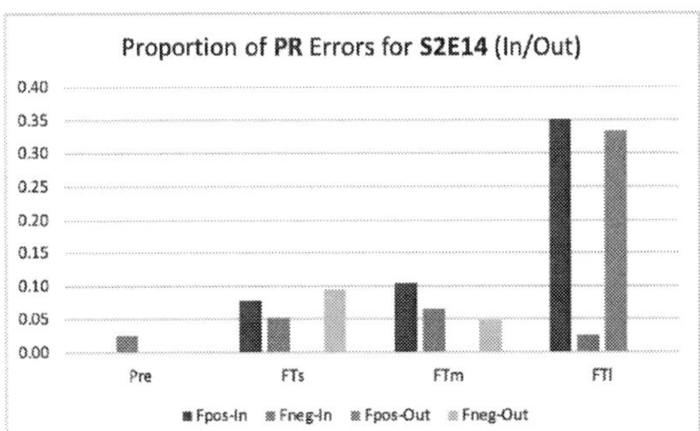

Figure 3

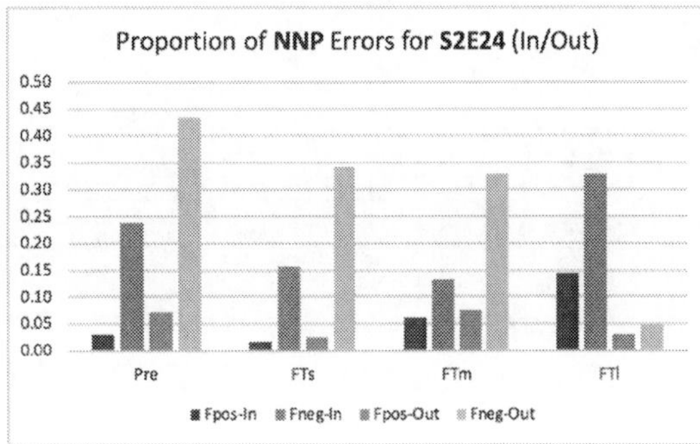

Figure 4

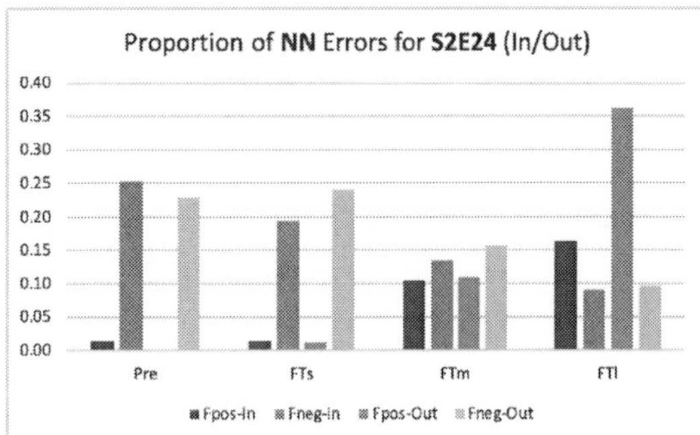

Figure 5

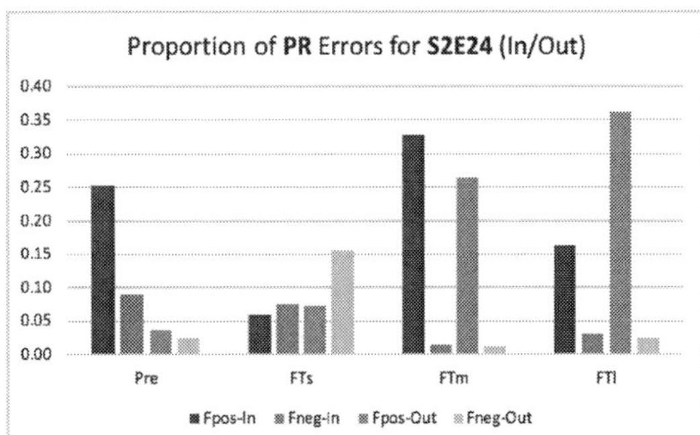

Figure 6

S2E14	Entity	#M	#V	#P	Variants
I	59	20	15	8	'Chandler': 5, 'man': 2, 'and': 1, 'an': 1, 'now': 1, 'even': 1, 'Well': 1, 'extra': 1, 'there': 1, "d'ya": 1, 'bud': 1, 'manager': 1, 'Bing': 1, 'Man': 1, 'Dude': 1
I	306	13	5	3	'Rachel': 5, 'she': 4, 'her': 2, 'waitress': 1, 'Rach': 1
I	335	13	9	3	'Ross': 5, 'dad': 1, 'man': 1, 'Geller': 1, 'yours': 1, 'date': 1, 'guy': 1, 'darling': 1, 'Jack': 1
I	183	12	7	6	'he': 3, 'man': 3, 'bud': 2, "n't": 1, 'it': 1, 'is': 1, ',': 1
I	248	10	7	4	'Monica': 3, 'her': 2, 'person': 1, 'darling': 1, 'sweetie': 1, 'she': 1, 'She': 1
O	55	6	3	3	'Casey': 3, 'he': 2, 'guy': 1
O	227	6	5	2	'he': 2, 'guy': 1, 'buddy': 1, 'him': 1, 'man': 1
O	78	3	3	2	'Dave': 1, 'Thomas': 1, 'founder': 1
I	271	3	2	2	'Judy': 2, 'mom': 1
I	30	2	2	1	'him': 1, 'he': 1
O	231	2	2	1	'Marcel': 1, 'Marceau': 1
O	352	2	2	1	'Steffi': 1, 'Graf': 1
I	51	1	1	1	'Carol': 1
O	137	1	1	1	'Gail': 1
I	145	1	1	1	'Gunther': 1
I	292	1	1	1	'she': 1
I	358	1	1	1	'Susan': 1
O	397	1	1	1	'woman': 1

Table 7: Statistics on the mentions, variants and their part-of-speech for the test case S2E14 with a 4/1 ratio for inner and outer entities. The first column differentiates inner circle (I) and outer circle (O) entities

S2E24	Entity	#M	#V	#P	Variants
O	60	33	8	3	'she': 10, 'her': 10, 'She': 4, 'girl': 3, 'guy': 3, 'person': 1, 'girlfriend': 1, 'woman': 1
I	306	22	7	4	'Rach': 6, 'Rachel': 6, 'she': 5, 'her': 2, 'honey': 1, 'Sweetie': 1, 'bride': 1
I	183	10	6	4	'Joey': 4, 'actor': 2, 'guy': 1, 'professional': 1, 'him': 1, 'Tribiani': 1
O	392	10	4	3	'Beatty': 4, 'guy': 3, 'Warren': 2, 'he': 1
O	29	9	4	4	'Barry': 5, 'him': 2, 'his': 1, 'Barr': 1
I	317	9	5	3	'Richard': 3, 'him': 3, 'sweetie': 1, 'He': 1, 'man': 1
O	215	7	6	4	'She': 2, 'Her': 1, 'Lola': 1, 'her': 1, 'she': 1, 'star': 1
O	242	7	6	2	'Min': 2, 'Mindy': 1, 'Mrs.': 1, 'Hunter': 1, 'Farber': 1, 'honey': 1
I	59	6	2	2	'Chandler': 5, 'guy': 1
I	30	5	3	3	'Benny': 2, 'he': 2, 'baby': 1
O	61	5	4	2	'husband': 2, 'his': 1, 'person': 1, 'guy': 1
I	168	5	2	1	'she': 4, 'her': 1'
I	335	5	4	4	'Ross': 2, 'his': 1, 'boyfriend': 1, 'She': 1
I	248	3	2	1	'Monica': 2, 'Honey': 1
O	252	3	3	2	'Mother': 1, 'Theresa': 1, 'mother': 1
O	228	2	2	2	'guy': 1, 'him': 1
I	292	2	2	2	'friend': 1, 'Phoebe': 1
O	17	1	1	1	'Angela': 1
O	32	1	1	1	'Man': 1
O	62	1	1	1	'secretary': 1
O	266	1	1	1	'Wineburg': 1
O	277	1	1	1	'Wineburg': 1
O	298	1	1	1	'friend': 1
O	372	1	1	1	'Tony': 1

Table 8: Statistics on the mentions, variants and their part-of-speech for the test case S2E24 with a 1/1 ratio for inner and outer entities. The first column differentiates inner circle (I) and outer circle (O) entities

Author Index

Chai, Haixia, 61

De Clercq, Orphee, 88
De Langhe, Loic, 88
Dobnik, Simon, 31

Gurevych, Iryna, 61

Hale, John, 1
Haug, Dag, 48
Hoste, Veronique, 88

Jørgensen, Tollef, 48

Kåsen, Andre, 48
Kobayashi, Hideo, 22
Kruijt, Jaap, 99
Kurohashi, Sadao, 74

Li, Jixing, 1
Loáiciga, Sharid, 31

Mæhlum, Petter, 48
Malon, Christopher, 22
Moosavi, Nafise Sadat, 61

Nøklestad, Anders, 48

Øvrelid, Lilja, 48

Rønningstad, Egil, 48

Schlangen, David, 31
Solberg, Per Erik, 48
Strube, Michael, 61

Ueda, Nobuhiro, 74

Vadász, Noémi, 38
Van Durme, Benjamin, 13
Velldal, Erik, 48
Vossen, Piek, 99

Xia, Patrick, 13

Zhang, Shulin, 1

Association for Computational Linguistics
209 N. Eighth Street
Stroudsburg, Pennsylvania 18360

ISBN 978-1-7138-6150-8

CURRAN ASSOCIATES INC. proceedings.com